O9-BTM-780

Some Time in the Sun

Hollywood Boulevard, 1936

Some Time in the Sun

Tom Dardis

Charles Scribner's Sons/New York

The James Agee letters to Dwight
MacDonald are reprinted by permission
of the James Agee Trust, Copyright ©
1962, 1976 by the James Agee Trust

Copyright © 1976 Thomas A. Dardis

Library of Congress Cataloging in Publication Data
Dardis, Thomas A. Some time in the sun.
  Bibliography: p. 253
  Includes index.
  1. Authors, American—20th century—Biography.
2. Authors, English—20th century—Biography.
3. Screen writers—Biography.   4. Moving-picture
industry—California—Hollywood.   I. Title.
PS129.D3   810'.9'0052   75-45083
ISBN 0-684-14563-4

1 3 5 7 9 11 13 15 17 19   v|c   20 18 16 14 12 10 8 6 4 2

Printed in the United States of America

For Jane, and for Tony, Anne, and Francis

Acknowledgments

This book would have been a very different one if the following individuals had not shared their knowledge so generously with me: Mia Agee, Leigh Brackett, Matthew J. Bruccoli, Alexander Clark, Daniel Fuchs, Edith Haggard, Nunnally Johnson, Jay Leyda, Helen Levitt, the late Kenneth Littauer, Dwight MacDonald, David MacDowell, Donald Newlove, Anthony Powell, John Sanford, Edward Simpson, and Donald Wolf.

A special note of thanks to my agent, John Cushman, who has been helpful in a great many ways. Finally, my editor at Scribners, Patricia Cristol, has been outstanding in the patience and care she has extended to this book.

Contents

I saw my first film when I was six; I suppose I've seen on average—and discounting television—a film a week ever since: let's say some two and a half thousand films up to now. How can so frequently repeated an experience not have indelibly stamped itself on the *mode* of imagination? At one time I analyzed my dreams in detail; again and again I recalled purely cinematic effects . . . panning shots, close shots, tracking, jump cuts, and the like. In short, this mode of imagination is far too deep in me to eradicate—not only in me, in all my generation.

—JOHN FOWLES

We are whores working in a brothel, a journal says of us, a journal noted generally for its civility and enlightened wit. We are regularly assailed, censured, pestered. "Did the Pope tell Michelangelo how to paint?" a big city newspapers asks, and they read out the roll of names: Fitzgerald and West and . . . and . . . and . . . who? I can rely on old friends to remind and reprove me; the correspondence doesn't slacken: What happened to you? Why have you fallen into silence? Why have you stopped writing? I write, in collaboration or alone, from my own original material, in the morning and in the night, on studio time and on my own time, until I fill shelves and prize reticence as the rarest of all jewels. But they don't mean movie writing. What they mean—they don't know what they mean, and the truth is they don't know as much about Hollywood as they believe they know. . . .

—DANIEL FUCHS

Introduction

Mr. Thalberg, I don't write lovely music . . .
—*Arnold Schoenberg, 1936*

This book originated in a chance conversation I had one night in London with Anthony Powell about F. Scott Fitzgerald and his years in Hollywood. To my considerable surprise, Powell had once spent the whole of a long afternoon there with Fitzgerald in the summer of 1937, shortly after his arrival in Los Angeles on his first visit to the United States. For a moment it was hard to accept the idea that such a meeting had ever in fact taken place, but it really had. Powell's extraordinary descriptive powers created a portrait of Fitzgerald in his final years that appeared to be very much in conflict with the one most of his biographers have succeeded in creating.

In the spring of 1937, some friends in London had informed Powell that Michael Balcon was going to produce a picture for the new firm of MGM-British. The film was to be shot entirely in England, but the script and casting were to be done in Hollywood. It was to be called *A Yank at Oxford,* with Robert Taylor as the Yank. Unemployed at the time, Powell decided to try his luck in California and see if perhaps MGM would agree to hire him to write the screenplay for this production—or any of their productions, for that matter. Although hard-pressed financially, Powell and his wife managed to get to Los Angeles after a four-week trip on a slow boat by way of Panama. Things started off very badly for them in California, for Powell's American agent had dropped dead on Hollywood Boulevard while they were still en route from England. He quickly acquired a new agent, who offered little hope of supplying any work at all for him in California, a soundly realistic view as it turned out.

In the course of the next few weeks, Powell went dutifully around to a number of the leading studios in Hollywood, including MGM, telling their chief executives his life story, but all to no avail. There were simply no jobs to be had. He did, however, make some friendships in Hollywood, and one of these was with a young Englishman, Elliott Morgan, who was working in MGM's research department in Culver City. He was then actively engaged in researching the background material for the very film that Powell had come all the way to California in hopes of working on, *A Yank at Oxford*. Morgan had recently been assigned to work with F. Scott Fitzgerald, who had just been given the task of revising the existing script for *Yank* as his very first job at MGM. When Morgan learned of Powell's interest in Fitzgerald's novels, he quickly arranged a luncheon, and a few days later Powell and his wife found themselves facing a highly animated Fitzgerald in the huge hangarlike atmosphere of the MGM commissary. Even then, by the summer of 1937, Fitzgerald had become something of a mythical figure: "It was almost as if he were already dead; at best risen from the dead, and of somewhat doubtful survival value."

Powell still recalls that long and delightful afternoon of July 20 with the utmost clarity. Here was someone very much alive, sober, and not at all the broken-down figure he might perhaps have expected to find there. They discussed at great length and in considerable detail the kind of dialogue to be written for the *Yank* film, the exact nature of the slang to be used. Powell was greatly surprised by this precise, almost donnish side of Fitzgerald's personality, especially when he launched into a long discussion of the differences in American and British life as reflected in their languages. At one point Fitzgerald drew for Powell a map of the United States on a scrap of paper, adorning it with arrows which were to indicate the three main directions by which culture had entered this continent. This was an element in Fitzgerald's character he would never have suspected, and it is one that few of his many biographers have stressed. Fitzgerald seemed to radiate a tremendous amount of enthusiasm for everything they discussed that afternoon, including his first impressions of his newfound way of making a living. They talked on in the vast, noisy eating place filled with throngs of other people on the MGM payroll. Spencer Tracy and James Stewart suddenly appeared, table-hopping their way around the immense area of the commissary. Fitzgerald pointed out Stewart to Powell, indicating that he too had attended Princeton.

As the afternoon advanced, the restaurant gradually emptied as people returned to work until finally there were only a few of the studio's "big shots" still talking at their tables in the center of the room. It was clearly time for Fitzgerald and his party to go, for these big shots were now staring with morose curiosity at this cheerful, talkative group of people who seemed utterly indifferent to MGM and all of its immense concerns. A few weeks later Powell returned to London, still jobless, and Fitzgerald continued on with his new life as a contract studio writer. That night, July 20, was the night of his first dinner with Sheilah Graham. It was truly the beginning of a new life for Fitzgerald. He and Powell never saw each other again.

This image of an apparently healthy and energetic Fitzgerald working in Hollywood is not the one usually encountered in much of the vast literature concerning him. The most common one is of a man engulfed in a continual state of despair, only slightly relieved by the presence of Sheilah Graham. It appeared that Fitzgerald's biographers, with a single interesting exception, hadn't much cared about the details of what he had done in California in these last three and a half years of his life. Acute misery was the key word in all these accounts, enlivened only by tales of some of his worst drinking escapades.

He had been paid a good deal of money, it would appear, as much as $1,250 a week, but what had he done to earn this kind of money? There had been some serious troubles for him at MGM, with people like Mankiewicz and Stromberg, and it seemed that he had earned only one screen credit in all the time he spent in Hollywood. This was the *Three Comrades* film of 1938, based on Remarque's novel, with Margaret Sullavan and Robert Taylor. He had worked on *The Last Tycoon,* published posthumously, the only book he wrote in the last five years of his life, the only sound in that long silence. It didn't really seem as if he'd done very much; and why had MGM ever hired him in 1937 if it were true that he was generally thought to be "finished" as a writer?

One biographer, Aaron Latham, whose book *Crazy Sundays* is devoted entirely to this period of Fitzgerald's life, has covered his screenwriting activities in considerable detail. The Fitzgerald of Latham's pages is, however, the same bleak and despairing man found in the Mizener and Turnbull biographies. For reasons that remain unclear, Mr. Latham tells us that Fitzgerald could do little that was wrong or downright bad as a film-writer, and his portrait of him in these years is that of a stricken, once noble figure much put upon by his gross, unfeeling employers. It is a puzzling picture in many ways, for his account is seriously marred by its lively descriptions of events that never occurred in fact, such as the details concerning Fitzgerald's collaboration with Aldous Huxley on the script of MGM's *Madame Curie.* Latham also recounts an episode in which Fitzgerald took Ernest Hemingway on a guided tour of the MGM lot, in the course of which Hemingway made some anti-Semitic remarks to Louis B. Mayer and Bernard Hyman before being forcibly ejected from the studio. There is not a word of truth in either of these stories.

Despite all of the details in Latham's 300 pages, I still found Fitzgerald's Hollywood years rather cloudy and contradictory. It was unclear how good or bad he was at his new profession. If he made $1,250 a week, how much was this salary compared with what the other writers at MGM or at the other major studios were getting at the time? If the state of our knowledge was as vague as this about Fitzgerald, perhaps the most carefully scrutinized figure in all of modern literature, what of all the other notable writers who had spent long stretches of time writing screenplays—Faulkner and Huxley and West? With these writers the available information was generally even scantier, for most of their biographers seemed to regard the work done in Hollywood as something just a bit shameful; they usually passed it over in their books as quickly as possible.

Some of the very greatest names in all of modern literature have spent considerable periods of their lives working as contract writers in Hollywood, with varying degrees of involvement. It was the case with most of them that their working in Hollywood became a matter of financial salvation for them, as even Bertolt Brecht found to be true when he arrived in Los Angeles in the summer of 1941:

> Every morning, to earn my bread,
> I go to the market, where lies are bought.
> Hopefully
> I join the ranks of the sellers.

Faulkner joined these ranks as early as 1932, but nearly all of the available information about his twenty-odd years in Hollywood has been either vague or inconclusive. There are many more unanswered questions about his work there than there are about Fitzgerald's. Almost all of the accounts of it have stressed the fact that Faulkner's visits to Hollywood were prompted by only temporary financial problems, that the work he performed there was done quickly and/or carelessly "just" for the money in it, and that the experience of Hollywood left absolutely no marks or traces on him as a writer. Not one of these assumptions is correct, for the necessity of Faulkner's becoming a professional screenwriter arose in time from financial burdens just as desperate as those of Fitzgerald's or perhaps even worse, for he had many more people to support. For twenty years Faulkner's finances were in a state of permanent crisis. In these years he wrote several dozen screenplays for the major studios, devoting weeks and even months to individual projects. In the early thirties it was at MGM, in the later thirties at Twentieth Century-Fox, and for nearly all of World War II at Warner Brothers. Just about everyone who has written about Faulkner has noted his contempt for much in Hollywood, but this fact is difficult to reconcile with his having found the origin of the novel he worked on for a decade in a screen treatment he wrote for a film that was never produced.

Joseph Blotner's recent massive biography of Faulkner has cleared up some, but scarcely all, of the confusion surrounding his years in Hollywood. It appears that Faulkner lacked confidence in himself as a screenwriter and always considered himself totally unfit for the work, once in desperation offering his services to any firm in Hollywood willing to pay him more than $100 a week. He was not joking, for by that time, in 1942, there was as little market for books by William Faulkner as there were for those by F. Scott Fitzgerald. If his lack of self-confidence for the work was that extreme, and if he was really all that unfit, why then did the director Howard Hawks keep requesting Faulkner's services as a writer on his films for over two decades? He used Faulkner as a collaborator on a half-dozen of his best films in very much the same way that Ingmar Bergman has used the same basic group of talents over and over again in his films. What did Hawks see in this tiny man who once rated himself as being worth only $100 a week?

2

Thank God for the movies. . . .

—*Nathanael West, 1939*

Whoever stayed in Mahagonny
Needed every day five dollars
and if he carried on more than most
he probably needed more than that . . .

In either case they lost,
But they got something out of it,
But they got something out of it,
But they got something out of it.

—*Bertolt Brecht,* Mahagonny

Jack Warner is once reputed to have snarled loudly that writers as a class were just "schmucks with Underwoods"; this attitude toward the writers he employed was perhaps reflected in the working quarters he gave them at his studio. At many of the major studios in the thirties and forties, the writers' building was more often than not a structure that had been originally designed to house something else on the lot, the kind of something that had finally managed to get new and better quarters—the publicity or advertising departments, for instance. In these years many of the writers discussed in this book occupied tiny cubicles in these small, slightly run-down buildings that many of them called rabbit-warrens. There, against the constant hum of electric fans, and in later years that of air conditioners, the writers typed out their daily quota of words.

The status of the screenwriter was considerably more ambiguous in the thirties and forties than it is today. If you were a Robert Riskin, a Dudley Nichols, a Nunnally Johnson, or ultimately a Ben Hecht, you were accorded lavish social and intellectual prestige, along with a salary commensurate with these graces. But below these lofty heights of enormous success most of the other screenwriters were looked down upon as hacks of one sort or another. When Fitzgerald wrote his series of short stories about Pat Hobby he was expressing some widely held views about hack-writing in Hollywood. Pat had graduated at the end of the twenties from the humble role of a writer of titles on silent films to a full-fledged writer of mediocre screenplays in the late thirties. He was the ultimate hack, and Fitzgerald seemed to derive some genuine pleasure from chronicling his behavior; most of his knowledge was derived from the observation of what went on around him in the course of his own daily work.

The "hack" epithet was accorded many of the writers who went to work in Hollywood, especially in the "politically conscious" thirties, and has been leveled against all five of the writers discussed in this book. Perhaps the most commonly held assumption about them is precisely this: that all the time they spent in Hollywood was lost, wasted time. With this also goes the general feeling that their work done in Hollywood is really best forgotten, left dead and buried in the story files of Metro-Goldwyn-Mayer and Warner Brothers.

Behind this basic assumption of wasted time and talent lies still another one, that *all* film-writing is by definition hackwork or simply work done with the left hand for the money and nothing else, the "don't ever look back" kind of work. With the single exception of Nathanael West's routine genre films for Republic, Universal, and RKO, the film-writing of the other four here—Fitzgerald, Faulkner, Huxley, and Agee—is of lasting interest as examples of what these extraordinary sensibilities could actually do in the film medium. While they may well have regarded their Hollywood work as indeed hack stuff, some of it has been done with such rare grace and ingenuity that the epithet "hack" no longer means very much.

All of which is by way of saying that neither Fitzgerald, nor Agee, nor Huxley were capable of turning out what is easily recognizable as the standard hack-work product of a Ben Hecht or a Jules Furthman. When Faulkner *did* try his hand at writing a purely commercial novel, he wrote *Sanctuary*. He applied himself to his screenwriting with just as much individuality as he approached everything else he touched. Although he despised some of the material he was assigned to work on, he performed his writing functions at Warner Brothers, as Daniel Fuchs has observed, as a good plumber might, doing the very best job he could, with some occasionally startling results.

The notion of it all being just hack-work is seriously challenged by the actual quality of some of the films these people wrote during all those years, films like *The Big Sleep, The Bride Comes to Yellow Sky, Jane Eyre, To Have and Have Not, Pride and Prejudice,* and *The Southerner*. Among the directors of these films were John Huston, Howard Hawks, and Jean Renoir, all of whom deliberately chose to obtain the services of these writers for the perfectly good reason that they were supremely talented to write the scripts for the films these three directors had in mind.

There is quite a lot about money in this book, for it was the money that had attracted these writers to Hollywood, and it was the money that kept them there for years on end. This is absolutely true of Fitzgerald, Faulkner, and West, all three of whom became financially dependent upon Hollywood to the point of absolute bondage. Huxley's and Agee's dependence upon making films for a livelihood was considerably less, but it is equally true that both men spent several years of their lives doing little else but thinking about film projects, and both of them had films on their minds at the very end of their lives.

There are those who have found it degrading that some of our greatest writers should have so demeaned themselves by writing for Hollywood. In the years with which this book is concerned, the thirties through the mid fifties, the phrase "selling out to Hollywood" became a standard cliché usually reserved for humorous exchanges in plays like *Once in a Life-*

time or *Clear All Wires.* But there were some who used it seriously, as if there were a special stigma about selling oneself on the West Coast that simply did not prevail in the East. But there is really nothing new about writers, even the very best ones, turning to something that might guarantee them some sort of a living.

At the beginning of the 1890s, Henry James entered a period of his life when he did little but write plays for the highly competitive theater world of London's West End. He did this for nearly five years, with no real measure of success at it, not returning to writing novels until the mid nineties. His principal reason was purely economic, for his novels almost never sold more than 3,000 or 4,000 copies, despite the fact that he was often considered to be America's most distinguished novelist. The world of the London theater promised him some money, of which he had once said, "About gold, I like a lot of gold." The novels that had not sold before the playwriting period were books like *The Princess Casamassima, The Bostonians,* and *The Tragic Muse.* The theatrical venture had absolutely no effect on James's sales after it had been concluded, for *The Awkward Age* and *The Wings of the Dove* sold no better than the earlier novels, but there were some decided changes in the technique of these later books.

There are some analogies here with the careers of both Fitzgerald and Faulkner, for they were also novelists whose literary eminence was far in advance of their sales. They both found they could not support themselves by writing the kind of novels that enjoyed a large sale, despite all their efforts to do so. Neither of the two ever thought of themselves as having very much dramatic ability, both *The Vegetable* and *Requiem for a Nun* giving little real pleasure to their authors. But film-writing was somehow different, somehow *possible,* as the Broadway stage was obviously not.

Fitzgerald had attempted a little film-writing in both 1927 and 1931, mainly as a source of supplementary income, but he never took these short visits to California very seriously, nor was there any need for him to do so. These were the years when his *Saturday Evening Post* market was still there at $3,000 and $4,000 per story. By 1937 things were very different for Fitzgerald, for the *Post* market had ceased to exist for him. His last published novel, *Tender Is the Night,* had sold after a fashion, but in nowhere near the large quantities he had hoped for as a compensation for the decade he had spent writing it. In the last year or so before going to Hollywood he had been through a truly terrible period in which he found that he could write almost nothing that was salable. As he wrote in his "Crack-Up" pieces for *Esquire* at the time, he felt that he had used up all of his literary capital. Working as a screenwriter in Hollywood in those last years restored a great many things to Fitzgerald, not the least of which was the slow but eventual return of his writing talent.

Faulkner had been able to support himself and his family in an uncertain fashion during the thirties, but he was always running a close, and eventually losing, race with poverty. He was burdened by bankrupt publishers, poor literary agents, and mostly disappointing sales for his novels. All through the thirties he was glad to take the money he earned in Hollywood as a supplement to his basic income, which he derived mainly from the sales of short stories, most often again to the *Post.* By the beginning of 1942 this was no longer possible, for by then all of his short story markets had dried up as completely as had Fitzgerald's five years earlier. To make matters still worse he now found himself further encumbered by the financial demands of his numerous impoverished relatives. All through the years of World War II, Faulkner's entire income consisted of his weekly paychecks from Warner Brothers, for by then all of his books were out of print. There were times in the mid forties when he regarded himself as condemned to be a "lifer" in Southern California, a place he did not like very much.

West's financial dependence upon Hollywood differs from that of Faulkner and Fitzgerald only in that it was total from the very beginning. At no time in his life as a professional writer did West have much of a market for the books he wrote; as a commercial writer West did not exist. It is quite clear that he could never have gone on with his writing at all if he had not had the financial support of his various writing jobs at the smaller Hollywood studios, where he undertook his assignments with an unmatched combination of wry humor and reasonably hard work. Of all the writers in this book he did the most to transform his working experiences in Hollywood to his own advantage as an artist. The result was *The Day of the Locust.*

Both Aldous Huxley and James Agee seem quite apart from Fitzgerald, Faulkner, and West, for neither of these men came to Hollywood looking for any sort of financial salvation. The chances of Huxley's writing screenplays in Hollywood had been on the low side, for his interest in the movies had always been decidedly minimal. When the sound film announced its arrival in 1927 with *The Jazz Singer,* Huxley denounced both in an essay he called "Silence Is Golden." He meant it at the time, but within a single decade he was writing some of the most literate dialogue that has been written for films in the history of the medium. The main thing about the money in Hollywood for Huxley was that as a happily confirmed lifetime settler in Southern California, the money was always there, waiting, very close, a temptation that in time became irresistible to him. He took on his writing tasks for the movies with apparent lightness, but the concern and care he showed for his *Alice in Wonderland* project for Walt Disney was quite genuine.

Unlike the other writers in this book, Agee became a screenwriter almost entirely on the strength of what he had felt and said about film-making, for films were his passion. He had left his reasonably comfortable job on *Time* as chief film critic in order to visit California and write a few longish essays for *Life* about certain of the film-makers he most admired at the time. All of this led to his working with John Huston for a few brief months, but the experience was so powerful that it changed the course of his life entirely, for he spent the rest of it writing for films in one way or another. The money he received for this work became in time his main source of income; things remained that way until the end of his life.

3

We heard that violin sonata of Handel which has the most beautiful of all larghettos; the Bach partita in eight movements; a quartet with oboe, which part was taken by a violin, by a Hungarian composer who was there for the performance. We dined with Charles Laughton, the uncannily amusing and slyly deep actor, who afterwards did a magnificent recitation from The Tempest *in his British English. Neither Paris nor the Munich of 1900 could have provided an evening so rich in intimate artistic spirit, verve, and merriment.*

—*Thomas Mann, Los Angeles, Summer, 1940*

The act of conjuring up the image of a Faulkner or a Huxley endlessly typing away on movie scripts in dingy writers' buildings in a vanished Hollywood is a difficult task for the imagination. In several cases it simply never happened this way, for a number of the directors who hired these writers were after something very different from just getting the services of a scriptwriter. If one reads the accounts of the working methods used by Howard Hawks and Faulkner, or talks with the people who worked with John Huston and Agee, it soon becomes quite evident that these two directors were often as not in quest of the physical presence or ambience of these writers, rather than just someone who typed out words on paper. Hawks put it as succinctly as he could when he once said of Faulkner, "It was awful nice having him around." He meant every word of it.

One of the most enjoyable virtuoso scenes in all of modern films is the famous tea-drinking sequence in Huston's *The African Queen*. This is the episode in which Katharine Hepburn and Robert Morley discover with a gradually increasing sense of horror that it is Bogart's gin-soaked stomach that is making the ferocious rumbling sounds. A great deal of improvisation seems to have gone into this scene, yet if one reads Agee's screenplay it will be seen that everything the actors have done appears on the printed page. The question is inevitable: If it was all down on paper, weren't Huston and his actors just carrying out Agee's instructions?

The answer is that both Huston and Agee shared a strong mutual interest in this scene, as well as many others like it, and they decided to make the most of it. If the Agee script had been given to another director the final result would have been totally different. The fact is that a great part of *The African Queen* is truly a joint effort by James Agee and John Huston.

Fitzgerald, Huxley, and West were not as lucky as Faulkner and Agee in finding directors with whom they could work so profitably, but all five of these writers found screenwriting in Hollywood to be at the very center of their lives for years. Some of the work these men did there is superb, and some of it is quite bad by any standard; but nearly all of it is interesting.

F. Scott Fitzgerald in Hollywood, 1939 (*Scottie Fitzgerald Smith*)

F. Scott
Fitzgerald

*What Do You Do
When There's
Nothing to Do?*

[1]

Nearly everyone who has ever written about Fitzgerald's final years in Hollywood, all three and a half of them, seems to paint pretty much the same sort of sad and grubby portrait of an artist in severe decline. It is a picture of failure all the way, and at the center of it is the image of Fitzgerald himself, wearily working away at all sorts of dismal movie projects that now seem entirely grotesque for a man of his talents and for which he was paid a weekly salary that was reputed to have been scandalously inadequate. A great deal of what we have commonly come to accept about this last period of Fitzgerald's life seems to be sad indeed.

This view of Fitzgerald's Hollywood years as a time of essentially unrelieved misery is one that was in part engendered by Fitzgerald himself, as when he wrote an admonishing but often quite self-pitying letter to his sixteen-year-old daughter, Scottie, in 1938: "You don't realize that what I am doing here is the last tired effort of a man who once did something finer and better. . . ."

All three of Fitzgerald's biographers have taken him very much at his word here; they have seen these final years as desperately unhappy and/or bitterly tragic ones and have written about them accordingly. The tradition of seeing Fitzgerald in Hollywood as a *suffering* man, a *failed* man, really began with Budd Schulberg's novel of 1950, *The Disenchanted,* and is still very much with us in Aaron Latham's recent account of Fitzgerald's film career, *Crazy Sundays*. There are a number of very good reasons for the prevalence of this view, not the least of which is Cyril Connolly's perhaps facetious characterization of Fitzgerald as ". . . an American version of the Dying God, an Adonis of letters, born with the century, flowering in the

18

twenties . . . quietly wilting through the thirties to expire—as a deity of spring and summer should—on December 21, 1940, at the winter solstice and the end of an epoch."

That Fitzgerald had some bad periods in Hollywood, even quite awful ones, admits of little doubt. His health was always a constant source of worry for him, as was frequently his job situation at the studios. His alcoholism was under control most of the time, but it had direct and lasting effects on both his health and the jobs he lost because of it. But what all his biographers have either omitted, distorted, or simply minimized are most of the really *good* things that happened to Fitzgerald in California. These must emphatically include the complete resurrection of his creative powers, seemingly either dead or dormant since 1935—Connolly's risen Adonis indeed. *The Last Tycoon* is very much admired, but the majority of Fitzgerald's chroniclers do not see that only someone who had been totally caught up in the daily life of actually *working* in Hollywood could ever have written such a book—an "insider's" book as much as *The Day of the Locust* and *The Slide Area.*

Fitzgerald's financial gains in Hollywood were considerable enough for him to finally manage getting himself out of debt with Harold Ober, his literary agent and chief financial "backer," as well as Maxwell Perkins *and* Scribners. The combined totals of all these debts were in excess of $40,000, and it took over a year and a half to repay all of them, but Fitzgerald was briefly free of debt for the first time in nearly a decade.

His love affair with Sheilah Graham was the first genuinely lasting sexual relationship he had been able to maintain with a woman since the onrush of Zelda's madness in 1930. The affair did much to restore his self-confidence, and it clearly made up for many of his other losses. Fitzgerald's life back in the East, as well as in the South, during much of 1935 and 1936 had surely been terrible, but his few brief years in California gave him a totally new and different kind of life—a life filled with hope—starting in July 1937 and lasting until the final day of his life.

[2]

. . . I am naturally disappointed about the Post's *not liking the Gwen story and must rest and go to work this afternoon to try to raise some money somehow though I don't know where to turn.*

  —Fitzgerald to Harold Ober, February 8, 1936

The lowest point in the tide of Fitzgerald's fortunes, both creative and financial, occurred during the years 1935 and 1936 and continued without much change into the first half of 1937. These were the years when he had good reason to fear that his writing talent had deserted him. For the first time in nearly two decades his stories were being rejected by editors as fast as he wrote them. These were also the years of his heaviest drinking, for it had become the kind of solitary drinking that would often lead him into the DT's, the attention of a good many doctors, and frequent hospitalizations. His most recent book, the *Taps at Reveille* of 1935, the very last to be published in his lifetime, had sold just under 3,000 copies; Zelda was now incarcerated in the Highlands Sanitarium in Asheville, North Carolina, presumably for the rest of her life. He had actually attempted suicide in September of 1936, shortly after the appearance of an unusually vicious story in the *New York Post* about the way he appeared to their reporter on his fortieth birthday—a shaky and half-hysterical ruin of a man.

The grimmest hour of his entire professional life as a writer may have been in March of 1937. Here is a portion of a letter he wrote from Tryon, North Carolina, to Harold Ober about a story he had just finished:

This will reach you with a story *The Vanished Girl*. It is I think, a pretty good story—at least it reads and isn't muffed, even if the conception isn't very full-bodied.

The point is that I have to sell it right away. I mean I'd rather have a little for it now than a lot in two weeks. On Monday there is income tax—thank God very little, Scotty to get out of school hotel bills + two doctors who are driving me frantic. On a guess I can get by with about $900.00. Do you think Costain would give that—I have absolutely no way to raise the money.

I know all this is poor policy and if I could struggle along until it could get a hearing I would, but it has been a struggle a plenty to get this out—a good eight hours a day for five weeks + This is the only one of four starts to come through at all. I am well, not pessimistic and doing my level best, including 2 mos. on the absolute wagon and the next one will as usual try to be a *Post* story but this just has to be sacrificed for immediate gold. . . . Isn't there some editor who would advance me that much on a delivered story. Tell them anything, tell them you've advanced me the limit but for God's sake raise me something on this story. . . .

The rising note of terror at the very end of this letter may have stirred Ober to do his very best, but he was unable to place the story with the magazine for which it had been written, the short-lived *American Cavalcade,* or with any other magazine, and it has never been published. The stories he wrote at this time were seldom taken up by his main market of the twenties, the *Saturday Evening Post,* but by such lower-paying ones as *Liberty, McCall's,* and *Redbook.* There were good reasons for this, for nearly all of Fitzgerald's fiction written during this period has a curiously weak and lifeless quality to it. It is fiction written by an exhausted man, desperate for sales, who has decided at forty to write in the manner of his twenty-five-year-old self. In their lack of energy, these stories are in extreme contrast to the superbly vivid writing found in his autobiographical pieces published in 1936 as "The Crack-Up" series in *Esquire.* Fitzgerald had not really lost his ability to write—what he needed most in 1937 was something new to write *about.*

This sharp decline in Fitzgerald's powers as a writer of fiction has an oddly similar parallel in the film career of Buster Keaton, whose own decline from both critical and popular favor took place at just about the same time as did that of the man who had published *Tender Is the Night* in 1934. Keaton's sound films of the early thirties for MGM, among them *Streets of New York* (1931), *The Passionate Plumber* (1932), and *What, No Beer?* (1933), are all pictures that feature Keaton simply as a comic actor, no longer the producer-director of his films. In all of these pictures he walked his way through his roles as a somnambulist might, tightly constrained in parts that were to- tally unsuited to him. He had become clodhopper "Elmer," a crude country-bumpkin type totally unlike the incredibly and specifically *precise* principal characters in *The Navigator* and *The General.* With equally catastrophic results, Fitzgerald at- tempted to write a long "medieval romance," *The Count of Darkness,* for *Redbook,* another attempt to recoup his fortunes and a book he never did finish. Both Fitzgerald and Keaton were facing very much the same pressures: sudden, violent changes in popular taste, equally strong emotional upheavals in their private lives, and alcohol operating simultaneously as the cause *and* effect of nearly everything they did.

Hollywood was very much in Fitzgerald's mind from the time of the publication of *Tender Is the Night* until the day of his departure for MGM in July of 1937. Despite widely held views to the contrary, the book was a success of sorts. In the year 1934 it actually sold 13,000 copies, easily earning a spot halfway up the best seller lists, where it remained for nine weeks. The serialization of the book in *Scribner's Magazine* just before publication greatly increased its readership, a fact not lost on Hollywood. There were immediate nibbles from a number of sources, finally settling down to a reasonably "serious" interest from both RKO Radio and Sam Goldwyn. It is more than likely that the other studios were frightened off by the incest theme that is at the heart of Nicole's illness. The people at RKO saw the book as a property for Katharine Hep- burn, as long as there were "some changes" made, but nothing ever came of their strong early interest. The Goldwyn organi- zation went further; they actually had a full treatment pre- pared by one of their own writers and then tentatively invited Fitzgerald to come out to Hollywood in early 1935 to rework it. Everything was rather vague, especially the money, and Fitzgerald was decidedly not anxious to go to Hollywood at that time—things simply weren't that bad yet. He wrote to Ober about the situation: ". . . the question of going to California. I hate the place with a sincere hatred. It will be inconvenient in every way and I should consider it only as an emergency measure." He did not care to tell Ober that he and Charles Warren, his young friend in Baltimore, had already collaborated on their own 10,000-word screen treatment of *Tender Is the Night* and that Warren had unsuccessfully peddled it all over Hollywood.

No one knew better than Ober that Fitzgerald's best hope for the future might lie in California. In December of 1935 he told Fitzgerald:

I have been talking to Merritt Hulburd, who is with Samuel Goldwyn, about the possibility of your doing some work in Hollywood. They have a Somerset Maugham book which Merritt says you might be interested to work on. . . . Do you think you would be well enough to go out there for a while early in the year? If you could do a really good job out there it might be the solution of your difficulties . . . let me know if you want to go to Hollywood and if you think you are well enough. I am sure that if you live quietly there and work hard and make a business of saving money that you could do a lot to get yourself out of the hole you are now in . . . there is no reason why you shouldn't get enough money ahead to give you freedom to write a novel when you get ready to write one. . . .

Fitzgerald's answer to Ober's letter is extremely revealing about what he really thought of Hollywood and his chances there, a full eighteen months before signing his contract with MGM:

I'd have gone to Hollywood a year ago last spring. I don't think I could do it now but I might. Especially if there was no choice. Twice I have worked out there on other people's stories * with John Considine telling me the plot twice a week and the Katherine Brush story—it simply fails to use what qualities I have. I don't blame you for lecturing me since I have seriously inconvenienced you, but it would be hard to change my temperament in middle-life. No single

---

* *This refers to Fitzgerald's 1927 and 1931 visits to Hollywood in connection with the unproduced* Lipstick *and MGM's* Red-Headed Woman.

man with a serious literary reputation has made good there. If I could form a partnership with some technical expert it might be done. . . . I'd need a man who knew the game, knew the people, but would help me tell and sell my story—*not his*. This man would be hard to find, because a *smart* technician doesn't want or need a partner, and an uninspired one is inclined to have a dread of ever touching tops. . . . I'm afraid unless some such break occurs I'd be no good in the industry.

In the year or so before he finally secured a contract with MGM, Fitzgerald's situation became progressively worse. He was often forced to wire Ober for money for his daily living expenses, with Maxwell Perkins occasionally coming to the rescue when Ober found himself unable to advance any further amounts. By May of 1937 Ober had been unable to place a Fitzgerald story in any magazine for nearly a year. Fitzgerald's royalty statements from Scribners were equally dispiriting; in 1936 his total earnings from *all* his books, and they were all in print, was $81.18. He was very nearly at the end of all his financial resources. With the death of his mother in September of 1936, he received a share of her small estate, but this only postponed the inevitable. His thoughts turned more and more frequently to Hollywood as the only real hope left open to him. Ober obligingly did his very best, but the prospects seemed slim:

I don't think you can count on anything from Hollywood at the present time. I think the days are over when an author with a good name can go out to Hollywood for a month or two and pick up a sizable amount of money. They would rather have a dramatist that has written a play that is a flop, whom they can get on a long contract at a moderate salary. . . .

Ober's letter may not have concealed the fact that Fitzgerald's name was not as good as it had once been, and that this was not entirely due to his present writing difficulties. In August of 1936, a picture deal with RKO Radio was held up "temporarily," and Ober was forced to tell Fitzgerald that it was ". . . because a friend of one of the men said he had seen you in New York when you had been drinking. I have assured them you have not been drinking this year and I think and hope things can be straightened out in a few days. . . ." They couldn't be, and the deal fell through in the end, with Fitzgerald returning to the writing of further unsalable stories. When be became utterly desperate, he would occasionally bypass Ober and send these stories off to the editors himself; it made no difference, they came back just as fast.

It was Edwin H. Knopf, at that time working for MGM in various capacities—director, producer, writer, and story editor—who managed to convince his colleagues at the studio that Fitzgerald would make a valuable addition to their staff of writers. This was not easy for him to do, for the publication of "The Crack-Up" pieces in *Esquire* in the spring of 1936 had done much to convince a great many people that Fitzgerald had become something of a hopeless case, both as a man and as a writer. Knopf refused to believe that this had happened, and it was actually his own reading of the pieces that made him painfully aware of the severity of Fitzgerald's problems. The two men had gotten to know each other in France at the end of the twenties, with Knopf always very much an admirer of Fitzgerald, both as a man and as a writer. So much so, that he still had enough confidence in his old friend to begin the extremely long and drawn-out negotiations that finally resulted in Fitzgerald's being hired by MGM after a great many delays and postponements. As month after month passed, there seemed to be an on-again, off-again quality to the hiring process that was particularly painful to Fitzgerald, causing him on one occasion to write Ober: "I'm anxiously waiting for news—no news is no doubt bad news. *Why don't I just go to the coast + let them see me.* I haven't had a drop in two months + feel fine. There's nothing I'd like better for immediate cash + a future foothold. . . ."

There were still further delays in Culver City, and Fitzgerald was soon forced to start sending wires like this one to Ober:

TO REMAIN HERE AND EAT MUST HAVE ONE HUNDRED AND THIRTY TODAY PLEASE ASK PERKINS.

Ober's reply was immediate:

MAX AND I WILL ARRANGE DEPOSIT BETWEEN US.

Ober finally arranged a lunch between Knopf and Fitzgerald in New York in June, with Knopf offering him a standard six-month contract at $1,000 a week, with an attached renewal option at $1,250 a week for the following year. It was everything Fitzgerald had hoped for, and he left for Hollywood, by train, in early July of 1937.

[3]

You either have credits, or you don't have credits.
—*Fitzgerald, 1937*

Work hard, Mr. Fitzgerald, work hard!
—*Joan Crawford, 1938*

Since Fitzgerald in his Hollywood years has most often been depicted as a trembling wreck of a man, it would be interesting to know how he actually appeared to the people around him at MGM, when he reported for work in Culver City that summer of 1937. There are a few such reports. Here is how Anthony Powell recalls Fitzgerald at the time of their lunch at the MGM commissary on July 20, about two weeks after Fitzgerald's arrival in Hollywood:

He was smallish, neat, solidly built, wearing a light grey suit and lightish tie, all his tones essentially light. Photographs—seen for the most part years later—do not do justice to him. Possibly he was a person who at once became self-conscious when before a camera. Even snapshots tend to give him a kind of cockiness he did not at all possess. On the contrary, one was immediately aware of an odd sort of unassuming dignity. There was no hint at all of the cantankerousness that undoubtedly lay beneath the surface. His air could be thought a trifle sad, but not in the least broken down, as he has sometimes been described at this period. . . .

This was Powell's only meeting with Fitzgerald, but he never forgot the quality of the joyous enthusiasm and curiosity about things and people that Fitzgerald displayed on that long afternoon. By chance, Powell's lunch at MGM took place on the day Fitzgerald first dined with Sheilah Graham. Here is the way she recalled her first real glimpse of Fitzgerald, at a dinner dance at the Coconut Grove, a week before that dinner:

I found him most appealing; his hair pale blond, a wide attractive forehead, gray blue eyes set far apart, set beautifully in his head, a straight, sharply chiseled nose. . . . He appeared to be in his forties but it was difficult to know, he looked half-young and half-old; the thought flashed through my mind, he should get out into the sun. . . .

She danced with him for the first time a few days later: ". . . on the floor he was like an American college boy. He was only a few inches taller than I but he was sinewy, strong, and firm, his step gay and youthful. . . ."

Both Miss Graham's and Powell's physical descriptions of Fitzgerald at this time, as well as those of his general manner, differ quite markedly from those of all three of his biographers, beginning with Arthur Mizener's *The Far Side of Paradise* in 1951. Neither Mizener nor Piper ever met Fitzgerald, while Turnbull's friendship with him was mainly confined to Turnbull's childhood and youth. When Mizener brought his biography up to date in 1965, to include information on Sheilah Graham, he chose to suggest Fitzgerald's appearance in Hollywood in 1939 by quoting at length from Budd Schulberg's 1960 *Esquire* piece on him, "Old Scott":

There seemed to be no colors in him. The proud, somewhat too handsome profile of his early dust-jackets was crumpled. . . . The fine forehead, the leading man's nose, the matinee-idol set of the gentle, quick-to-smile eyes, the good Scotch-Irish cheekbones, the delicate, almost feminine mouth, the tasteful Eastern (in fact, Brooks Bros.) attire—he had lost none of these. But there seemed to be something physically or psychologically broken in him that had pitched him forward from scintillating youth to shaken old age.

An earlier, much shorter, but essentially the same sort of description had appeared in the pages of Schulberg's *The Disenchanted*—the book that is the ultimate source for all these "ruined, shattered man" descriptions, most of which are usually accompanied by discussions of Fitzgerald's "failure" in Hollywood. If Fitzgerald did not in fact strike other observers as being as badly off as Schulberg would have us believe, we may reasonably wonder why Schulberg wrote the way he did, why this constant emphasis on the word "failure." There are a number of perfectly plausible reasons, perhaps the main one being that Schulberg's most vivid recollection of Fitzgerald is surely that of his playing nursemaid to him on their ill-fated, disastrously drunken trip to Dartmouth College for the film *Winter Carnival* in February of 1939. Besides nearly costing him his job with Walter Wanger, this experience furnished Schulberg with the only convincing scene in his novel.

There may be still other reasons. Fitzgerald had put his knowledge of Schulberg's childhood and youth in California, as well as his general sensibility, to good use when he created the character of Cecilia in *The Last Tycoon*. It is quite possible that Schulberg, for quite understandable reasons, may never have really forgiven Fitzgerald for this "borrowing" of his feelings. There was always a certain rivalry at work between them, with Fitzgerald, however, having sharp reservations about the nature of Schulberg's literary talent. Although perfectly willing to endorse Schulberg's *What Makes Sammy Run?* for Bennett Cerf of Random House, Fitzgerald's own private view of the book was scarcely enthusiastic. His final summation of Schulberg as a writer was tersely expressed in his *Notebooks:* "*Budd, the untalented.*"

Actually, Fitzgerald didn't really need Budd Schulberg to proclaim him a failure after his death, for he had done a pretty good job of that himself in "The Crack-Up" pieces for *Esquire,* published over a year before his arrival in Hollywood. In those pages he allowed himself what proved to be a prophetic look at certain aspects of film-making:

I saw that the novel, which at my maturity was the strongest and supplest medium for conveying thought and emotion from one human being to another, was becoming subordinated to a communal art that, whether in the hands of Hollywood merchants or Russian idealists, was capable of reflecting only the tritest thought, the most obvious emotion. It was an art in which words were subordinate to images, where personality was worn down to the inevitable low gear of collaboration. As long past as 1930, I had a hunch that the talkies would make even the best-selling novelist as archaic as silent pictures . . . there was a rankling indignity, that to me had become almost an obsession, in seeing the power of the written word subordinated to another power, a more glittering, a grosser power. . . .

Fitzgerald regarded this "grosser power" of the film with a great deal of suspicion and even fear, obviously feeling it was a medium that surely threatened his own. His intense dislike of collaboration in any form, perhaps the one thing that plagued him most of all in his MGM days, originated in his having had to work with Marcel de Sano in 1931 on their ill-fated version of *Red-Headed Woman* for Thalberg. There is also in this passage from "The Crack-Up" a note of what seems to be downright hostility to films, no matter who made them or for what purpose—a sort of total distrust. He may well have felt that film was the perfect medium for "failures."

A "failure" in Hollywood would not really be expected to make very much money there, but Fitzgerald made quite a bit. He earned a weekly salary of $1,000 at MGM for the last six months of 1937 and $1,250 per week for all of 1938, the second year he spent under contract to MGM. During this second year he worked an actual total of forty-five weeks and was paid a total of $68,000 by the studio. By the standards of the seventies, this last sum would approximate a salary of $200,000 a year—all this at a time when income taxes were either tiny or nonexistent.

To give some concrete idea as to just where Fitzgerald fits into the earning hierarchy of Hollywood screenwriters of this period, I have reproduced the table in Leo C. Rosten's classic sociological account of life in Hollywood at the very end of the thirties: *Hollywood: The Movie Colony, the Movie Makers.*

In his weekly earnings at MGM Fitzgerald fell somewhere between the eighty-third and the ninety-first percentiles at the top of the scale; out of a total of the 228 writers surveyed *not more than a maximum of 18 were paid more than he was.* From

WEEKLY SALARIES OF WRITERS AT
THREE MAJOR HOLLYWOOD
STUDIOS: 1938

	Number	Percent
Less than $250	93	40.8
$250–$499	52	22.8
$500–$749	36	15.8
$750–$999	17	7.5
$1,000–$1,249	11	4.8
$1,250–$1,499	5	2.2
$1,500–$1,749	7	3.1
$1,750–$1,999	3	1.3
$2,000–$2,249	—	—
$2,250–$2,499	—	—
$2,500–$2,749	3	1.3
$2,750–$2,999	—	—
$3,000–$3,249	1	.4
Total	228	100.0

Note: The survey is based on an analysis of the payroll data of
Twentieth Century-Fox, Warner Brothers, and Columbia Pictures Corporation.

all this, there can be little doubt that Fitzgerald's earning
power as a writer was among the highest possible in all of
Hollywood for 1938. He always received a great deal more
than did many of his famous contemporaries who had gone
out there just "for the money." Faulkner, as will be shown,
could only command a weekly salary of $300 at Warner
Brothers as late as the mid forties; Nathanael West received
$350 from Republic Pictures, but only after he had worked
for them for nearly four years. While it is true that
Fitzgerald's Hollywood earnings fell off sharply after MGM
failed to renew his contract at the end of 1938, his pay scale at
Universal, Paramount, and Twentieth Century-Fox remained
pretty much in line with his original MGM salary. His low
point as a screenwriter was the $300 a week he received from
Lester Cowan in 1940 while working on his own "Babylon
Revisited" script.

When Sheilah Graham first met Fitzgerald in 1937 she

thought his $1,000 a week salary an absolute "fortune." She had good reason to think so, for despite the fact that she was nationally syndicated by the North American Newspaper Alliance, she was earning $160 per week. She may well have wondered what this quietly withdrawn man did with all his money, but the answer was simple enough, for he was rarely able to keep more than half the money he was paid.

At the beginning of his first MGM contract he had agreed to send Ober $600 each week in order to pay him back what he owed him plus the weekly commissions due him for having gotten him the job. The remainder of the $600 was to be used to repay his personal loan from Maxwell Perkins as well as his debt to Scribners. In addition, Ober also agreed to set up various bank accounts so that Fitzgerald could pay his income taxes and provide for his vacations. The remaining $400 per week was to pay his current living expenses, including all those entailed in having a young daughter at Vassar, as well as those incurred by the monthly hospital bills for Zelda in North Carolina. When he was not drinking, which was most of the time, he lived quite frugally, driving an old secondhand Ford to work each day.

Fitzgerald's only real extravagance during this first year or so in Hollywood was the $400 a month rent he paid on his apartment at the Garden of Allah Hotel on Sunset Boulevard. Now demolished and reduced to the status of a large parking lot, just one of many in Los Angeles, the "Garden" was thought at the time to be a lavishly exotic place to live. Fitzgerald would defend the expense as a necessary one by telling people that his professional status as a writer demanded such an address, for in the late thirties the Garden was the main congregating place for many of the Eastern writers in Hollywood. It had been built originally as the residence of the twenties film star Alla Nazimova, a collection of bungalows clustered around a large swimming pool constructed in the shape of the Black Sea—its owner's birthplace was Yalta. Robert Benchley lived there for years, and it was at his bungalow that Fitzgerald first met Sheilah Graham.

He lived at the Garden from the time of his arrival in Hollywood until November of 1938. Sheilah Graham was the one responsible for finally getting him away from the place, she being well aware that the steady company of the heavy drinkers there was bad for him. As for the rest of his money, during the entire course of his time in Hollywood Fitzgerald spent a great deal of it on nurses and doctors, some of this because of his hypochondria, but most of it connected with his alcoholism. He wrote Ober in 1939 that every trip East he had taken in 1937 and 1938 had wound up in a binge that eventually required his being hospitalized.

After his salary was raised to $1,250 per week at the beginning of 1938, basically the same sort of financial arrangements were followed with Ober, but they became less rigid, with Fitzgerald tending to keep more and more of his salary as his debts slowly faded away back East. This was the first extended period of genuine financial security he had known since Zelda's first breakdown in 1930. When it became seriously threatened at the beginning of 1939, he took it very badly, for he had become totally accustomed to these weekly paychecks. The loss of this money eventually drove him back into his former relationship with Ober, actually a form of living on credit.

With his ever-recurrent family expenses, as well as his own, Fitzgerald found it unbearable to consider any serious reduction in his earnings. It was only when screenwriting jobs became scarce or nonexistent that he finally settled down to writing The Last Tycoon. Even then his financial demands were high. In the course of his ultimately unsatisfactory negotiations with Kenneth Littauer of Collier's for the serialization rights to The Last Tycoon, Fitzgerald clearly indicated that the notion of receiving $15,000 for four months' work on the book was simply not enough for him to get by on at that time—he needed at least $20,000 or $25,000 from them. He wrote Perkins in October of 1939, telling him just why he needed so much: "But (without taking such steps as reneging on my income tax, letting go my life insurance for its surrender value, taking Scottie from college and putting Zelda in a public asylum) I couldn't last four months on that. Certain debts have been run up so that the larger part of the $15,000 has been, *so to speak,* spent already.* This quietly expressed "so to speak" meant just what it said—that although he was again in debt, he could still command a relatively high price for his work, even risking the loss of $15,000.

Merely citing the fact that Fitzgerald had the ability to earn quite a lot of money in Hollywood would never suffice to acquit him of all the familiar "failure" charges: Is he not, after all, the author of that famous phrase, "I talk with the authority of failure"? Didn't he himself often consider his screenwriting career as another of his failures? He certainly did, especially after any sort of defeat. Fitzgerald's entire life can be seen as a never-ending series of these success/failure fluctuations in which there was never a middle ground, only violent extremes. If he couldn't impress Hollywood as a living composite of Robert Riskin, Jules Furthman, Ben Hecht, and Anita Loos, then it was surely clear to everyone that he was a total, absolute failure at screenwriting—or so he liked to tell people.

This constant habit of putting himself down is quite similar to what he had apparently felt in the early twenties when Hemingway first appeared on the scene; a feeling that his own efforts as a writer had been made strangely *unnecessary.* In a memorial tribute written just a month or so after Fitzgerald's death, Glenway Wescott remembered what he called this "morbid belittlement," recalling that Fitzgerald had

felt that Hemingway was inimitably, essentially superior. From the moment Hemingway began to appear in print, perhaps it did not matter what he himself produced or failed to produce. He felt free to write just for profit, and to live for fun, if possible. Hemingway could be entrusted with the graver responsibilities and higher rewards such as glory, immortality. . . .

In 1925, when Hemingway and his wife, Hadley, were invited to lunch at the Fitzgeralds' gloomy and airless furnished apartment on the Rue Tilsit in Paris, Fitzgerald showed them his ledger, an experience Hemingway recalled thirty-five years later:

* *Italics added.*

Scott also showed us a large ledger with all of the stories he had published listed in it year after year with the prices he had received for them and also the amounts received for any motion picture sales, and the sales and royalties of his books. They were all noted as carefully as the log of a ship and Scott showed them to us with impersonal pride as though he were the curator of a museum. Scott was nervous and hospitable and he showed us his accounts of his earnings as though they had been the view. There was no view.

[4]

From now on I go nowhere and see no one because the work is hard as hell. . . .
—*Fitzgerald to Anne Ober, July 1937*

Everything I have ever done or written is me. . . .
—*Fitzgerald to Harold Ober, July 1939*

. . . you know about Fitzgerald weeping because Jos. Mankiewicz fiddled with his work, rewriting it, which gives you an idea how seriously these folk took the work, how tortured and tortuous the work was. . . .
—*Daniel Fuchs to Tom Dardis, May 1975*

During his year and a half with MGM Fitzgerald was assigned to a total of six different film projects. Of these six, one was a partial rewriting of another MGM writer's original script, *A Yank at Oxford*, actually a polishing or patching job. Four of the assignments resulted in his writing screenplays based on the literary works of other writers: *Three Comrades, Infidelity, The Women,* and *Madame Curie.* The other assignment, *Marie Antoinette*, lasted for only a few days before he was transferred to work on *The Women*. All the films he worked on, with the exception of *Infidelity*, were eventually produced, but Fitzgerald managed to earn only one actual screen credit at MGM, that for his work on *Three Comrades*.

A Yank at Oxford was unusual in that it was produced entirely in England by Michael Balcon (now Sir Michael) as the very first "MGM-British" joint production effort, a short-lived experiment that utilized the combination of MGM's money and British producers to make such films as *The Citadel* and *Goodbye, Mr. Chips*. The idea to make a comedy about the adventures of an American Rhodes Scholar at Oxford had been an MGM story department "project" for years, until the day L. B. Mayer made his deal with Balcon, at which time it was given priority for immediate production as a vehicle for the rising Robert Taylor.

Besides being generally regarded as the discoverer of Hitchcock, Balcon is best known as the producer of such diverse films as *The Thirty-nine Steps, Next of Kin, Dead of Night, Kind Hearts and Coronets,* and *Tom Jones,* as well as for heading up such English firms as Gaumont-British, Ealing Films, and Gainsborough Pictures. In his recent autobiography, *A Lifetime of Films,* Balcon refers pretty consistently to L. B. Mayer as "the unspeakable Mayer," making it quite clear why he could simply not work for Mayer under any circumstances; MGM-British was dissolved within two years of its creation, with *A Yank at Oxford* one of the very few reminders that it ever existed.

Balcon claims that Ben Hecht was MGM's first choice to write the script for *Yank,* but that Hecht declined because he "knew nothing of college life," an unlikely story knowing Hecht's history as a screenwriter. Herman Mankiewicz, the co-author of *Citizen Kane* and another reputed Hollywood "failure," was the next in line, but he proved to be unavailable because of "drink." The assignment was finally placed in the hands of Frank (Commander) Wead, an MGM staff writer. He had nearly completed his version of the script when Fitzgerald arrived for work; Wead's script was immediately placed in the hands of the man who had written *This Side of Paradise*. Balcon's memories of Fitzgerald's part in the making of *Yank* are understandably hazy, for these are recollections about a man he had met once thirty years previously, but who had somehow turned out to be an important writer. He concludes his account this way: "To my regret he could work up no interest in *A Yank at Oxford,* although he had written about university life and the reason for putting him on the script was that he 'understood' young people. . . . I found all this very sad indeed."

None of this was true, for he did work up quite an interest in the subject, as can be seen from the pages and pages he wrote about it. Nor was it all that sad, for this was actually the easiest task given to Fitzgerald in all his time at MGM. He was told to add some sort of a "collegiate gloss" to Wead's nearly complete script, and he did so, demonstrating a good deal of knowledge and enthusiasm for the job. The plot of *Yank* concerned the initial disdain young Lee Sheridan (Taylor) feels for both Oxford and England and his slowly changing state of mind about them, mainly as a result of his feelings about two female students, played by Vivien Leigh and Maureen O'Sullivan. One of Fitzgerald's intentions was to sharpen the characterization of the woman played by O'Sullivan by writing some new dialogue for her, explaining his intentions in long memos to all concerned.

He also set himself the task of convincing Balcon and the other people at MGM that his new dialogue was better than Commander Wead's. He tried to prove it by rewriting the scene in the railway coach, en route to Oxford, in which Molly (O'Sullivan) has her first encounter with Lee Sheridan, who is in the company of her brother Paul. Fitzgerald handed in his new dialogue typed up side by side with that written by Wead (Fitzgerald's is on the right), prefaced by his "Here is the scene as written and as it might be":

MOLLY

I thought I'd have some coffee with you.
(she discovers Lee, and pauses with a startled look)
Oh!

PAUL (with an ironical smile)
Quite!
(his tone changing)
This is Lee Sheridan of America entering Cardinal—my sister.

MOLLY

Room for one more?

(She discovers Lee)

PAUL

This is Lee Sheridan of America, entering Cardinal—my sister, *of St. Cynthia's.*

MOLLY (Reserved, but curious)
How do you do?
(Lee is regarding her with evident admiration)

LEE
Glad to meet you Miss Beaumont. Very glad.
(Turning to Paul)
Say—is your sister a fair sample of English girls?

PAUL (A flicker in his eye)
Oh, I think we can do better than that.
(Molly makes a face at him.)

MOLLY (reserved but curious)
How do you do? *American?*

LEE (regarding her with evident admiration)
Glad to know you. *How'd you know I was American?*

MOLLY
Second sight.
(to the others)
Are you putting him on to things?

PAUL
We're doing our best.

Fitzgerald spent between two and three weeks on this, and some of his original dialogue can still be heard at screenings of *A Yank at Oxford,* but he received no screen credit for his work—nor, for that matter, did Commander Wead. Officially, the screenwriting was the work of Malcolm Stewart Boylan, Walter Ferris, and George Oppenheimer, all of whom had been assigned to the film after Wead and Fitzgerald; in the screen-credit business, it was often best to be last. Besides learning again the rudiments of screenwriting, probably the best thing about the whole experience for Fitzgerald was the apparently delightful lunch he had one day with Maureen O'Sullivan.

More has been written about Fitzgerald's work on *Three Comrades* than any of the other films he worked on at MGM, and there are good reasons for this. Most of his biographers have singled out his bitter quarrel over the rewriting of his script by Joseph L. Mankiewicz as being perhaps the most devastating thing that happened to him in Hollywood, the thing that jaundiced him about the *control* other people now had over his work as a writer. There is certainly some justifica-

tion for this belief, for it is a fact that Fitzgerald wrote a total
of seven different versions of this script for Mankiewicz,
whom he later liked to refer to in letters as "Monkeybitch,"
and that he took six months of his time at MGM to do so.
There is little doubt that he considered the script he had written to be both good and "serious" work on his part, and that
he regarded Mankiewicz's cavalier treatment of it to be a savage desecration of what he had done. There is a generous
amount of surviving correspondence about the writing of
Three Comrades, most of it from Fitzgerald's point of view, and
over the years the quarrel has taken on the familiar aspect of
the serious artist in conflict with the philistine boors of com-
merce. The truth of the matter is a lot more tangled than this,
and the whole episode shows pretty clearly what Fitzgerald
had let himself in for when he signed his MGM contract.

The traditional villain of the controversy is Joseph L. Mankiewicz, who started out in Hollywood in the late twenties as a
screenwriter at Paramount, the studio where his older
brother, Herman, had established himself some years earlier.
While at Paramount he wrote the scripts for such films as
Million Dollar Legs in 1932 and for their *Alice in Wonderland* the
following year. By the mid thirties he had become a producer
at MGM, with such films as Fritz Lang's *Fury* and George
Cukor's *Philadelphia Story* to his credit. After the war Mankiewicz began writing and directing his own pictures, some of
them quite well-known indeed: *Letter to Three Wives* and *All
About Eve.* A bit on the magisterial side, at least as seen in his
occasional television appearances as well as in a number of published interviews, he has remained tirelessly urbane, a professional maker of movies for nearly fifty years. It was Mankiewicz who was sent to Rome in 1962 to salvage the $20 million
that Twentieth Century-Fox had invested in its *Cleopatra.*

When general interest in Fitzgerald was reawakened in the
early fifties, Mankiewicz was suddenly faced with a much more
difficult problem than that of Michael Balcon. The publication
of Fitzgerald's letters about the writing of *Three Comrades* became a source of profound embarrassment to him. One letter
in particular was extremely distasteful to Mankiewicz, and he

was able to dissuade Edmund Wilson from printing it in the 1945 *Crack-Up* collection. However, Mizener did print it, and it has since become one of the most reprinted of all Fitzgerald's letters. After having received the pages containing all of Mankiewicz's revisions of *Three Comrades,* Fitzgerald wrote him a detailed criticism, concluding his letter on this note:

My only hope is that you will *have a moment of clear thinking.* That you'll ask some intelligent* and *disinterested* person to look at the two scripts. Some honest thinking would be much more valuable to the enterprise right now than an effort to convince people you've improved it. I am utterly miserable at seeing months of work and thought negated in one hasty week. I hope you're big enough to take this letter as it's meant—a desperate plea to restore the dialogue to its former quality—to put back the flower cart, the piano-moving, the balcony, the manicure girl—all those touches that were both natural and new. Oh, Joe, can't producers ever be wrong? I'm a good writer—honest. I thought you were going to play fair. Joan Crawford might as well play the part now, for the thing is as groggy with sentimentality as *The Bride Wore Red,* but the true emotion is gone.

Mankiewicz has always insisted that he never received this letter, and he may be telling the truth, but it would have made no difference if he had gotten it. He has consistently reacted to questions about what happened early in 1938 in about the only way he could, by simply claiming that he thought he was right then, and that he still thinks so today:

I personally have been attacked as if I had spat on the American flag because it happened once that I rewrote some dialogue by F. Scott Fitzgerald. But indeed it needed it! The actors, among them Margaret Sullavan, absolutely could not read the lines. It was very literary dialogue, novelistic dialogue that lacked all the qualities required for screen dialogue. The latter must be "spoken." Scott Fitzgerald wrote very bad spoken dialogue.

The novel on which Fitzgerald based his disputed screenplay was Erich Maria Remarque's best seller of 1937, a book that dealt with the lives of three young veterans of World War I in the inflation-cursed Germany of the early 1920s. As

---

* Fitzgerald's emphasis.

filmed, the three were portrayed by Robert Taylor, Franchot Tone, and Robert Young, with Margaret Sullavan as the mortally ill girl in love with Taylor.

Fitzgerald was assigned to prepare a treatment for Mankiewicz of *Three Comrades* on August 4, 1937, and after having completed this was given the go-ahead to write the final shooting-script by himself, apparently doing so by the first of September. By the middle of October he had been given a collaborator in the person of E. E. (Ted) Paramore, an old acquaintance of Fitzgerald's from his early days in New York, but never much of a friend. Why was Paramore brought in at this point? Mankiewicz seems to have felt that Fitzgerald required a helping hand on the project, although he was perfectly well aware of Fitzgerald's dislike of such help. At one point Mankiewicz denied he had any intention of bringing in another writer:

I HAVE READ THE STUFF AND THINK IT SIMPLY SWELL WHERE DID YOU GET THAT BUSHWAH ABOUT ANOTHER WRITER BEST WISHES FOR A HAPPY THIRD ACT AND COME BACK AS SOON AS YOU CAN.

The need for a collaborator arose after Mankiewicz had read the first draft of Fitzgerald's script. It included sequences that disquieted not only Mankiewicz but perhaps others as well. At one point in the draft, Bobby (Robert Taylor) is attempting to place a telephone call to the girl Pat (Margaret Sullavan) whom he has just met the previous night. As written, the scene may have been Fitzgerald's attempt at what used to be known as the "Lubitsch Touch":

54   A SWITCHBOARD—
     —with a white winged angel sitting at it
          Angel (sweetly)
     One moment, please—I'll connect you with heaven.
                                             CUT TO:
55   THE PEARLY GATES
     St. Peter, the caretaker, sitting beside another switchboard.
          St. Peter (cackling)
     I think she's in.
                                             CUT TO:
56   BOBBY'S FACE
     —still ecstatic, changing to human embarrassment as Pat's voice says:

PAT
Hello
57   A SATYR, who has replaced the angel at the switchboard—
     —pulling out the plug with a sardonic expression.
                                              CUT TO:

How could Fitzgerald write something quite as bad as this? Was Mankiewicz perhaps right in thinking that Fitzgerald had a good deal to learn about screenwriting—that only a rank amateur could have come up with a scene so absolutely wrong for the film? Fitzgerald had always brought a certain arrogance to almost everything he had ever attempted, and the movies were no exception. He seems to have regarded them as a trade like any other and to have felt that a close study of the medium would guarantee success. After all, in 1919 he had studied the *Saturday Evening Post* carefully, and it had worked. During his first few months in Hollywood, Fitzgerald gave himself up to what amounted to a crash course in screenwriting. He had the studio screen dozens of MGM's greatest hits of the previous fifteen years; he typed up hundreds of file cards containing the plot lines of all the successful films ever made by the studio. When Faulkner was exposed to his first screening of an MGM film he fled the room in horror, but Fitzgerald sat calmly through all of them, constantly taking notes on everything he saw and heard. There was an ingrown quality to all this study; he was constantly looking back at things that had been done in the past. This tendency to do things the "way they were supposed to be done" was something that plagued almost all his work for the movies, even that work that meant the most to him emotionally.

There is a quite well-known letter of Fitzgerald's to his daughter, written on board the train taking him to California, which spoke of his two previous visits to Hollywood and of his resolve not to make the same mistakes again:

I want to profit by these two experiences—I must be very tactful but keep my hand on the wheel from the start—find out the key man among the bosses and the most malleable among the collaborators—then fight the rest tooth and nail until, in fact or in effect, I'm alone on the picture. That's the only way I can do my best work. Given a break I can make them double this contract in less than two years.

All his arrogance is certainly here, but there is also his clearly stated intention to work with film producers rather than with film directors, here downgraded to the rank of "collaborators." Actually, Fitzgerald seems to have had no use whatsoever for directors as such. On several occasions he referred to Frank Borzage, his director on *Three Comrades,* as "a glorified cameraman." From a purely self-serving point of view Fitzgerald could have justified his working with the ultimate power in the studio, but there is no doubt that by avoiding contact with the directors at MGM he missed a lot about the really workaday side of film production. All his major contacts at the studios he worked for were with the men of power: Mankiewicz, Stromberg, Wanger, and, toward the end, Nunnally Johnson and Lester Cowan.

There should not have been the slightest doubt in Fitzgerald's mind that Mankiewicz was in fact the producer of *Three Comrades,* and that he obviously did not like what he had seen of Fitzgerald's attempt to go it alone on the script. It was predictable that Fitzgerald would not get along with his enforced collaborator, E. E. Paramore, and that they would be quarreling bitterly within a week or so after their first encounter. They had never really gotten along very well in the past, and now they were both trying hard to impress Mankiewicz with very different viewpoints about the direction his production should take. Fitzgerald naturally tended to have the more "adventuresome" approach of the two, with Paramore wishing to play it safe. Or at least this is the way Fitzgerald saw the situation, despite the fact that his approach to the problems of the script was not really adventuresome *enough* for Mankiewicz, and that his work was occasionally either stodgy or overly romantic in the worst sense. Here is an excerpt from a scene in which Pat and Bobby are riding in a flower wagon, discussing their affair:

> BOBBY
> (puts his arm around her with a passion that belies his words)
> But you'd better not get lost in here, because I'd never be able to pick you out from the other flowers.
> (His arm around her—she lies closely to him.)

PAT
I'm not this kind of flower. I'm afraid I'm the hothouse variety.
   (she picks up a blossom and addresses it rather sadly)
I'd love to be like you, my dear

   BOBBY (holding her close to him; passionately)
Oh you are—you are!

Despite Fitzgerald's violent objections, Mankiewicz removed this scene from the final script, apparently believing it to be entirely too romantic for the film he had in mind. In his first draft Fitzgerald had written a very brief scene in which Pat talks with Bobby about going home from the sanatorium when she has recovered her health:

   PAT (shading her eyes)
Is that the road home?

   BOBBY
Yes.

   PAT
How far is it?

   BOBBY
About five hundred miles. In May you'll be starting back along that road. Otto and I will come and get you.

   PAT
In May, My God, in May!

                                        FADEOUT

In the final script this scene has become greatly expanded, and Pat and Bobby are depicted as talking in a hospital room in the snowy mountains of a place like Davos or Gstaad:

   PAT (a pause, then she turns to him smiling)
This isn't what we're supposed to say, this first time together.
   (he looks at her puzzled)
All these months I'd figured out what you would say and I would say—word for word. Do you want to hear?
   (he nods, smiling)
We'd be sitting here on the foot of the bed like this, and I'd ask, is that the road home? And you'd say yes. It's four hundred miles. And I'd say, that doesn't matter, now. We love each other beyond time and place now. And you'd say, that's right and you'd kiss me—
   (and he kisses her gently)

And you'd say, ought I to be in this room now? Aren't we breaking the rules? And I'd say must I start now—not breaking them—
   (he looks into her eyes, unsmiling)
Because I can't let you go and then suddenly it would be so real it would stab my heart and—
   (they embrace each other fiercely)

The CAMERA trucks over their heads to the window, until the window frames disappear and only the snow-covered mountains stand before us.

Pat's dying words remained almost unchanged in the final script:

It's right for me to die, darling—and its not hard—when I'm so full of love—like a bee is full of honey when it comes home in the evening.

As the months passed the working situation between the two collaborators became so heated that Fitzgerald, apparently not trusting himself to simply talk things over with Paramore, instead wrote a letter of several pages to him in some attempt at a reconciliation. Here is part of that letter of October 24, 1937, selected more to show Fitzgerald's state of mind about his working status on the picture than his feelings about the actual work itself:

. . . I totally disagree with you as to the terms of our collaboration. We got off to a bad start and I think you are under certain misapprehensions founded more on my state of mind and body last Friday than upon the real situation. My script is in a general way approved of. There was not any question of taking it out of my hands—as in the case of Sheriff. The question was who I wanted to work with on it and for how long. *That was the entire question* * and it is not materially changed because I was temporarily off my balance.
   At what point you decided you wanted to take the whole course of things in hand—whether because of that day or because when you read my script you liked it much less than Joe or the people in his office—where that point is I don't know. But it was quite apparent Saturday that you had and it is with my faculties quite clear and alert that I tell you I *prefer to keep* * the responsibility for the script as a whole.

* Fitzgerald's emphasis.

This candid reference to what surely must have been one of his drinking episodes indicates another problem that Mankiewicz, and Hunt Stromberg after him, had to cope with in their dealings with Fitzgerald. There were actually very few of these drinking bouts while he was at MGM, for by that time they almost always cost him some time away from the job, and he was clearly determined to keep this job. Almost no one at MGM seems to have been entirely ignorant of Fitzgerald's problems with alcohol; it was something they had faced when they had decided to hire him, for his reputation had preceded him. He was certainly not the only offender working for the studio at that time. With the single exception of his trip to Chicago with Sheilah Graham in late 1937, the one described in *Beloved Infidel,* as well as a few trips East to visit Zelda, Fitzgerald managed to keep himself sober for weeks and months on end. Among his many good reasons was the especially urgent one of his desiring to have his contract renewed at the end of the year.

Besides being so frank about his drinking and subsequent behavior on that Friday, Fitzgerald's letter to Paramore shows that he was quite adamant about refusing to give in to Paramore's wishes, and that he still regarded himself as the prime or senior writer on the script who looked to his collaborator mainly for technical assistance. The writing of the letter must have worked, for the two men apparently made up and got on with the writing of *Three Comrades.* They dutifully turned in their first complete version on November 5 to Mankiewicz, who seems to have been patient as the months passed. Neither their first script nor the subsequent versions dated December 7, December 13, December 21, and January 21 appeared to please Mankiewicz, for it was at this time that he undertook his own drastic revisions of the script, finally OKing it for production on February 1, 1938.

As previously indicated, Fitzgerald took Mankiewicz's revisions of his work very badly. In his long letter of protest there were indications that he was attempting to frighten Mankiewicz by suggesting that the picture would be a box-office disaster if it was filmed Mankiewicz's way:

To say I'm disillusioned is putting it mildly. I had an entirely different conception of you. For nineteen years, with two years out for sickness, I've written best-selling entertainment, and my dialogue is supposedly right up at the top. But I learn from the script that you've suddenly decided that it isn't good dialogue and you can take a few hours off and do much better.

I think you now have a flop on your hands—as thoroughly naive as "The Bride Wore Red" but utterly inexcusable because this time you had something and you have arbitrarily and carelessly torn it to pieces. . . . My God, Joe, you must be intelligent enough to see what you've done.

When *Three Comrades* finally entered production in February, Fitzgerald gave his daughter his first impressions of what he had seen: *"Three Comrades* is half-way through. I have seen some of the shooting and some of the 'rushes' (where they run off what they've shot that day) but you can't tell much from either. To my mind, the producer seriously hurt the script in rewriting it. It may be that I am wrong."

He may have been, for the picture opened to extremely favorable reviews, with Frank Nugent of the *New York Times* selecting it as one of the Ten Best Pictures of the Year, and with Margaret Sullavan receiving an Academy Award nomination for Best Actress of the Year. All this was great news to Mankiewicz, but his final triumph was achieved when the picture became a success at the box office. The long battle over *Three Comrades* continued to rankle Fitzgerald, who felt no better about it when he saw the completed film at the preview. Sheilah Graham remembered his anger:

When *Three Comrades* opened, Scott and I drove into Hollywood to see it. "At least they've kept my beginning," he said on the way. But as the picture unfolded, Scott slumped deeper and deeper in his seat. At the end he said, "They changed even that." He took it badly. "That s.o.b.," he growled when he came home, and furiously, helplessly, as though he had to lash out at something, he punched the wall, hard. "My God, doesn't he know what he's done?"

Just what had Mankiewicz actually done? He had exercised his legitimate function as the producer of *Three Comrades,* overriding the objections and feelings of his chief scriptwriter, F. Scott Fitzgerald, who never forgave him for it. It is now impossible to say what kind of film would have resulted if Fitzgerald's final version of his script had been the one that was shot; all we have to consider is the completed film that was released in the autumn of 1938. An examination of the seven versions of the script prepared for Mankiewicz clearly indicate that Fitzgerald kept changing his mind about all sorts of things in the story; whether this was because of the influence of Mankiewicz or Paramore or both is now not clear. What is clear is that Mankiewicz needed an acceptable shooting-script for the beginning of 1938, felt he didn't have one, and undertook the job himself.

How good was *Three Comrades* then, and how good is it now? The most common response I've met with from people who've seen it recently is, "Well . . . it was OK," which may mean just that, or it may be a way of saying that it was a reasonably typical example of the smooth and glossy films turned out by MGM in the late thirties. Nearly everyone who now sees the film does so for only two reasons, the first one being that it starred an actress of remarkable charm and grace, Margaret Sullavan. There is a much smaller group that sees it because it is the only time Fitzgerald's name can be seen on the credits of a film as screenwriter. To Fitzgerald, a lastingly important fact about *Three Comrades* was that halfway through this troublesome job for "Monkeybitch" his option was picked up by the studio and his weekly salary was increased to $1,250 per week.

5

"Well, you can stop right now. I don't want a word on paper—I repeat, not a single word—until we've found the answer to the question."

"The question?" I repeated uncertainly.

"That's right," he said. "The all-important question your story raises—namely, should a woman tell?"

There was a short, pregnant silence, approximately long enough to consume a slice of poppyseed strudel, and my wife leaned forward. "Should a woman tell what?" she asked with almost Japanese delicacy.

"Why, the truth about her past," returned Thalberg, like one addressing a child. "In short, should a beautiful, sophisticated woman confess her premarital indiscretions to her fiancé?"

—*S. J. Perelman, 1957*

Listen, young man, when I say a gag won't play, it won't play. I, more than any single person in Hollywood, have my finger on the pulse of America. I know *what people will do and what they won't do.*

—*Irving Thalberg, 1935*

Although Irving Thalberg had been dead for nearly a year when Fitzgerald arrived at MGM in 1937, his guiding spirit remained very much alive at the studio, especially about what must now seem some rather curious ideas about sex and marriage. From the day of his death a kind of "he once lived among us" attitude was perpetuated by many of his former associates—Mayer, Stromberg, Sidney Franklin, Edgar Mannix, Bernard Hyman—so that a great deal of Thalberg's habitual way of thinking went on pretty much as it always had in his lifetime. S. J. Perelman worked briefly for Thalberg in the mid thirties and found a pronounced "moral" quality to his way of thinking that was doggedly, even ferociously, simplistic, and this quality of Thalberg's mind went on thriving at MGM long after his death. Both Hunt Stromberg and Fitzgerald were very much aware of this when they undertook the production of *Infidelity* at the beginning of 1938.

Fitzgerald and Stromberg appeared to get along well together from the very start, so much so that by the middle of March Fitzgerald was writing to friends about his new producer in this way: ". . . this time I have the best producer in Hollywood, a fine showman who keeps me from any amateur errors, and I hope to finish the picture alone." In addition to his much higher rank in the MGM hierarchy, Stromberg was even more of an old experienced hand at producing money-making pictures than Mankiewicz had been at that time. He had started at MGM with the famous Garbo and Crawford silents of the twenties, *The Torrent* (1927) and *Our Dancing Daughters* (1928), and entered the sound era with such films as *Red Dust* in 1932, *The Thin Man* in 1934, and *Naughty Marietta* in 1935. In the later thirties his chief productions included *The Great Ziegfeld* (1936), *Marie Antoinette* (1938), and *Idiot's Delight* and *The Women,* both 1939. The quality of his films of the forties and fifties dropped off with almost dramatic suddenness. An extremely tall, bespectacled man, he is often described as resembling American university professors as they were then imagined to be. Fitzgerald described him to Perkins as "a sort of one-finger Thalberg, without Thalberg's scope, but with his intense power of work and his absorption in his job."

Despite many claims to the contrary, including those by Fitzgerald himself, *Infidelity* was not an "original," for its origin was a *Cosmopolitan* short story by Ursula Parrot, a popular writer for the women's magazines of the thirties. It concerned a young and wealthy married couple, Althea and Nicholas Gilbert, and what happens when Althea discovers that her husband has betrayed her on a single occasion with his young and beautiful secretary. After prolonged talk of divorce, the young Althea finally comes to her senses, forgives Nicholas, and there is a happy ending. While this is the kind of plot that proves to be completely uninteresting if summarized in either

30 or 300 words, it is also the kind of story that Thalberg would probably have liked. Fitzgerald's job was to make this material interesting enough to sustain a 75-minute movie and yet bland enough to get by the hostile eye of the Breen Office that looked down on the very title of *Infidelity* as a strong affront to the American Home. The Breen Office was the administrative arm of the Hollywood Production Code of the twenties, thirties, and forties, the industry's self-imposed censorship body. It was also known as the Hays Office and the Johnson Office.

The project had been originally conceived as a vehicle for Joan Crawford, an actress noted mainly for her intensity but not much of anything else except her strong will. Fitzgerald began his work on *Infidelity* by screening three of her biggest hits of the early thirties, *Chained, Possessed,* and *Forsaking All Others.* He then began to write analytic breakdowns of these films, dividing them up into acts and scenes in order to get at their dramatic structure. After this effort, he then made up a dramatic "plan," or scenario, for his *Infidelity,* showing how the plot would work out in terms of acts and sequences. He did all this *by the book,* and it is quite possible that no screenwriter in Hollywood ever did things quite so carefully or methodically. The only other important writer of this century who seems to have undertaken dramatic writing with quite this degree of laborious seriousness is Henry James, who devoted several years of his life concocting completely unsuccessful plays for the West End theaters of London.

Like James the playwright, Fitzgerald took his work on *Infidelity* with the utmost seriousness, dealing with Stromberg in a "strictly business" manner, as is shown in one of his early letters to him:

So much for the story. Now, will the following schedule be agreeable to you? The script will be aimed at 130 pages. I will hand you the first "act"—about fifty pages—on March 11th, or two weeks from Friday. I will complete my first draft of the script on or about April 11th, totalling almost seven weeks. This is less time than I took on THREE COMRADES, and the fact that I understand the medium a little better now is offset by the fact that this is really an original with no great scenes to get out of a book. Will you let me know if this seems reasonable? My plan is to work about half the time at the studio but the more tense and difficult stuff I do better at home away from interruptions. Naturally I'll always be within call and at your disposal.

He had wished to work alone on *Infidelity*, and he got his wish, for Stromberg had a great deal of faith in Fitzgerald's abilities to write a screenplay that would be equally acceptable to MGM and the Breen Office. This proved to be difficult, and Fitzgerald began an apparently endless series of revisions of what he had written. Some of the dialogue he wrote for the film was occasionally quite charming. Here is a scene between Althea and Nicholas, occurring before the breakup when she is about to leave on a trip to Europe by herself:

NICHOLAS
You're not going away. Listen, did you read in the papers about the dog they froze up in a cake of ice—

ALTHEA
Poor dog.

NICHOLAS
Wait a minute—

ALTHEA (near tears anyhow)
I'm afraid I'm going to weep over that dog.

NICHOLAS
Wait! They thawed him out after a month, and he came to life again. That's how it'll be with us.

ALTHEA
But what'll I think about in my cake of ice?

NICHOLAS
Oh, you look out and see the Italian scenery and watch your mother get well and write me letters.

ALTHEA (desolately)
Here are some letters.
(she hands him a package—six letters, each addressed to Nicholas Gilbert, Esq.)
This is for the time I'm on the boat. You're to open one every day.

Fitzgerald continued his "freezing" motif on the next page, for Nicholas attempts to turn on the water faucet in Althea's cabin:

NICHOLAS
I guess they don't go until the boat starts. Even ice water.

ALTHEA
You can freeze me right now.

NICHOLAS
No, not yet

ALTHEA
Yes.

Fitzgerald kept revising his script for *Infidelity* all through the spring of 1938, attempting over and over again to create a screenplay with strong box-office values while placating the official Production Code of the thirties, which frowned on the subject of adultery. He found that he was being asked to perform an impossible task, for he could not please Stromberg *and* the Breen Office at the same time. Stromberg took him off *Infidelity* in May, after the Breen Office had finally decided that the intrinsic theme of the picture was entirely inimical to the values of its Production Code. To get around these values, Stromberg and Fitzgerald had hit on the expedient of calling their picture *Fidelity*, but this ruse failed as had everything else they devised.

It is highly possible that Stromberg felt a certain irritation about Fitzgerald's inability to complete a satisfactory script on *Infidelity* after four months' work, and that this may have had something to do with MGM's refusal to renew his contract at the end of 1938. Fitzgerald thought so a year and a half later, in a letter to the agent Leland Hayward, in which he noted that Stromberg ". . . liked the first part . . . so intensely that when the whole thing flopped I think he held it against me that I had aroused his hope so much and then had not been able to finish it. It may have been my fault—it may have been the fault of the story but the damage is done."

There is little to say about Fitzgerald's work on Stromberg's *Marie Antoinette,* for he remained on the picture for only a week or so and was reassigned to *The Women* by mid May of 1938. This was to be another major Stromberg production, based on Clare Booth Luce's Broadway play of the same year,

which featured the novelty of having a cast composed entirely
of women. Fitzgerald again started off alone on the script, but
he was soon given the director Sidney Franklin as his co-
worker on the project. This arrangement lasted several weeks,
but apparently did not work out to Stromberg's satisfaction,
for Fitzgerald was then given still another collaborator in the
person of his old friend from St. Paul, Great Neck, and Paris,
Donald Ogden Stewart.

Stromberg's decision to team Fitzgerald with Stewart may
well have come about from his certain knowledge that Stewart
was a real pro at writing *successful* film scripts, and that the experience of working with him was just what Fitzgerald badly
needed in the summer of 1938. As to his professionalism,
Stewart was responsible, either wholly or in part, for the
screenplays of *Laughter* (1930), *Dinner at Eight* (1933), *The Barretts of Wimpole Street* (1934), *Holiday* (1938), and *The Philadelphia Story* (1940). At the time of his reunion with Fitzgerald on
The Women, Stewart had been at MGM for the better part of a
decade and had not laid eyes on Fitzgerald for a good deal
longer than that. He recently recalled his feelings about being
assigned to the film:

The only worrisome thing about *The Women* was the fact that I was
expected to work on it with Scott Fitzgerald. Our paths had separated widely in the eighteen years since our St. Paul friendship at the
dawn of our careers. . . . As I entered the gates of the new Irving
Thalberg Memorial Building I didn't quite know what to expect,
especially as I had greatly disliked his confessional "The Crack-Up,"
probably because it was a little too close to home. My own crack-up
as a writer had been, in many respects, quite as reprehensible and as
disappointing to those early 1920 hopes as had Scott's. But now, I
felt, I was back on my feet, still capable of fulfilling my promise.

To my great surprise and delight, so was Scott. He wasn't drinking, and he was, in fact, much more understanding than before, and
infinitely more human. In our month together our old friendship
came back, and it was like those starry-eyed days in St. Paul when he
was reading Masefield to me in front of the fire in his living room.
"Be with me, beauty, for the fire is dying." But, the fire still wasn't
dying—in either of us. . . .

Somewhat the same sort of situation developed on *The
Women* as there had on *Infidelity*. Here again there was a strong

possibility of interference from the Breen Office, for Mrs. Luce's satire was considered quite daring in 1938. Despite all of Stewart's professional know-how, he and Fitzgerald found it impossible to please Stromberg, and it is quite possible that from about this time Fitzgerald began to doubt that he would. In a letter to Ober, written a year later, he may have been referring to this: "You now have plenty of authors who produce correctly and conduct their affairs in a business-like manner. On the contrary, I have a neurosis about anyone's uncertainty about my ability that has been a principal handicap in the picture business."

Fitzgerald occasionally liked to express his feelings about people in light verse, and while engaged in the writing of *The Women* he invoked Stromberg's name at least twice; this one was scrawled on a piece of torn paper:

> Stromberg, the name is like a solemn drum
> Beaten upon an ice flow in the north
> Grant that we shall not always rest here dumb
> Give us a date, let us for god pour forth
> The woes of pretty faces
> The mistakes.

Like Thalberg, Stromberg kept people waiting for a long time before seeing them, and Fitzgerald was no exception. More importantly, Stromberg was constantly changing his mind about the direction his writers should take on the properties he had assigned them. *Marie Antoinette* had been something of a mess from the very start, and Fitzgerald recalled that

> Stromberg sent for Poppa, though Papa hadn't et
> To do what Jesus couldn't—
> Save Marie Antoinette. . . .

Fitzgerald spent a total of four months working on *The Women*, but Stromberg had never seemed satisfied with anything Stewart and he had attempted to do with this story of all these women who talked and talked. Toward the very end of their assignment, both Fitzgerald and Stewart had developed what amounted to a sullen apathy for the entire project, a fact that perhaps did not go unnoticed by Stromberg. At the beginning of November, Fitzgerald was abruptly reassigned to *Madame Curie.* It was quite significent that *Madame Curie* was not a Stromberg picture; it was to be a Sidney Franklin production. It is quite possible to conjecture now that Stromberg had by this time become disillusioned with Fitzgerald, feeling perhaps that he would never deliver the script he had in mind. More importantly, he may also have come to the conclusion that Fitzgerald was not worth all the money he was being paid by MGM, and that the transfer to *Madame Curie* was simply one of convenience, something to keep him occupied until the expiration of his contract.

As was the case with *A Yank at Oxford,* some of Fitzgerald's original lines are on the soundtrack of the film released by MGM in 1939, but the official credits for *The Women* were given to Anita Loos and Jane Murfin. This situation left Fitzgerald in the awkward position of having to explain why he had not received any screen credit after four months' work.

Presumably one of the reasons for Fitzgerald's working for Franklin was that they had gotten along so well together in the past, but this was not much help to either of them on *Madame Curie,* a film project with a long history. Originally conceived as a vehicle for Garbo with Cukor as director, absolutely no one at MGM had managed to come up with anything resembling an adequate screenplay about the Curies. Aldous Huxley had turned in his version of the story at the end of September, but it was thought to be entirely too "scientific" and bloodless, and apparently no one really liked it very much. Fitzgerald was assigned to the picture shortly after Huxley's attempt, but there would appear to have been no very good reason why he would have been expected to do any better with *Madame Curie* than had Huxley. He took on his new assignment with a certain amount of guarded enthusiasm, writing to Zelda that

Madame Curie progresses and it is a relief to be working on something that the censors have nothing against. It will be a comparatively quiet picture—as was *The Barretts of Wimpole Street,* but the more I read about the woman the more I think about her as one of the most admirable people of our time. I hope we can get a little of that into the story.

Sidney Franklin had directed the extremely successful *Barretts of Wimpole Street,* a sensitive film about Elizabeth and Robert Browning, in 1934 for MGM, and he hoped the studio could duplicate that success in 1939 with *Madame Curie.* Just the reverse of Mankiewicz, Franklin had gone from directing films (*Private Lives* and *The Good Earth*) to producing them (*Mrs. Miniver* and *The Yearling*). When he undertook the production of *Curie* in November of 1938, it was the first time he worked on a film as producer. The film itself was not released until 1943, and it had Greer Garson and not Garbo in the title role.

Franklin and Fitzgerald attempted to come up with some equation by which *Madame Curie* could be simultaneously an MGM "love story" and a reasonably accurate biography of the famous French woman scientist—in other words, a typical Paul Muni–Warner Brothers biography film with the kind of uplift and love interest that would sell lots of tickets. The man they had to please was Bernard Hyman who, along with Stromberg, had been one of Thalberg's chief assistants and who was now in charge of the production unit for *Madame Curie.* Hyman saw the film as essentially a love story (time has proved him right) and told Fitzgerald to stress this element over the Great Moments in Science aspect of the Curies' lives.

The work went ahead, but Hyman kept saying no to nearly all of Fitzgerald's and Franklin's various proposals about the way the story should be told. This caused Fitzgerald occasionally to fall into a slight state of panic, as may be seen in this letter to his daughter:

I am intensely busy. On the next two months, during which I finish the first part of *Madame Curie,* depends whether or not my contract will be renewed. So naturally I am working like hell. . . .

He had gotten about halfway through the script when he was abruptly informed by Hyman, at Christmas, that his contract was not being renewed. In effect, he had been fired by MGM after working for them for eighteen months. He was completely on his own again.

6

> *He had simply wandered away from the field where he was
> a master and was sludging around in an area for which he
> had no training or instinct.*
> —*Nunnally Johnson to Tom Dardis, December 1974*

Fitzgerald never quite knew why he had been fired from
MGM, or at least he told people he didn't. He had immediately wired Ober of the news:

METRO NOT RENEWING TO MY GREAT PLEASURE BUT WILL FINISH CURIE
THERES LOTS OF OTHER WORK OFFERED STOP HOWEVER PLEASE SAY
NOTHING WHATEVER TO PERKINS OR TO SCOTTIE WHO WOULD NOT UN-
DERSTAND AM WRITING.

Within another day or so he kept his word and wrote to Ober
about the perplexity he felt about the firing:

As I wrote you the contract wasn't renewed. Why I don't know—but
not on account of the work. It seems sort of funny—to entrust me
alone with their biggest picture, *continue* me on it with a "your services will not be required". Finally Eddie said that when I finished it
he hoped he'd have good contract for me. O.K. If *Curie* is a hit I'd
go back for $2000 a week. Baby am I glad to get out! Ive hated the
place since Monkeybitch rewrote 3 Comrades!

The "Eddie" Fitzgerald mentions is Edwin Knopf of MGM,
the man who had originally gotten Fitzgerald the job at the
studio. Ober had lunch with Knopf in New York and wrote
Fitzgerald what Knopf had said about the reasons for the
firing:

He told me that the only reason that they were not renewing your
contract was that they weren't paying anybody $1500 if they could
help it. He said you had done fine work on THREE COMRADES
and admitted Metro had made a mistake in not doing the picture the

57

way you wrote it. If you want to work in Hollywood, after the expiration of the Metro contract, I feel sure that you can do so. . . .

This explanation conceals more than it reveals. Aside from
the fact that technically the contract had expired, there are at
least two other reasons for Fitzgerald's being let go by MGM at
this time. The first reason is purely economic. Screenwriting is
a "business" like any other, and Fitzgerald was being paid a lot
of money with really very little to show for it. In a period of
eighteen months he had managed to obtain only one screen
credit, and this only after months of endless bickering, not
only with Mankiewicz, but with almost everyone else connected
with the film. His full year with Hunt Stromberg was rather
different, but in the end there was nothing to show for it. His
final months with Sidney Franklin on *Madame Curie* had
seemed to promise pretty much the same story all over again.
As was suggested earlier, it may have been decided not to
renew Fitzgerald's contract in early November, at just about
the time he left Stromberg. All of this raises the question of
just how "good" Fitzgerald's work was at MGM.

The answer to this question might best take the form of "He
was good—but not that good," if "that good" is equated with
the sum of $1,500 per week, the amount MGM would have
had to pay him if they had kept him on their payroll. In a
recent letter to me, Nunnally Johnson indicates that Fitzgerald's main trouble as a screenwriter, at MGM as well as in
all his later jobs, was simply the amount of money he received: "His biggest misfortune, which I doubt that he ever
realized, was that they paid him fat money at the very beginning. And even though he blew his chances with inadequate
work he believed that he should continue to draw such salaries
or even larger ones. . . ."

Johnson speaks from the professional point of view of a
man who has spent forty years in the film business, and it is
difficult not to agree in part with him about Fitzgerald's abilities as a screenwriter, at least on the basis of what can be
learned from the people Fitzgerald worked for and with.
Johnson believes that Fitzgerald lacked the basic equipment a
screenwriter might be expected to possess:

The explanation for his continual failure as a screenwriter is that he was simply unable to understand or turn out dramatic work . . . he wasn't the first novelist who was unable to master the technique of dramatic writing. But Scott didn't think of that. He saw dozens of inferior writers being paid fat sums out here and although I don't think he ever had any genuine interest in screenwriting he could see no reason why he shouldn't get in on it and help himself out of his financial slump.

The other main reason for MGM's nonrenewal is bound to remain extremely conjectural. Fitzgerald did very little drinking while working for them, but the few times he did were catastrophic, inevitably causing lost time away from the job. At $1,250 per week, this state of affairs may be bearable to an employer, but only when the employee is turning out good enough work to warrant the indulgence—surely not the case with Fitzgerald.

Fitzgerald did not spend the final two weeks of his MGM contract working on *Madame Curie*. Instead, he was loaned out by MGM to David O. Selznick for some last-minute work on the script of *Gone with the Wind*. By January of 1939 Selznick had utilized the talents of at least a dozen screenwriters before becoming satisfied that his final shooting-script was as close to the spirit of Margaret Mitchell's novel as was humanly possible. Fitzgerald had been borrowed by Selznick to do a little polishing job on this script—by now a palimpsest—just before the actual shooting, but it was an unusual kind of polishing. Several weeks later Fitzgerald wrote to Perkins about the kind of work Selznick had demanded:

It is wonderful to be writing again instead of patching—do you know in that "Gone With the Wind" job I was absolutely forbidden to use any words except those of Margaret Mitchell, that is, when new phrases had to be invented one had to thumb through as if it were Scripture and check out phrases of her's which would cover the situation!

Fitzgerald had been hired more as a critic of the working script than as a writer, and he obediently marked up the script with his comments and questions. He contributed so little to what had gone before that apparently no one can now recall just what it was. Selznick let Fitzgerald go after working two weeks on the picture, replacing him with still another polisher.

Fitzgerald had told Ober that he expected lots of offers of employment, but this was wishful thinking. In February of 1939 Fitzgerald set himself up seriously as a free-lance screenwriter, utilizing the services of H. N. Swanson ("Swannie") and, later, Leland Hayward as his agents. There had been some talk of jobs, but there were no concrete offers, and he became quite nervous about his situation in Hollywood. It will be recalled that his working price ($1,500 per week) was considered high for the time, but Swanson managed to get it for him almost immediately, on the very first job he secured for him. This was the Walter Wanger production of *Winter Carnival,* a rather undistinguished film designed for Ann Sheridan, cast as a waitress posing as the bogus guest of a college boy at the annual Dartmouth Winter Carnival—essentially a "college romance" picture. Fitzgerald's participation in the making of this film was a personal disaster for him and became the material from which a great many legends have been made.

Wanger had hired the twenty-four-year-old Budd Schulberg, a Dartmouth alumnus, to write the screenplay for his *Winter Carnival* but apparently had found Schulberg's efforts inadequate and, after becoming aware of Fitzgerald's availability, decided to hire him as a collaborator on the job, very much for the same reasons that MGM had placed him on *A Yank at Oxford.* All the details of what happened in Hanover, New Hampshire, in that snowy week in February 1939 have been told a great many times, and only the barest outline will be attempted here. Fitzgerald flew east with Wanger and Schulberg in order to "experience" the actuality of the Dartmouth Winter Carnival; a full camera crew was brought along to take background shots for the film. Fitzgerald started drinking on the plane eastward, managed to get quite drunk very quickly, and stayed that way, off and on, for the next ten days. There were a number of unfortunate "incidents," with Fitzgerald often in a state of near collapse.

Wanger put up with a good deal of this behavior before finally telling both Schulberg and Fitzgerald to get out of town and return to New York; in effect, they were both fired. With Schulberg acting as his reluctant nursemaid, the still drunk Fitzgerald was brought back to New York on the train, by now suffering from what appeared to be pneumonia. The hotels they went to took a jaundiced view of their physical appearance, the result of several days of intensive drinking, and denied them accommodations. Fitzgerald had become virtually comatose, and only with the assistance of Sheilah Graham was he finally admitted to Doctors Hospital. He spent the next week there, in a state of complete physical and spiritual collapse. Schulberg was eventually rehired by Wanger in order to complete the script, but this was not the end of the episode.

None of what happened in New Hampshire would have counted as much as it finally did in the formation of the legend of what Fitzgerald was really like in his Hollywood years had it not been for Budd Schulberg's account of it in his novel *The Disenchanted*. Written a full decade later, and based on a very slight acquaintance with Fitzgerald, his portrait of Fitzgerald is very far from being, in any real sense, a picture of the way he appeared to those who knew him a lot better than Schulberg. The portrait of Manley Halliday in this book is the portrait of a man who was anything *but* a writer, a person totally lacking in the personal dignity that Fitzgerald never seemed to lose even in the worst of circumstances. Schulberg was given a great deal of assistance in writing this novel by Arthur Mizener, who allowed him access to all the early biographical material he had unearthed about Fitzgerald for the book that became *The Far Side of Paradise*. Conversely, Mizener's book borrows freely from Schulberg's novel, as well as from his various magazine pieces, in anything related to Fitzgerald's time in Hollywood. This is especially true in the 1965 revised edition of the biography, which deals much more openly with that part of his life than had the earlier one. Each of the two books tended to reinforce the other, and the picture of Fitzgerald as a shattered wreck of a man, as something of a drunken sot, became firmly established.

Here is the way Arthur Mizener has Fitzgerald talking to Schulberg in their hotel room in New Hampshire:

"You know," he said, "I used to have a beautiful talent once, Baby. It used to be wonderful feeling it was there. . . ."

Schulberg had done it this way in *The Disenchanted:*

". . . Baby, no one'll ever do it any better. Had a talent once, Baby. Got enough left for one more book. Two or three if I pace myself. . . ."

Despite Andrew Turnbull's doubts as to the real nature of Schulberg's feelings toward Fitzgerald, he nevertheless has him thinking aloud in that same hotel room at the Hanover Inn:

"You know, I used to have a beautiful talent once, Baby. It used to be a wonderful feeling to know it was there, and it isn't all gone yet. I think I have enough left to stretch out over two more novels. I may have to stretch it a little thin. . . ."

Fitzgerald was never one to waste material, and the trip to New Hampshire was no exception. Months later, while writing *The Last Tycoon,* he made this note about the character called Robinson:

I would like this episode to give a picture of the work of a cutter, camera man or second unit director in the making of such a thing as *Winter Carnival,* accenting the speed with which Robinson works, his reactions, why he is what he is instead of being the very high-salaried man which his technical abilities entitle him to be. I might as well use some of the Dartmouth atmosphere, snow, etc. being careful not to impinge at all on any material that Walter Wanger may be using in *Winter Carnival* or that I may have ever suggested as material to him.

The man who wrote this is obviously not the kind of man who appears in the pages of *The Disenchanted,* a man who could never have written much of anything.

The Dartmouth fiasco was a costly one for Fitzgerald, financially as well as spiritually. His drinking periods became much more frequent than they had been in the previous year of enforced sobriety. No longer having a regular job to go to each day, and with none in sight, his drinking soon took on the frightening proportions it had assumed in the worst days of 1934 and 1935, when everything had seemed hopeless. This sudden resumption of constant, heavy drinking now required the care of expensive doctors and nurses, often on an around-the-clock basis. Everyone who knew him at this time agrees that the months following the New Hampshire trip were the most difficult ones Fitzgerald had to endure in his entire stay in California. A deep sense of gloom and personal defeat, which was further exacerbated by his daily intake of gin, seemed to have overwhelmed him all through the spring and summer of 1939. These were the months that Sheilah Graham thought Fitzgerald was trying quite seriously to kill himself by drinking; he came close, and he may well have owed his life to her constant care and sympathy.

There were some good reasons for his despair. Although he was able to pick up a short working assignment at Paramount for a film to be called *Air Raid* in the middle of March, he had by then become more than half-convinced that the news of his behavior in New Hampshire had gotten around sufficiently to have him blackballed by the film industry. A year and a half later, and in a much better frame of mind, he wrote Zelda about these terrible months of early 1939: "I don't know what the next three months will bring further, but if I get a credit on either of these last two efforts things will never again seem so black as they did a year ago when I felt that Hollywood had me down in its books as a ruined man—a label which I had done nothing to deserve."

Air Raid was finally canceled as a film project by Paramount, and he was again without work. He then decided to take an ill-advised trip to Asheville, North Carolina, and then to Cuba with Zelda, who had been allowed a brief holiday from the Highlands Sanitarium. Fitzgerald had left Hollywood in a rage after a particularly bitter and drunken quarrel with Sheilah Graham, and he continued to drink heavily all the way eastward, just as he had done earlier in the year. The entire Cuban trip seems to have been a total disaster, with Fitzgerald continuing to drink all the way there and back again. He had gotten into a violent fight in Havana and still another one in New York with a cab-driver after their return flight there. The trip came to an unpleasant end at the Algonquin Hotel, where Fitzgerald finally collapsed in a state of total exhaustion. Zelda placed him in Doctors Hospital again, where he was forced to remain in bed for two weeks. Perhaps the saddest thing about the trip was that this was the very last time Zelda and Scott Fitzgerald ever saw each other.

When he finally returned to California he then had to remain in bed for several more weeks, and it was nearly two months before he was at all able even to consider any further screenwriting work. When he did, he found there was little enough available, and the only film assignment he received in the next few months was a one-week job at Universal in August on a project identified as "Open That Door." By that time, however, his money worries had become so great that he had actively resumed the writing of short stories, something he had not done for over a year.

Although all of his nine published titles were still in print, their total combined sales for the year 1939 amounted to a total of 114 copies, producing royalties of exactly $33. He could not have received these figures from Scribners until the middle of 1940, but the ones for 1938 had been even worse, with a total sale of only 96 books for that year. With no screenwriting job anywhere in sight, the choice to write short stories at this time was not really a free one—it was a matter of utter desperation, for he now had absolutely no other form of income.

7

I am not a great man, but sometimes I think the impersonal and objective quality of my talent and the sacrifices of it, in pieces, to preserve its essential value has some sort of epic grandeur.
—*Fitzgerald to his daughter, October 1939*

I knew Scott only during his last few years and whenever he was not drinking he seemed to me as thoroughly alive and alert as anybody I ever knew.
—*Nunnally Johnson to Tom Dardis, November 1974*

All of Fitzgerald's biographers have tended to deemphasize his social life in Hollywood, often giving the impression that he passed most of his time in lonely isolation, except for what he spent with Sheilah Graham. This is not in accord with the facts, for although he was scarcely the rabidly eager party giver of the twenties—whether in Paris, New York, or Great Neck—Fitzgerald remained very much a social being. He no longer cared for large, glittering parties but now preferred to entertain people in small, relatively intimate groups or have them entertain him in the same way. Among the people he often saw in this manner were S. J. Perelman and his wife, Laura, Ogden Nash, Frances and Albert Hackett, Nunnally Johnson and his wife, Nathanael West and the Eileen he married, and that other "ruined" man, Herman J. Mankiewicz. The only point in mentioning these names is to indicate that Fitzgerald was scarcely a social recluse in Hollywood, as Faulkner very definitely was.

In the spring of 1938 Sheilah Graham had rented a beach house for him at Malibu, and this is where he briefly lived after leaving the Garden of Allah. The climate there proved to be unsuitable for the winter months, and in the fall of 1938 both he and Miss Graham rented a house together in the San Fernando Valley. It was located in Encino on the estate of the actor Edward Everett Horton; they liked the place immensely, despite Fitzgerald's aversion to its nickname of "Belly Acres." He lived there for a total of eighteen months, not leaving it until the spring of 1940, when he finally rented a small apartment on North Laurel in Hollywood, mainly to continue being close to Miss Graham, whose work required her being in the heart of town.

It was just as impossible to live in Greater Los Angeles without an automobile in 1939 as it is today. Fitzgerald managed to get around in a car that a number of writers have usually identified as something terribly decrepit, but it was in fact a 1937 Ford, originally the property of S. J. Perelman, who had sold it to him in 1938. He ate out quite a lot, and for this the car was an absolute necessity. His taste in restaurants was similar to that of Faulkner and West, for he too became a regular patron of Musso & Frank's restaurant, a place highly esteemed by a number of Hollywood writers for both the quality of its food and the credit it extended.

The kind of life that Fitzgerald led in Hollywood in 1939 and 1940 was in every way more satisfactory than the lonely, frightened one he had endured in Baltimore and Tryon in the early and mid thirties; he was now seeing people, working hard, and gradually beginning to feel the return of his creative powers.

The short stories he wrote for the *Saturday Evening Post* and *Collier's* at this time were not taken by their editors, and Fitzgerald soon fell back into his old and familiar habit of asking Ober for advances against the stories to tide him over until they did sell. Ober reluctantly complied with the first of these requests, but to Fitzgerald's complete astonishment he flatly refused the second one. One main reason for Fitzgerald's shock was that by now he had fully repaid Ober all the money he had borrowed over the years. He flew into a rage and sent this wire to Perkins on July 3:

HAVE BEEN WRITING IN BED WITH TUBERCULOSIS UNDER DOCTORS
NURSES CARE SINCE ARRIVING WEST. OBER HAS DECIDED NOT TO BACK
ME THOUGH I PAID BACK EVERY PENNY AND EIGHT THOUSAND COMMIS-
SION. AM GOING TO WORK THURSDAY IN STUDIO AT FIFTEEN HUNDRED
CAN YOU LEND ME SIX HUNDRED FOR ONE WEEK BY WIRE TO BANK
AMERICAN CULVER CITY. SCOTTIE HOSPITAL WITH APPENDIX AND AM
ABSOLUTELY WITHOUT FUNDS. PLEASE DO NOT ASK OBERS COOPERATION

Although Perkins seems to have supplied the $600 at this
time, the "Thursday" job did not materialize until another six
weeks had passed. Fitzgerald did not take defeat easily, for on
July 13 he sent one of his more desperate wires to Ober:

STILL FLABBERGASTED AT YOUR ABRUPT CHANGE IN POLICY AFTER 20
YEARS ESPECIALLY WITH STORY IN YOUR HANDS STOP MY COMMERCIAL
VALUE CANT HAVE SUNK FROM 60 THOUSAND TO NOTHING BECAUSE OF A
SLOW HEALING LUNG CAVITY STOP AFTER 30 PICTURE OFFERS DURING
THE MONTHS I WAS IN BED SWANSON NOW PROMISES NOTHING FOR
ANOTHER WEEK STOP CANT YOU ARRANGE A FEW HUNDRED ADVANCE
FROM A MAGAZINE SO I CAN EAT TODAY AND TOMORROW STOP WONT
YOU WIRE.

Ober did, and his answer was as final as it had been two weeks
earlier:

SORRY COLLECTIONS SLOW AND IMPOSSIBLE MAKE ADVANCE NOW
SUGGEST ASKING SWANSON GET ADVANCE ON JOB.

Fitzgerald's reaction to this wire was to scrawl across the bottom part of it these words: "The insult to my intelligence in
the phrase 'collections slow' makes me laugh."

Ober's refusal precipitated a more or less final break in their
close author-agent relationship of nearly twenty years' stand-
ing. Why did Ober choose this particular time to refuse
Fitzgerald's demands? The answer seems to be that he knew
all too well that giving money to Fitzgerald at that time would
simply inaugurate another borrowing cycle that might run on
for months or even years. By July 19 Fitzgerald realized that
he could not sway Ober from his decision and wrote him a
long letter, some of it on the self-pitying side, but a great deal
of it quite honest and direct. At very nearly the end of this letter he acknowledged the need for a break between them: "Everything I have ever done or written is me, and who doesn't

choose to accept the whole cannot but see the wisdom of a parting."

This should have marked the end of these discussions, but it didn't, for Fitzgerald had counted very much on the mere fact of Ober's support as a kind of confidence in him both as a writer and as a human being. On August 2 he again wrote to Ober, still expressing his shock:

Your reasons for refusing to help me were all good, all praiseworthy, all sound—but wouldn't they have been equally so any time within the past fifteen years? And they followed a year and a half in which I fulfilled all my obligations.

If it is of any interest to you I haven't had a drink in two months but if I was full of champagne I couldn't be more confused about you than I am now.

This full realization that he could no longer count on Ober for any further financial support was a terrible blow, for now he realized that he had only himself to depend on for the future.

There were a few scattered film-writing jobs for him in the fall of 1939, but not many, and they didn't last very long. Twentieth Century-Fox hired him to create "ideas" for a Sonja Henie ice-skating picture, but this job lasted exactly one day. Another September assignment was Sam Goldwyn's hiring him to rewrite a script he was about to shoot for his production of *Raffles,* starring David Niven, but after only a single week's work on the script there developed a quarrel between Goldwyn and his director, Sam Wood, and Fitzgerald's services were then deemed unnecessary. With this film, his quasi-official rate of pay in Hollywood had dropped to $1,000 per week.

After his break with Ober, Fitzgerald became his own not terribly good literary agent, with *Esquire* as his main market. It was at about this time that he began writing his long series of stories about Pat Hobby, of which he wrote a total of seventeen for the magazine. They all concern a rather stupid forty-nine-year-old "hack" screenwriter who is something of a holdover from the days of the silents, a man who had been originally hired to write titles, and who now in the early forties is depicted as scrounging his way around the various studios hoping to be hired at *his* price—$250 or $350 per week. There are those who have thought that perhaps one reason for Fitzgerald's writing stories about people like Pat Hobby and his friends was to exorcise the spirit of what he saw himself becoming as he too cadged screenwriting jobs at *his* new price. Arnold Gingrich of *Esquire* paid Fitzgerald $250 per story in the series, which began running at the beginning of 1940, finishing up in May of 1941. These stories are "light fiction" in the worst sense of the word, but Fitzgerald's main purpose in writing them was financial survival, and in this he was successful.

In March of 1940, Fitzgerald sold the film rights to what is perhaps his most often reprinted short story, "Babylon Revisited," to Lester Cowan, an independent producer, best known today for such films as *My Little Chickadee* and *The Story of G. I. Joe.* Fitzgerald's share of the purchase price was only $800, but he was also to be paid $300 per week while working on the screenplay for Cowan, for a total price of $5,000. He accepted the offer immediately. His encounter with Cowan had come at a very good time, for he had again begun to think of himself as perhaps unemployable as a screenwriter. In February he had written Zelda, "At the moment I am hoping for a job at Republic Studios, the lowest of the low, which would among other things help to pay your hospital bill."

There was something speculative about Cowan's deal from the very beginning, and Fitzgerald wrote to his daughter about this aspect on the day before he was to begin work on the script:

I go to cinema work tomorrow on a sort of half-pay, half-"spec" (speculation) business on my own story "Babylon Revisited." Which is to say Columbia advances me living money while I work and if it goes over in installments with the producer, the company, the releasing people, I get an increasing sum. At bottom we eat—at the top the deal is very promising.

Besides advancing Fitzgerald $300 a week of Columbia's money, Cowan also permitted him to work at home, which was now his new apartment on North Laurel just around the corner from Sheilah Graham. He continued to utilize the services of Frances Kroll as his secretary. She had to be literally on call, day and night, for whatever might occur. She was particularly helpful in the endless typing and retyping of the curriculum of his program of continuing education for Sheilah Graham, who has written a charming memoir about it called *College of One.*

It is now not at all clear why either Cowan or Fitzgerald ever thought a story like "Babylon Revisited" could be transformed into a feature-length film script. Fitzgerald did just this, but only at the cost of losing whatever feeling his story originally possessed, creating in its stead a rather cheap and glossy melodrama, filled with embezzlers, hired assassins, last-minute rescues, and kindred types of outlandish villainy in high places. He is perhaps unique among modern writers whose work has been "savaged" by Hollywood in that he did it all by himself in cold blood and while quite sober. As indicated earlier, Fitzgerald had some very fixed ideas about what he thought Hollywood would accept as entertainment. What had been an extremely affecting story about Charlie Wales's pathetic efforts to regain the custody of his nine-year-old daughter, Honoria, who has been legally adopted by the family of her dead mother, becomes utterly transformed into a rather predictable screenplay about lost millions in Wall Street and paid assassins.

It seems likely that Cowan and Fitzgerald had both Shirley Temple and Cary Grant in mind for the leading roles before Fitzgerald ever wrote a word of all this, but at one point he thought rather differently, as in this letter to Cowan: "The writing on the wall is that *anybody* this year who brings in a good new story *intact* will make more reputation and even money, than those who struggle for a few stars. I would rather see new people in this picture than Gable and Temple. I think it would be a bigger and better thing for you."

Cowan's leaning toward Miss Temple must have prevailed, for in this scene between Wales and Honoria, who has become Victoria, one can almost hear the voice of that prodigal child star. Wales has been telling her about some friends of his:

VICTORIA
Who are they?

WALES
Parasites.

VICTORIA
From Paris.

WALES (in a stage whisper)
No, a parasite is something you find everywhere.
  (whispering again)
They want something you've got.

VICTORIA
What do they want?

WALES
Sometimes it's your happiness.

VICTORIA
How do they get to be that?

WALES
Oh, they begin by not doing their lessons.

VICTORIA (with a sigh)
I knew there'd be a moral in it.
  (pause)
I wish there was some person who could talk to you without always
ending up with a moral.

WALES
Darling, from now on, word of honor, that'll be me.
  (They dance in silence a moment)

VICTORIA
I suppose this is just the happiest that you can ever get, isn't it?

WALES
I suppose so. Just about.

VICTORIA (sorry for everybody else)
I hope those parasites have found somebody to annoy, because they
might as well be happy, too.

Fitzgerald spent the better part of a day in July at the home
of the twelve-year-old Miss Temple in order to encourage the
child's mother to permit the rapidly aging young star's partici-
pation in the proposed film. He wrote to his daughter about
this visit:

Max Perkins writes me that Jane and three classmates are coming here and want to see something of the movies. I don't know who to introduce them to except Shirley Temple with whom I spent the day yesterday. (Her mother was there so it was all right.) She really is a sweet little girl. . . . I don't know whether she's going to do my picture or not.

She eventually didn't, and it would appear that her appearance in it was an absolute necessity to secure the financial support it required. Her final decision was a long time in coming, but Fitzgerald kept working away on successive drafts of *Honoria,* first calling it that, then *Babylon Revisited,* and finally *Cosmopolitan.* He continued to work on the project for several months after his weekly payments had stopped. He seemed to be happy doing this work, for he wrote to Zelda at one point, "My movie progresses and I think it's going to be damn good." Although he continued to be concerned with *Cosmopolitan* until the very end of his life, neither the stars nor the financing could ever be obtained in the right combination, and the film was not produced.

He began to believe that his work on this screenplay had done him a lot of good in the film community, telling Zelda in August, "I have my fingers crossed but with the good Shirley Temple script behind me I think my stock out here is better than at any time during the past year." In late September he again mentioned his hopes for the script: ". . . the Shirley Temple script is looking up again and is my great hope for attaining some real status out here as a movie man and not a novelist."

It took Lester Cowan more than a full decade before he recouped his investment in *Cosmopolitan* by finally selling the script to MGM for a reported price of $100,000. MGM then had Fitzgerald's screenplay completely rewritten for the film that became, in 1954, *The Last Time I Saw Paris,* starring Elizabeth Taylor and Van Johnson as the parents of the little girl, Honoria-Victoria.

All the readings *Cosmopolitan* received indicate that Fitzgerald may have been right about his improved status in the film community, for he was hired by Twentieth Century-

Fox for a very brief stint of work on a film project of theirs about Old New York, Boss Tweed, and the Brooklyn Bridge, but this was soon canceled. Almost immediately after this he was given a ten-week job by Zanuck and Nunnally Johnson of revising their script for Emlyn Williams's London stage success, *The Light of Heart*. This was a sentimental play about a broken-down alcoholic actor who has become a department-store Santa Claus. Fitzgerald's job was to develop the actor's moral rehabilitation at the hands of his club-footed daughter—no mean task. For his work on this picture his rate of pay was $700 per week, but he was extremely glad to get it, for his only real income was still from the monthly Pat Hobby stories he was writing for *Esquire*. Fitzgerald's version of *The Light of Heart* script was considered to be unacceptable—"too glum." Two years later Nunnally Johnson rewrote it completely for Zanuck as *Life Begins at Eight-Thirty*, starring Monty Woolley. This was Fitzgerald's final film assignment in Hollywood; the $7,000 he received for his work on the picture was a windfall for him at this time, but it was earned at the cost of neglecting the novel he had quietly and cautiously begun in the previous year: *The Last Tycoon*.

[8]

> . . . *I'm not going to perish before one more book.*
> —*Fitzgerald to Corey Ford, July 1937*

> *My room is covered with charts like it used to be for* Tender Is the Night, *telling the different movements of the characters and their histories. However, this one is to be short, as I originally planned it two years ago, and more on the order of* Gatsby.
> —*Fitzgerald to Zelda, October 19, 1940*

As early as July of 1937, the month of Fitzgerald's arrival in Hollywood, Ober had written to him about the possibility of his writing some sort of novel after he had left California, telling him that "when you are through you will be able to write the novel you want to write without financial worries." But these money worries never really stopped, and in April of 1938 Ober was prompted again to mention the writing of a novel, this time in connection with the size of Fitzgerald's bank account: "I hope that during the rest of this year you can build this up to a really good-sized amount so that when you want to get to work on your novel you will be able to do so without worrying about money."

For a long time he was quite consciously secretive about the book he was writing, even willing to lie about it. One of the first specific references to what became *The Last Tycoon* appears in a letter he wrote to Perkins in May of 1939, in which he flatly denies that the novel he had described to Charles Scribner, Sr., several weeks previously was in fact about Hollywood:

He [Scribner] seemed under the full conviction that the novel was about Hollywood and I am in terror that this mis-information may have been disseminated to the literary columns. If I ever gave any such impression it is entirely false: I said that the novel was about some things that had happened to me in the last two years. It is distinctly not about Hollywood (and if it were it is the last impression that I would want to get about).

The parenthetical material at the end may have been enough to tell Perkins that the novel was indeed all about Hollywood, despite all the stout denials in the first part. His daughter was not informed of his plans about the novel until October: "Look! I have begun to write something that is maybe great, and I'm going to be absorbed in it four or six months. It may not make us a cent but it will pay expenses. . . ."

It was not until that same month that Fitzgerald made a formal submission of an outline of *The Last Tycoon* to Kenneth Littauer of *Collier's,* who had shown a strong interest in the idea of Fitzgerald's writing a serial for them with Hollywood as the background for the story. Everything went well at the beginning, with Fitzgerald using Perkins's services as his unofficial agent in New York, going out of his way to exclude Ober

from the negotiations. There were some serious misunder-
standings, for both Perkins and Fitzgerald were convinced
that *Collier's* would pay a total price of $30,000 for the serial
rights to the book, but it turned out that they were only prepared to pay $15,000, a figure that, as mentioned earlier, was
simply not acceptable to Fitzgerald at that time.

He was quite nervous about showing the opening pages of
The Last Tycoon to almost everybody, even old friends like John
O'Hara, but he finally did one Sunday afternoon at the very
end of 1939, when O'Hara had been invited for lunch.
Fitzgerald kept postponing things for a long time, but finally

. . . he suddenly said, "Would you like to read what I've written, but
first promise you won't tell anyone about it. Don't tell them anything. Don't tell what it's about, or anything about the people. I'd
like it better if you didn't even tell anyone I'm writing another
novel." So we went back to the house and I read what he had written. He saw that I was comfortable, with pillows, cigarettes, ash trays,
a Coke. And sat there tortured, trying to be casual, but unhappy
because he did not know that my dead pan was partly due to my
being an extremely slow reader of good writing, and partly because
this was such good writing that I was reading. When I had read it I
said, "Scott, don't take any more movie jobs till you've finished this.
You work so slowly and this is so good, you've got to finish it. It's
real Fitzgerald." Then of course, he became blasphemous and abu-
sive, and asked me if I wanted to fight. I saw him a few times after
that day, and once when I asked how the book was coming he only
said, "You've kept your promise? You haven't spoken to anyone
about it?"

In November Fitzgerald submitted the first 6,000 words of his
manuscript—what is now the first chapter of the book and
part of the second—to Littauer who found them insufficient
to make a final judgment. This decision threw Fitzgerald into
a rage, and instead of simply writing another 5,000 words or
so for Littauer he instructed Perkins to suspend all dealings
with *Collier's*. He then instructed Perkins to submit the material to the *Saturday Evening Post*, which expressed absolutely no
interest. This was his last effort to sell the serial rights. Despite
the constant interruptions of his film work throughout 1940,
Fitzgerald continued to work on the manuscript until the end

of his life, fully confident that Perkins really liked the book, and that Scribners would eventually publish it.

The final weeks of Fitzgerald's life were spent almost uninterruptedly on writing *The Last Tycoon,* some of them actually in bed, but it was a happy time for him, as he wrote Zelda: "I am deep in the novel, and it makes me happy . . . two thousand words today and all good." On December 13, eight days before his death, he again wrote to Zelda about the book's progress.

The novel is about three-quarters through and I think I can go on till January 12 without doing any stories or going back to the studio. I couldn't go back to the studio anyhow in my present condition as I have to spend most of the time in bed where I write on a wooden desk that I had made a year and a half ago. The cardiogram shows that my heart is repairing itself but it will be a gradual process that will take some months. It is odd that the heart is one of the organs that does repair itself.

The night that Sheilah Graham informed Ober by telephone of Fitzgerald's death in Hollywood she mentioned the existence of the manuscript of *The Last Tycoon.* Ober wrote down what she told him about it: "She has will and papers and rough draft of ⅔ of novel. Sheilah Graham says Scott intended to rewrite the first part entirely—*he wouldn't want it seen as it is*—" * This is just the way the pages of Fitzgerald's unfinished novel *were* read, however, creating certain problems about his intentions that have never been answered to everyone's satisfaction. A few of them can be briefly mentioned here. All the surviving outlines for the book envision a short, compact work in the tradition of *The Great Gatsby* that would run, as did that book, to about 50,000 words. However, the existing six chapters alone of *The Last Tycoon* run close to 45,000 words, with less than one-half of the outline covered in them. If all the outline material is closely examined, it would appear that Fitzgerald had all the basic materials for a novel that would perhaps have run to the length of *Tender Is the Night,* or about 125,000 words.

* *Italics added.*

It would seem that Fitzgerald's main problem in writing his novel was the choice of the right point of view for his narrative. His choice of the young producer's daughter, Cecilia Brady, was an awkward one in many ways, for she really couldn't be in all the places she'd have to be. The book comes most completely alive at the very moment when Fitzgerald drops both her and any pretense of her existence and carries on with the narrative by himself. This is especially true of all the scenes showing Monroe Stahr at work in the studio, the conference scenes, which have never been seriously rivaled by any writer in their sharp, brilliant ring of truth about the way some movies got produced in the thirties.

When Fitzgerald said that the sacrifice of his talent, "in pieces, to preserve its essential value has some sort of epic grandeur," he was very close to the truth, with perhaps "heroic" grandeur more in order than "epic." For despite all its inherent contradictions and curious puzzles, *The Last Tycoon* is a heroic book to have written, a fascinating work that established beyond any question that Fitzgerald had indeed regained his ability to write as well as he ever had in the past. He contributed nothing noteworthy to the history of the American film, but his place in its history is perhaps secured by our interest in the courageous efforts he made to conquer an alien medium as just one part of his struggle to regain his lost creativity. Although he certainly had no intention of ever having it taken as his last will and testament, *The Last Tycoon* is undeniable proof that Fitzgerald enjoyed a second brief, brilliant rebirth in Hollywood.

William Faulkner, Oxford, Mississippi, April 1931 (*Cofield Studio, Oxford, Mississippi*)

William Faulkner

"They're Gonna Pay Me Saturday, They're Gonna Pay Me Saturday"

[1]

---

*You surprise me when you say he spent four years out here.
I would never have guessed it. Admittedly Bill needed the
money and if Hawks wanted to give it to him, why not?*
    —Nunnally Johnson to Tom Dardis, November 1974

*Faulkner . . . wrote his best on the scripts, I know and
don't care what anyone says to the contrary, even Faulkner
himself. He was the kind of man who would do a bang-up
job of work if he came to your house to fix the plumbing.*
    —Daniel Fuchs to Tom Dardis, May 1975

Faulkner spent much more of his life working as a
screenwriter in Hollywood than is generally imagined. He actually accumulated a total of over four years' work out there,
the time being split up into segments of various lengths, long
and short, starting in 1932 and not ending until 1955. This is
a lot of time spent working at something he is supposed not to
have taken very seriously, and it raises a lot of questions. What
did he actually do all those years? Why was he ever there at
all, and why did he keep on going back there?

An answer to the first of these questions may be had by con-
sidering one of Faulkner's best-known efforts at screenwriting
for Warner Brothers, *The Big Sleep*, released in 1946. This film
is an extremely popular rerun on television and is still
frequently shown in film houses, usually as one-half of a
Humphrey Bogart double-bill. Bogart's name alone would
guarantee its lasting popularity, but there are other reasons as
well. It was directed by Howard Hawks, who has become
regarded as one of the great American directors. The picture
was based on a crime novel by Raymond Chandler, still another figure of lively interest. And finally, there is the pres-

ence of Faulkner himself, who is credited as the coauthor of the screenplay, along with Jules Furthman and Leigh Brackett.

The opening sequence of the film is justly famous. Chandler's Philip Marlowe, played by Bogart, is having a strange sort of job interview with the old, rich, and ailing General Sternwood. The general has two daughters, one of whom is being blackmailed by someone unknown. This entire scene takes place in a huge greenhouse on the general's estate, where he indulges his hobby of growing rare orchids. It is stiflingly hot in there, and Marlowe is sweating profusely. The general is dressed completely in white and is confined to his wheelchair. He tells Marlowe all about his orchids and the corruption of his two daughters in what amounts to a series of monologues:

STERNWOOD
A nice state of affairs when a man has to indulge his vices by proxy. You are looking at a very dull survival of a rather gaudy life, a cripple, paralyzed in both legs. There's very little I can eat, and my sleep is so near to waking that it is hardly worth the name. I seem to exist on heat like a newborn spider. . . .

MARLOWE
Yeah?

STERNWOOD
And the orchids are an excuse for the heat. Do you like orchids?

MARLOWE
Not particularly.

STERNWOOD
They are nasty things. Their flesh is too much like the flesh of men, and their perfume has the rotten sweetness of corruption. . . .

Marlowe asks the General about his daughters:

MARLOWE
Are they alike? Do they run around together?

STERNWOOD
I think not. They are alike only in having the same corrupt blood. Vivian is spoiled, exacting, smart, ruthless. Carmen is still the child who likes to pull the wings off flies. I assume they have always had the usual vices, besides new ones of their own invention. . . .

Sternwood's dialogue here has a decidedly Faulknerian ring to it—of all the scenes in the picture, this is the one that seems most likely to have been written by him. Surprisingly enough, the entire scene, almost word for word, is taken over directly from the pages of Chandler's novel. Where, then, is Faulkner? If he didn't write any of this, just what did he do? The answer probably lies in the fact that a film like *The Big Sleep,* like all films for that matter, is a collaborative work, and that Faulkner's precise function here may be hard to isolate.

Another look at this particular scene reveals a certain oddness—it manages both to look and to sound unlike all the rest of the picture; it almost seems to exist independently. The film critic Manny Farber has noticed this specific quality:

All the unbelievable events in *The Big Sleep* are tied together by miserable time jumps, but, within each skit, there is a logic of space, a great idea of personality, gesture, where each person is. Bogart's sticking shirt and brain-twisting in front of a princely colonel, which seems to have a present-tense quality, is typically out of touch with other events and probably dropped into its slot from a facetious memory of Faulkner.

Farber may well be right, that it was actually Faulkner who dropped the scene into "its slot." It would appear that often Faulkner's specific function as a screenwriter in the various films on which he worked was the exact determination of "what goes where." An illustration of this is an earlier Hawks and Faulkner collaboration, *To Have and Have Not* (1944). In a rather famous scene, the girl Marie (Lauren Bacall) is trying to indicate that she's easily available. When she tells Harry Morgan (Bogart) that all he has to do whenever he wants her is just to whistle, he looks puzzled. She then shows him how to whistle by saying, "You just pucker up . . . and blow. . . ." These lines were actually written by Hawks himself, as part of a screen-test for Bacall, but he could find no way to use them in the picture. Faulkner hit on the idea of moving the couple into the hotel room and having them talk there, where the scene "worked." The only *writing* Faulkner did for the scene was in supplying the characters with the preliminary dialogue that led up to Bacall's delivery of Hawks's lines.

Leigh Brackett was one of the three writers on *The Big Sleep*. I once met her at a writers' conference held on the West Coast in the mid sixties, and I asked her if she could remember much about Faulkner's part in the writing of the script. Since it had been the very first picture she had ever worked on, she recalled the experience clearly, and with great amusement. Faulkner had been excessively polite to her—so polite that his usual manner with her had seemed to be a parody of the way in which a Southern gentleman might treat a nice young lady on her very first job. Twenty years later she still found it funny, and rather touching.

She told me that a great deal of their time had been spent in trying to clarify Chandler's extremely complicated plot. The three writers had shuffled and reshuffled its strands, desperately attempting to make the story coherent. The motivations of the characters kept baffling them: *Why* did X kill Y if Z really didn't know all along that X actually . . . ? This involved a seemingly endless juggling of the individual scenes, with Faulkner functioning as the chief juggler. At the end of nearly three months of hard work, they had a screenplay that still worried them, but not Howard Hawks. He had told them that if they just kept things happening fast enough, it wouldn't make very much difference. Hawks was right; it really didn't.

All this tinkering and shuffling may sound very much like glorified hack-work, and there is not much doubt that Faulkner himself often considered it to be just that and nothing else. It was something to be equated with a weekly paycheck: so many words, so many dollars. But Faulkner's work in Hollywood (mostly with Hawks) led to some quite curiously delightful films, and it is interesting to see that time has treated them a lot more kindly than it has the more "thoughtful" or "serious" films of the thirties and forties. *The Big Sleep* and *The Maltese Falcon* are a lot more tolerable today than many of the more ambitious films of the time, which were once highly touted as "art": *The Informer, Wuthering Heights,* and *The Best Years of Our Lives.*

This brief look at *The Big Sleep* hasn't really answered too many of the questions raised previously. For any reasonably clear picture of Faulkner's long and sometimes bitter involvement with Hollywood, it is necessary to go back to the very beginnings of his career there.

[2]

It was his almost complete failure to make any money as a writer that brought Faulkner to Hollywood, and it was this continued failure that kept bringing him back there again and again. Only one of his earlier books had any real success, and it was this that got Faulkner his first job as a screenwriter. The book was *Sanctuary,* which enjoyed a relatively good sale— good, that is, for a Faulkner novel. His first four books, including *The Sound and the Fury,* had an average sale of about 2,000 copies per title. Three different publishers had brought these books out to a variety of responses from the reviewers and critics of the time: admiration, bewilderment, and resounding indifference. The reading public's response was the last of these, four times in a row.

In the late 1920s Faulkner didn't seem to care very much about making money from writing books. He had gotten by with doing odd jobs as a sort of general handyman in his hometown of Oxford, Mississippi: house-painting, carpentry, and even golf instruction. He had also lived intermittently on the Gulf Coast in Pascagoula, Mississippi, where he did a little rum-running, as well as working on shrimp trawlers. It seemed to be enough for him.

His feelings about money underwent a marked change after his marriage in 1929 to Estelle Franklyn, who had brought with her two children by her first marriage. Now, with a family to support for the first time, Faulkner decided that it was about time he made some money from his writing. *Sanctuary* was to be the book, and Faulkner later wrote an account of just why he had written it:

I began to think of books in terms of possibly money. I decided I might just as well make some of it myself. I took a little time out, and speculated what a person in Mississippi would believe to be current trends and invented the most horrific tale I could imagine and wrote it in about three weeks and sent it to Smith, who had done *The Sound and the Fury* and who wrote me immediately, "Good God, I can't publish this. We'd both be in jail."

Faulkner claimed that he had then proceeded to forget all about *Sanctuary,* but that his publisher had not. Some time in the next year, 1930, Harrison Smith changed his mind about the book and sent Faulkner a set of galleys for his correction. Faulkner was appalled when he read them:

Then I saw that it was so terrible that there were but two things to do: tear it up or rewrite it. I thought again, "It might sell; maybe 10,000 of them will buy it." So I tore the galleys down, and rewrote the book. It had already been set up once, so I had to pay for the privilege of rewriting it, trying to make out of it something which would not shame *The Sound and the Fury* and *As I Lay Dying* too much and I made a fair job and I hope you will buy it and tell your friends and I hope they will buy it too.

A fairly large number of people did buy it, and it would be pleasant to think that Faulkner had been successful in his efforts to make some of the money he sorely needed. But things turned out rather differently than he had expected: Harrison Smith's firm went bankrupt within six months after *Sanctuary* was published early in 1931, and Faulkner received almost nothing in the way of royalties from the sale of the book at that time. The only money to come from *Sanctuary* was to come from Hollywood.

It came in two ways—by the sale of the film rights to Paramount Pictures, and by Faulkner's securing a contract as a screenwriter at Metro-Goldwyn-Mayer. Despite its rather limited commercial success, *Sanctuary* became something of a controversial book, even a notorious book, and its impact was clearly felt in Hollywood. New writers were always in demand there, but especially so in the early days of the sound film. The early talkies needed talk, a lot of it, and the studios were literally desperate for writers who could supply it. Writing talents were recruited wherever they seemed likely to emerge, from the popular magazines, from the Broadway stage and, above all, from among the younger novelists. No one was considered too good or too "pure"—if Henry James had been around in the early thirties he too might well have been offered a contract. So while it may seem unlikely today that Faulkner and Nathanael West could secure writing jobs on the basis of books like *Sanctuary* and *Miss Lonelyhearts,* it must be recalled that both of these novels contained a good deal of what was then considered to be toughly realistic dialogue, a highly desired product in the years of *Scarface, Little Caesar,* and *The Public Enemy.*

By the end of 1931 Faulkner was quite aware that his talents might command some sort of a price in Hollywood. He had met the agent Leland Hayward on a visit to New York in the autumn of that year, and Hayward agreed to represent him on the West Coast. On December 18, Hayward received a telegram from Sam Marx, the head of the MGM story department in Culver City, that read:

DID YOU MENTION WILLIAM FAULKNER TO ME ON YOUR LAST TRIP HERE. IF SO IS HE AVAILABLE AND HOW MUCH. BEST REGARDS

Absolutely nothing came of this, for Faulkner was not at all eager to go to California at that time. He had apparently agreed to write some sort of an original story for Miss Tallulah Bankhead, an old school friend of his wife, Estelle, but nothing ever seems to have come of this either; in any case, the work would have been done at home in Oxford. All through the early months of 1932 he was counting on receiving the accrued royalties earned by the sales of *Sanctuary* to bail him out of the financial difficulties he now found himself in, largely caused by his purchase the previous year of the house and land that he later called Rowan Oak.

When it became apparent that MGM was seriously interested in hiring him, Faulkner began to show a strong reluctance about actually going to California, but his economic plight made it hard to refuse their various offers. Early in 1932 Harrison Smith was placed in involuntary bankruptcy proceedings by his disaffected English partner, Jonathan Cape, thus depriving Faulkner of the approximately $4,000 due him at that time. When it became quite clear that he would never receive any of this money, he found it nearly impossible to reject MGM's offer. Although he had just completed *Light in August* that spring, the book did not promise much in the way of any real money. Harrison Smith was soon back in the publishing business, under still another of his many imprints, but his advance for the book was necessarily a very small one. So in May of 1932 Faulkner went out to Hollywood in urgent quest of money, for the first of his many visits.

At the very start, it might be best to attempt some clear picture of how he struck the people he met at MGM. A very small man, scarcely over five feet in height, he was usually dressed in impeccably pressed but worn tweeds and had a pipe constantly clenched between his teeth. His social graces were as absent in California as they were in Mississippi or New York. His habitual manner was nearly always reserved to the point of what seemed to some downright rudeness; he was so distant that he made a lot of people uneasy. It took a long time to break down his famous reserve, and there were many who never did.

His very speech presented a special problem. It was quite literally true that it was often difficult to understand what Faulkner was actually *saying*—his low-pitched Mississippi drawl made him very nearly unintelligible to many of his fellow workers at the studio. When they could understand him, they often didn't especially like what they heard. For he really seemed to be somewhere else most of the time, certainly not in the hectic swirl of daily story conferences. His social life in Hollywood was confined to the extent of his almost not having one. And then there was all that booze: his drinking capacity was legendary from the time of his arrival. None of these things were to help him much in Hollywood, and they offer at least a partial explanation of why his pay scale remained so low during the time he spent there.

There were also those who fully appreciated his genuine warmth and charm—the fantastic wit and humor that accompanied his frightening powers of observation. He usually said very little, but when he did speak he could be devastating. Despite the relaxed manner, there was nothing casual about him.

Unlike Nathanael West, Faulkner never worked for the smaller studios such as Republic or Monogram whose product was entirely *schlock*. He started out at what was then the very top: the MGM of Irving Thalberg and Louis B. Mayer, the studio with the highest pretensions to culture, always tempered by the best cost accountants in the business. The depression had spared only MGM and Warner Brothers and by 1932 they were the only major studios to have remained financially solvent. Paramount, Fox, and Universal had all either declared bankruptcy or were in some form of receivership. All studio production costs were being cut to the bone, and the writers were among the first to feel it. He had come to Hollywood at a very bad time.

Faulkner's original contract with MGM was not especially lucrative either by today's standards or by those of 1932. The contract was for a very short time, really a trial period of six weeks' work at $500 per week. This was a lot of money to Faulkner, actually ". . . more money than I had ever seen, and I thought it was more than there was in all Mississippi."

Almost from the very moment of his arrival at MGM he began to create legends about himself. He had found his first impressions of Hollywood quite unnerving, so unnerving that during his very first week there he decided to quit immediately and was reported to have fled in panic from the studio, spending several days wandering around in the wilds of Death Valley: "The truth is that I was scared. . . . I was scared by the hullabaloo over my arrival, and when they took me into a projection room to see a picture, and kept assuring me that it was going to be very easy, I got flustered." Why Death Valley? It is curious that two film directors, von Stroheim and Antonioni, although separated in time by over forty years, should both share the same sort of hypnotic fascination with the place. Both *Greed* and *Zabriskie Point* * use Death Valley as the

* *They were both MGM films.*

"escaping place" for their main characters, and perhaps this is why Faulkner fled there—to the most desolate spot of earth in all of North America.

Faulkner quickly returned to the studio—all was forgiven—and he was soon given a chance to see what MGM actually produced. After sitting through about ten minutes of a screening of one MGM picture, he is supposed to have emerged from the projection room, muttering over and over to himself, "Jesus Christ, it ain't possible!" On still another of these occasions, he is reported to have requested the projectionist to stop the picture very soon after its beginning, as he knew only too well how it would all come out.

There have been a great many stories told about Faulkner's seemingly total ignorance of both films and the whole world of film-making. Most of these stories are probably apocryphal, but some of them display a certain guile on Faulkner's part, as when he is reputed to have asked Sam Marx, the head of MGM's story department, if they had anything to do with Mickey Mouse—if they did, Faulkner would be only too happy to supply them with some ideas for the series. When Marx politely told him that MGM was not in the cartoon business, he then wondered if they might like him to write newsreels. Behind these country-bumpkin antics lay the simple fact that Faulkner knew perfectly well what he was supposed to do in Hollywood. He was just pretending he didn't, but not for very long.

During the single year he remained on MGM's payroll, Faulkner worked on a total of nine "projects" for them, originals and adaptations of both his own and other writers' work. These covered a wide range, running from twenty-page treatments to full-length screenplays. In essence, they were fairly competent imitations of the sort of picture 'MGM was then turning out: "problem" pictures set in "mythical Latin-American kingdoms," aerial combat stories of World War I, and just plain love stories. Only two of these efforts were ever produced, but they were written during the period of Faulkner's second and final MGM contract. The original one had expired at the end of June 1932, with MGM refusing to pick up its renewal option, and this might well have been the end of Faulkner's career as a screenwriter. He had earned $3,000 in weekly paychecks, as well as another $3,000 from MGM for the film rights to his famous *Saturday Evening Post* story of World War I torpedo boats, "Turn About." He hadn't really made the grade in Hollywood and later said that ". . . it ain't my racket. I can't see things . . . I can only hear." He had agreed "to do an honest day's work according to what the man said." The $6,000 was more money than he had ever had in his life. If MGM didn't want him around anymore, he was perfectly happy to leave California, and that seemed to be the end of it.

Within a month or two of his return to Oxford there was a sudden change. It had been the director Howard Hawks who had bought "Turn About" for MGM, and he now wanted Faulkner's services for the writing of the screenplay for what became *Today We Live*. Faulkner was reluctant, and a certain amount of persuasion was required: "He [Hawks] sent for me—called me at home in Oxford. I said to him, 'Now why the hell should I get out there? Here I am—I had $6000 . . . —with more money than any man in the state of Mississippi. . . .'" The phone call worked, and Faulkner returned to Culver City the following month. MGM was still cutting its costs, and his salary dropped to $250 per week.

Faulkner and Hawks struck up an immediate and close relationship that was to last until Faulkner's death in 1962. They shared a common interest in hunting and flying and, most of all, in story-telling. Curiously enough, both men had younger brothers who had been killed in freakish plane crashes. Faulkner liked to think of Hawks as a "broken-down aviator" like himself, while Hawks regarded Faulkner as a vital force in the kind of pictures he wished to make. He was to continue thinking this way for the next twenty years.

The relationship with Hawks was the most important, as well as the most lasting, one that Faulkner was to make in all his years in Hollywood. It was quite unlike the usual one between writer and film director, for Hawks was like no other director in the Hollywood of 1932.

Hawks's career as a film-maker has been unique in Hollywood. He began directing films in 1926 and was still at it as late as 1970. But it has not been simply the longevity of his career that has made Hawks the subject of such intense interest to us today. Hawks has had, almost from the very beginning, a degree of *control* over his films that has been virtually unmatched by any other Hollywood director. This degree of tight control has given his films a consistency of tone and attitude, a personal style that is unmistakably his own in whatever he has chosen to do. There are a number of very good reasons for this relative independence from the more usual rigidities of Hollywood film-making, beginning with the simple fact that nearly every Hawks film has shown a profit. Strong box-office receipts can often guarantee a fairly high degree of artistic freedom.

Another factor of perhaps equal importance is that Hawks was something of a writer himself, contributing regularly to the scripts he both produced and directed. He had written the original stories on which were based the scripts of his early silent films such as *The Road to Glory* (1926), *Fig Leaves* (1926), and *A Girl in Every Port* (1928). He was the coauthor of the script for his own *Dawn Patrol* (1930), and a number of his later sound films were based on his own stories: *The Crowd Roars* (1932), *Only Angels Have Wings* (1939), and *Red Line 7000* (1965). Although officially uncredited for the work, he seems to have had a hand in the writing of the script for Von Sternberg's *Underworld*. His improvisational abilities as a writer are apparent in every one of his films.

Hawks's attitude toward his own work is often startlingly similar to Faulkner's. When asked by critics in various interviews about his meanings or intentions in a given film, he frequently replies to the questions in this fashion: "Oh, I listen to them, and I get open-mouthed and wonder where they find some of the stuff they say about me. *All I'm doing is telling a story.*" *

As a director, Hawks was in the rare position of being able to tell a writer just what he wanted, an ability he did not share with many other Hollywood directors, either then or now. This talent was to prove invaluable in his working relationship

---

* *Italics added.*

with Faulkner, who was to find that Hawks was the one man he could work for and with in his screenwriting career, and just about no one else. Faulkner was to function primarily as a technician in Hollywood—a writer, yes, but one who mainly contented himself with carrying out his various assignments as best he could. At no time did Faulkner envision himself as enriching the possibilities of film as a creative medium, as Fitzgerald had occasionally hoped to accomplish in his embittered years as a screenwriter. As a Hollywood "worker," Faulkner was much closer in outlook to Nathanael West, who also refused to take his work there very seriously. Both men regarded Hollywood as a place to earn the money to support their own not very profitable writing careers. Working with Hawks was to be fun, but profitable fun.

Films had lost a certain amount of their basic fluidity with the advent of the sound film in the late twenties, although this fact has been greatly exaggerated by some film historians, as a quick look at the opening sequences of Wellman's *The Public Enemy* of 1931 will attest. Camera movement had become somewhat limited by the heavy but extremely sensitive recording equipment, and some motion pictures moved very slowly for several years. Talk was the thing, and people talked as they never would again, with crippling effects on the medium. Hawks's predilection for movement in his films turned him in the direction of the "action" film, but when he did direct "talk" films, the talk was faster and funnier than anyone else's in the business: *Twentieth Century* (1934) and *His Girl Friday* (1940).

At the time of his first meeting with Faulkner in 1932, Hawks had directed three of these "action" films: *Scarface, Tiger Shark,* and *The Crowd Roars* (all 1932). They all had one thing in common: a speed and a compulsive drive in the *telling* that singled them out from most of the films of the early sound period. They were produced very quickly, and their only purpose was entertainment; they were in every way possible the complete antithesis of the "serious" or "art" film. They were nearly always based on clichés of one sort or another, but they did possess the supreme virtue of *movement.*

In the United States, it was probably Manny Farber who

first singled out Hawks, along with Raoul Walsh (*They Drive by Night, White Heat, High Sierra*) and William Wellman (*The Public Enemy, Roxie Hart*), as the really important directors in Hollywood, as opposed to the award-winning, "serious" type of director such as William Wyler and George Stevens. Here is Farber's view:

Hawks and his group are perfect examples of the anonymous artist, who is seemingly afraid of the polishing, hypocrisy, bragging, fake educating that goes on in serious art. To go at his most expedient gait, the Hawks type must take a withdrawn, almost hidden stance in the industry. Thus, his films seem to come from the most neutral, humdrum, monotonous corner of the movie lot. The fascinating thing about these veiled operators is that they are able to spring the leanest, shrewdest, sprightliest notes *from material that looks like junk* and from a creative position that on the surface seems totally un-committed and disinterested. With striking photography, a good ear for natural dialogue, an eye for realistic detail, a skilled inside-action approach to composition, and the most politic hand in the movie field, the action directors have done a forbidding stenography on the hard-boiled handyman as he progresses through the years.*

If this can be taken as a fairly accurate description of the way in which Hawks went about making his films, it should be obvious that a writer like Faulkner would be extremely helpful in making them. *Sanctuary* itself was filled with passages that may have been appealing to the director of *Scarface*. The fu-neral service for the gangster Red has turned into a drunken brawl, and his coffin has been knocked to the floor:

When they raised the corpse the wreath came too, attached to him by a hidden end of wire driven into his cheek. He had worn a cap which, tumbling off, exposed a small blue hole in the center of his forehead. It had been neatly plugged with wax and was painted, but the wax had been jarred out and lost. They couldn't find it, but by unfastening the snap in the peak, they could draw the cap down to his eyes.

This was certainly visual enough, but the demands of "Turn About" were quite different. Hawks had wanted Faulkner for the film because he believed that Faulkner could write con-

---

* *Italics added. In London, in the summer of 1972, Huston's* Key Largo *was considered pre-tentious and vapid, while Hawks's* The Big Sleep *drew cheers.*

vincing British dialogue. Faulkner did "just what the man said" and wrote the entire script in clipped, staccato Britishese, almost all of which was to be spoken by American actors. When *Today We Live* was released in 1933, this relentless dialogue amused many of the critics:

"Make a hit?"
"Yes."
"Glad. Been waiting."

At their very first meeting, Hawks had told Faulkner just what he wanted: stick to his original story as closely as possible. Faulkner told him he'd have the script ready for him in five days. He did just that, establishing for the first time that he could turn out a script faster than just about anyone else in Hollywood. Irving Thalberg is supposed actually to have read this script himself and to have given his formal blessings to the project, but everything changed with the sudden "availability" of Joan Crawford for the film. The addition of a heroine entailed a complete rewriting of the script, and the result was a lugubrious love triangle, with Crawford in love with both Gary Cooper and Robert Young. The action sequences were the only good thing about the picture; it failed with the critics and had a very modest financial success.

The relative failure of *Today We Live* did not diminish Hawks's faith in Faulkner. There really doesn't seem to be much doubt that it was Hawks's continuing belief in Faulkner that enabled him to keep coming back to Hollywood. It might even be claimed that Hawks's influence made Faulkner a viable commodity in Hollywood, or that at least Hawks tried his best to make him one.

It was the association of Hawks and Faulkner on *Today We Live* that gave birth to what is perhaps the most famous of all the stories about Faulkner in Hollywood. This is the "I'm working at home" story, of which there are at least a dozen versions. It is such a good story that in one form or another it has turned up in many recent books about Hollywood; Mel Gussow's book on Zanuck, *Don't Say Yes, Until I Finish Talking,* has it taking place at Twentieth Century-Fox in the late thirties, while Jack Warner's "autobiography," *My First Hundred Years in Hollywood,* locates it at Warner Brothers in the mid forties. The actual events of the story took place at MGM in 1932.

During the rewriting of *Today We Live,* Faulkner's father died suddenly, and Faulkner returned to Oxford where he remained for several months. The work on the script continued, largely by telephone. When it was finished, Hawks suggested that if Faulkner ever needed movie work again, the door would always be open to him at MGM. A knock on that door was soon necessary, and Faulkner informed Hawks that he was ready to start work whenever Hawks wanted him. The weekly paychecks, now increased to $600, started arriving immediately and continued to do so until May of 1933. There was a clear understanding between them that Faulkner could work at home if he wanted to, just as he had done in the past. It was only when someone at the studio, who was not privy to this arrangement, made an attempt to contact Faulkner that the trouble began. Working at home was not unusual, but when "home" proved to be 2,000 miles away, a legend was created that grew as the years passed, with Faulkner helping all the way.

In his usual tall-tale manner, Faulkner told many conflicting versions of what had actually happened, sometimes even denying the whole thing by claiming it was all "a pure lie by some press agent fella." The way he usually told it was that he had been getting $600 a week from MGM for doing absolutely nothing. In 1956, in his famous *Paris Review* interview with Jean Stein, he told it this way: *

About six months later I wired my director friend that I would like another job. Shortly after that I received a letter from my Hollywood agent enclosing my first week's paycheck. I was surprised because I had expected first to get an official notice or recall and a contract from the studio. I thought to myself the contract is delayed and will arrive in the next mail. Instead, a week later I got another letter from the agent enclosing my second week's paycheck. That began in November 1932 and continued until May 1933. Then I received a telegram from the studio. It said: *William Faulkner, Oxford, Miss. Where are you? M.G.M. Studio.*

* *From* Writers at Work, *The Paris Review Interviews edited by Malcolm Cowley, First Series. Copyright © 1957, 1958 by The Paris Review, Inc. Reprinted by permission of The Viking Press, Inc.*

I wrote out a telegram *M.G.M. Studio, Culver City, California. William Faulkner.*

The young lady operator said: "Where is the message, Mr. Faulkner?" I said, "That's it." She said: "The rule book says that I can't send it without a message, you have to say something." So we went through her samples and selected I forget which one—one of the canned anniversary greeting messages. I sent that. Next was a long distance telephone call from the studio directing me to get on the first airplane, go to New Orleans and report to Director Browning. I could have got on a train in Oxford and been in New Orleans eight hours later. But I obeyed the studio and went to Memphis where an airplane did occasionally go to New Orleans. Three days later one did.

I arrived at Mr. Browning's hotel about six P.M. and reported to him. A party was going on. He told me to get a good night's sleep and be ready for an early start in the morning. I asked him about the story. He said, "Oh, yes. Go to room so and so. That's the continuity writer. He'll tell you what the story is."

I went to the room as directed. The continuity writer was sitting in there alone. I told him who I was and asked him about the story. He said: "When you have written the dialogue I'll let you see the story." I went back to Browning's room and told him what had happened. "Go back," he said, "and tell that so and so—never mind, you get a good night's sleep so we can get an early start in the morning."

So the next morning in a very smart rented launch, all of us except the continuity writer sailed down to Grand Isle, about a hundred miles away where the picture was to be shot, reaching there just in time to eat lunch and have time to run the hundred miles back to New Orleans before dark.

That went on for three weeks. Now and then I would worry a little about the story but Browning always said, "Stop worrying. Get a good night's sleep so we can get an early start tomorrow morning."

One evening on our return I had barely entered my room when the telephone rang. It was Browning. He told me to come to his room at once. I did so. He had a telegram. It said: *Faulkner is fired. MGM Studio.* "Don't worry," Browning said. "I'll call that so and so up this minute and not only make him put you back on the payroll but send you a written apology." There was a knock on the door. It was a page with another telegram. This one said: *Browning is fired. MGM Studio.* So I came back home. I presume Browning went somewhere too. I imagine that continuity writer is still sitting in a room somewhere with his weekly paycheck clutched tightly in his hand. They never did finish the film. . . .*

* *They actually did:* Lazy River, *MGM, 1934.*

The actual circumstances leading to Faulkner's being let go by MGM at this time were more prosaic than he was willing to admit in 1956. The studio had wanted Faulkner to return to Culver City for some additional work on the script after the completion of the location photography in New Orleans. Partially because of his concern about the recent birth of his daughter Jill, Faulkner was adamant about not returning to California at that time. The result was inevitable, and here is the actual telegram he received from Sam Marx of MGM:

OWING TO NECESSITY BROWNING SCRIPT BEING COMPLETED HERE AT STUDIO AND YOUR INABILITY TO RETURN HERE I BELIEVE IT BEST WE RELIEVE YOU OF YOUR ASSIGNMENT STOP MANY THANKS FOR ALL YOU HAVE DONE STOP STUDIO FEELS THIS METHOD OF WORKING IS NOT FEASIBLE CONSEQUENTLY WE WILL BE MOST HAPPY TO CONTINUE YOU ON STAFF HERE AT ANY TIME YOU WILL COME TO CALIFORNIA STOP I HAVE ASKED HOWARD HAWKS TO WRITE YOU. . . .

This is a lot more friendly than the crude "Faulkner is fired" telegram that he referred to in the 1956 interview, but the message is quite clear that the working-at-home system was finished for good. In actual fact, Faulkner had turned out a number of treatments and screenplays for MGM that spring of 1933, not one of which was ever produced. As to why he so strongly wished to indicate that he had been taking MGM's money for nothing, it may be that while he had done the writing they had asked him to do, they in turn had refused to make use of it—which in his view was clearly taking money for nothing. Besides the difficulties of determining his actual whereabouts, MGM couldn't afford the further luxury of spending $600 a week for a writer whose scripts were never produced.

Working with "Director Browning" had not been much of a help to Faulkner's career at MGM, for this was the Tod Browning who had directed a great many of the Lon Chaney horror films of the twenties and, more recently, *Dracula* (1931) and MGM's *Freaks,* released in 1932. For reasons that are now obscure, the studio had conceived the notion of pairing him with Faulkner on this "Southern" property about Cajuns and lazy bayous in Louisiana. At the time of this New Orleans venture, Browning's stock as an MGM director was at an all-time low, largely because of the repercussions from his *Freaks,* which he had made for them in the previous year. This was perhaps the most genuinely "disturbing" feature film ever released in the United States. Nearly the entire cast of the picture was quite literally composed of "freaks" of every possible description—Siamese twins, dwarfs, a living torso, an armless wonder, and several bearded ladies. The film built up to a climax in which Olga Baclanova, playing the part of a villainous trapeze-artist, was carved up by the flashing knives of the freaks into what seemed to be a human chicken. The picture was shown at a disastrous preview in Los Angeles, during the course of which a woman was said to have run screaming up the aisle of the theater. After its formal release, the film was recalled from distribution almost immediately, as many of the exhibitors absolutely refused to book it. This was still very much the era of "You're only as good as your last picture," and in 1933 the relative failure of *Today We Live* and *Freaks* was sufficient grounds for firing almost anyone.*

Hawks himself was not faring too well at MGM at this time either and was replaced on the next picture he directed for them, *Viva Villa!* in 1934. After this, he worked out various combined production-direction deals with virtually all of the major studios, never accepting the role of a "house" director at any one of them. He and Faulkner did not work together again until late in 1935, at Twentieth Century-Fox.

Faulkner accepted his second firing philosophically enough: he had come only for the money, and he had gotten it. Hollywood had made him angry most of the time, and he had absolutely no intention of ever going back there. He hadn't much liked the work, the climate, or most of the people he had met out there. He wrote only one story with a Hollywood setting, "The Golden Land," and he depicts it, as did Nathanael West, as a place for burning:

. . . that city of almost incalculable wealth whose queerly appropriate fate it is to be erected upon a few spools of a substance whose

---

* *Dan Talbot exhumed* Freaks *at his New Yorker Theater in the early sixties, and it has become an "underground classic" of sorts.*

value is computed in billions and which may be completely destroyed in that second's instant of a careless match between the moment of striking and the moment when the striker might have sprung and stamped it out.

[3]

Faulkner . . . worked on a script for me once but I never thought for a moment that he had the slightest interest in either that script or anything else in Hollywood. A director named Howard Hawks kept bringing him out here for reasons that I can only guess at. It may be that he simply wanted his name attached to Faulkner's. Or since Hawks liked to write it was easy to do it with Faulkner, for Bill didn't care much one way or the other. . . .
—*Nunnally Johnson to Tom Dardis, November 1974*

Faulkner returned home to Oxford and got back to his writing. He was there for good, or so he thought. He may have been worried about his writing, for he wrote to a friend late in 1933: ". . . I have written three short stories since I quit the movies, so I have not forgotten how to write during my sojourn downriver." The writing itself was mainly his *Absalom, Absalom!* (1936), with which he had great technical difficulties, abandoning it temporarily to work on *Pylon,* a short novel about a group of impoverished flyers attending a competitive racing meet in New Orleans, which was based partially on some actual events that Faulkner had observed there at the opening of Shushan Airport in February of 1934. It was quite unusual for Faulkner to write a novel about racing pilots in New Orleans, and I think that only his recent involvement with Hawks and Hollywood can explain his ever having written such a book. In a curious sort of way, it may be regarded as Faulkner's "homage" to Howard Hawks, just as Fitzgerald's *The Last Tycoon* was surely his to Thalberg.

A novel about the life of high-speed racing pilots in the mid thirties had close parallels to the kind of picture Hawks was making in these years—the auto-racing of *The Crowd Roars,* the flying in *Ceiling Zero* and *Only Angels Have Wings.* Like many of these Hawks films, *Pylon* is mainly concerned with the ethos of people engaged in dangerous occupations, with the ultimate criterion being simply "How good are you at what you do?" The characters in this book display all the typical Hawksian virtues of professional competence before danger, combined with stoical endurance, qualities equally esteemed by Faulkner.

Nearly all of *Pylon* is seen through the eyes of an unnamed newspaper reporter who befriends a "family" of racing pilots. This family is made up of Roger Shuman, the pilot, Jack Holmes, a parachute jumper, and Laverne, the wife they share between them. There is also Jiggs, the book's wonderful comic relief of sorts, whose sole desire is the possession of an expensive pair of boots. Laverne has a small child and has married Shuman on a throw of the dice to give the boy his name. With her powerful, overriding sexuality, her sheer toughness in the face of disaster, she is the dead center of the book, and the only reason for the reporter's fascination with the group. She bears a certain resemblance to a number of Hawks's later heroines—Hildy Johnson in *His Girl Friday,* "Slim" in *To Have and Have Not,* and the girl called "Feathers" in *Rio Bravo.* Like all Hawks's "tough" women, Laverne has a certain strain of pseudomasculinity about her, although she remains totally and obsessively desirable to all the men around her. This quality of hers disappeared almost entirely in the role played by Dorothy Malone in Douglas Sirk's film of *Pylon,* which he called *The Tarnished Angels.*

There is a very definite "movie" quality about this book that resembles a great many films of the early thirties—pictures like *Hell Divers, The Front Page,* Hawks's *The Crowd Roars* and *Tiger Shark*—all of them rough and tough, fast-talking films about people in "dangerous" occupations. Totally unlike all of Faulkner's previous novels, the people in *Pylon* are not depicted inwardly; they are always seen from the outside, a mandatory device in films. The characters even talk the way the people did in these films, for they keep barking "yair" to each other over and over again, never a simple "yes." Faulkner had been continually cautioned to keep things visual in his screenwriting, and he may have kept this in mind with a vengeance when he wrote the scene in which Laverne and Shuman copulate in mid-air just before she makes her first parachute jump—she believing that it may be their last time together.

Faulkner seems to have had some real hopes of selling *Pylon* to Hollywood when he wrote it in 1934, but there were no takers at that time, not even Howard Hawks. The book was pretty much of a commercial failure, and he soon found himself in debt to his publisher, Harrison Smith, whose firm found it financially impossible to advance Faulkner very much of the money he needed to complete *Absalom, Absalom!,* to which he had now returned. In the fall of 1935 Smith did advance him some money, but there were some strings attached about repaying it.

Faulkner had spent the better part of a month working at Universal for $1,000 a week in July of 1934, mainly on an unrealized project of Howard Hawks called *Sutter's Gold;* it is most likely that this short visit produced his only piece of fiction about Hollywood: "The Golden Land." Smith recalled this profitable trip and suggested that another like it might be in order to solve Faulkner's money problems. Smith enlisted the help of the well-known literary agent Harold Ober, who somewhat later became Faulkner's agent for all his writing. On this occasion, Ober's task was solely to secure him some sort of work on the West Coast, but nothing very much came from his efforts. In early December of 1935, Faulkner wrote to his then literary agent, Morty Goldman, that he was desperate for a contract: "About movies, I don't care how I get a contract, just so I do. I had rather it came through you. . . . My feeling about the movie contract is, as you know, that I don't particularly want to go at all but am doing so as part of my agreement with Smith: so let them find the way to farm me out, if that's what they want."

In the course of this same letter to Goldman, Faulkner mentioned that the earlier efforts of Harold Ober had failed to produce any offers: ". . . I understand that he returned and told Hal Smith what I had already told him that they were not going to contract for Shakespeare himself 3 months ahead, but that he [Ober] left strings out for later." Perhaps the strings worked, for he finally got his contract that very same month. It was again Howard Hawks who had gotten it for him, this time at Twentieth Century-Fox, where he had just signed a single-picture deal with the newly created firm. Hawks had convinced Darryl F. Zanuck that Faulkner was just the man for the writing of the screenplay on what was released as *The Road to Glory* in 1936.

Twentieth Century-Fox had come about through the merger, or rather takeover, of the once mighty but now moribund Fox Film Corporation by Joseph M. Schenck's new Twentieth Century Pictures, with Darryl F. Zanuck in charge of all production. At the time of Faulkner's employment, the new firm had been in existence for about six months. Zanuck was somewhat more generous with money than MGM had been in 1932–33; he offered a salary of $1,000 per week, and Faulkner accepted immediately. He left for Los Angeles in November of 1935 and remained out there, with occasional trips home between assignments, until the late summer of 1937.

Zanuck was in fact very much in charge of all production at Twentieth Century-Fox, and *The Road to Glory* was one of the very few Hawks pictures supervised by others. Hawks had gotten Faulkner his contract with Zanuck, but after their first picture together Faulkner was strictly on his own, with some occasionally painful results. Hawks himself did not remain long at Twentieth Century-Fox and did not return to work there again for nearly twenty years. Zanuck seems to have been aware that Faulkner was still pretty much of a novice at screenwriting and insisted that he be given a collaborator on *The Road to Glory*. He got one in the person of Joel Sayre, a young novelist who was best known for his college novel, *Ricketay-Rax*. Again, unlike Fitzgerald, Faulkner was quite happy to have a collaborator, and the two writers started work on their assignment for Hawks and Zanuck. Sayre and Faulkner became close friends during this time and remained so during Faulkner's later years in Hollywood.

Faulkner was a heavy drinker in these years, and there are

many legendary accounts of his drinking while working at Twentieth Century-Fox. The most common one is centered around his first meeting with Nunnally Johnson, who had been delegated by Zanuck to be the coproducer of *The Road to Glory*. Roark Bradford was a professional teller of tall tales, and his version of this story is perhaps the most extreme one, but it is amusing enough to relate here. Johnson, a fellow Mississippian, had decided to roll out the red carpet and receive Faulkner in the most awe-inspiring circumstances possible. He was supposed to have done this in a huge room, over one hundred feet long, with three levels of flooring. When one entered this sanctum, one walked the entire length of the room and descended two flights of marble steps to reach the throne of Mr. Nunnally Johnson himself:

"Are you Mr. Johnson?"
"I am. Are you Mr. Faulkner?"
"I am."
There was an awkward silence. During this silence Faulkner fished into his hip pocket, took out a pint of whiskey and began uncorking it. This act was complicated by the fact that the bottle had been sealed with heavy tinfoil. Bill dropped his hat on the floor and went to work with both hands. In the process, he cut his finger on the tinfoil. He attempted to staunch the flow of blood by wetting the wound with his tongue, but it was too deep a cut for that. Next, he looked around for a suitable drip pan. The only thing in sight was the hat at his feet. Holding the bleeding finger over the hat, he continued to work, methodically and silently, until the bottle was finally uncorked. He then tilted it, drank half its contents, and passed it to Johnson.
"Have a drink of whiskey?" he offered.
"I don't mind if I do," said Johnson, finishing off the pint.
This, according to the legend, was the beginning of a drunk which ended three weeks later, when studio sleuths found both Faulkner and Johnson in an Okie camp, sobered them up, and got them to work.

Johnson himself, still another teller of tall tales, relates a much more subdued version of all this. He stresses the fact that Faulkner had insisted on telling him in great detail the circumstances of his youngest brother's tragic death and burial just a month before Faulkner's return to Hollywood. In 1933, with the aid of the MGM money, Faulkner had bought himself a small Waco cabin plane, which he and his youngest brother, Dean Swift Faulkner, flew occasionally. Dean had crashed to his death in the Waco, while giving flying lessons. The face of his brother had been so badly mangled that it was virtually unrecognizable. So Faulkner had worked at the funeral home in Oxford for one entire night with wax, and a bottle of whiskey beside him, rebuilding his dead brother's face, piece by piece, He had done this for the sake of Dean's young and pregnant wife. "And I did a pretty good job," he finished. "Because she just cried." Faulkner was to tell this story obsessively to a number of the people he worked with at Twentieth Century-Fox.

He never made any real attempt to hide his drinking habits and frequently told stories on himself about his escapades. One such story has him attending a polo match, drinking heavily, borrowing a pony, and riding it out onto the field where he finally fell off in a stupor. On awakening, he found himself ". . . starin' right into Darryl Zanuck's teeth bendin' over me. It was such a feelin' of horror that I became instantly sober."

Nunnally Johnson is also responsible for still another story involving Faulkner and Zanuck. There had been

an early conference in which Faulkner had sat for three hours without opening his mouth. Toward the close Mr. Zanuck, presiding, inquired: "Are there any further questions?" Mr. Faulkner sat up and cleared his throat. "Yes, sir."

"What did you have in mind, Mr. Faulkner?" asked Mr. Zanuck, hopeful of some great creative suggestion. "Please," answered Faulkner, "may I have an office?"

He got the office, and he and Sayre went on with their screenplay for *The Road to Glory*. It was to be a war film, in the vague tradition of such pictures as *The Big Parade, All Quiet on the Western Front, Journey's End,* and Hawks's own *Dawn Patrol,* but with a difference. The task of Faulkner and Sayre was to write a screenplay for Hawks that could somehow utilize several thousand feet of excellent combat footage that Zanuck had bought from the producers of a French war film called *Les Croix des Bois*. Without this existing footage, *The*

Road to Glory would probably never have been produced. Calling their script *Zero Hour,* they finished it early in 1936, and the picture went into immediate production.

What they came up with was a love story about the rivalry between a brandy-drinking infantry captain and his young lieutenant over the affections of a pretty nurse, set against the background of trench warfare in the France of 1918. The three roles were played by Warner Baxter, Fredric March, and June Lang. Captain LaRoche endures the horrors of war by living on a straight diet of cognac and aspirin, but is constantly defended by his loyal sergeant as being "the finest officer in the entire Army." The captain's ancient father (Lionel Barrymore!) suddenly joins his company as the oldest private in the French Army, a veteran of the Battle of Sedan in 1870. The picture concludes with a huge French attack in which both father and son are totally blinded. Captain LaRoche and his father deliberately sacrifice themselves, with the father blowing his bugle again as he had done at Sedan. LaRoche's self-sacrifice is motivated by the effect of his blindness on the girl—he does not want her pity—and he chooses to die and leave her to the lieutenant.

The bare bones of this story are certainly maudlin enough, but Hawks was able to bring much of it off in his usual style of extreme understatement. This was particularly true of the scene in which the French troops listen intently as the German sappers dig away beneath their trenches. The dialogue, however, is decidedly mawkish, especially when Monique (the young nurse) talks with Lieutenant Denet about the necessity of going on with the war:

MONIQUE
What sense does it make just to be brave? Why do you all have to die?
DENET (comforting her)
That question has been asked as many times as men have died—but the answer hasn't satisfied anybody or stopped men from killing each other.

Nunnally Johnson has claimed that he rewrote the entire script of *The Road to Glory* himself. He may very well have done so, but there seem to be very definite signs of Faulkner in this film, especially in the scenes between the drunken captain and his loyal sergeant, as well as in the type of dialogue just quoted. At the time he was working on *The Road to Glory*, he was often capable of turning in as much as thirty-five pages of manuscript per day, each one of them neatly written out in his minute handwriting, a daily nightmare for his typists. A good many of these pages remained in the final shooting-script, despite the continually warring pressures of Zanuck, Johnson, and Hawks.

Faulkner may have found the work on the picture either tiring or boring, or both, for he went off on a week's drinking binge just before the script was quite finished. Or he may just possibly have been celebrating his completion of *Absalom, Absalom!*, one of his greatest novels. To have gone on with the writing of such a book while handing in his self-imposed quota of thirty-five pages a day on *The Road to Glory* is astonishing. The fact that he could do this for months on end indicates something about the way in which he regarded his screenwriting—simply a job to be done. Unlike Fitzgerald, Faulkner was able to distinguish clearly his screenwriting from his own writing, the writing in which he became personally involved. Fitzgerald was unable to make this vital distinction—there are pages in *The Last Tycoon* that could almost have been written *for* Thalberg, a love letter of sorts. Faulkner had never felt the kind of infatuation for the movies that Fitzgerald occasionally had; he always knew that his talents belonged elsewhere. Which is not to say that these talents did not show up in odd ways in the pictures he worked on, or that he didn't feel the pressures of working for Zanuck and, much later, Jack Warner.

The binge cost him some time in a hospital. His principal French translator, Maurice Edgar Coindreau, visited Faulkner in his Beverly Hills home in the early summer of 1937 and has this to say of Faulkner's drinking at that time:

He drank. That was no secret to anybody. He did not try to hide it, nor did he boast of it like certain other writers of the "lost generation." He would go through tragic periods, but would emerge from his crises just as a strong swimmer succeeds in escaping from the undertow that carries him away. Personally I never saw him give any embarrassing signs of drunkenness. While I was staying at his home, he drank constantly, but without seeming to be affected by it. . . .

Faulkner quickly recovered and was back at work at the studio by the end of February 1936. He was then assigned to write some dialogue sequences for a picture called *Banjo on My Knee,* a love story filled with the local color of Mississippi bargemen. One of Faulkner's continuing troubles in Hollywood was the *kind* of dialogue he wrote; he was often accused of writing dialogue that actors would have considerable difficulty speaking. Here is a speech written by Faulkner for *Banjo on My Knee,* in which the heroine (Barbara Stanwyck) is explaining why she has been abandoned by her lover:

PEARL
Then he left me before we were even married. He fixed it so that his people could say the things about me they wanted to say. Then he left me, because when I left I wasn't running from him. I was running after him. If he had loved me he would have known that. If he had loved me he would not have left me. If he had loved me he would have followed me and overtaken me. He could have because no woman ever runs too fast for the man she loves to catch her, but he didn't. All he was after was to catch the man he thought had offered to give me what he had denied to give me. So that even this man would have to leave me just as he had left me.

Although this is rhythmically simple, it is easy to believe that it would have given any competent actress, including Stanwyck, some real trouble. It is also likely that Zanuck and Johnson were worried that audiences simply wouldn't accept convoluted speech like this; they were probably quite sure that shantyboat girls didn't—really *shouldn't*—talk this way in a film, for none of Faulkner's scenes were used in the picture.

He next became involved with a rather curious film called *Slave Ship,* for which he received screen credit in this manner: "Story by William Faulkner." There is some confusion as to just what this means, since he did not write either the actual screenplay or the original material on which the picture was based, which was a novel called *The Last Slaver* by George S. King. He may have written an extended treatment based on this novel, parts of which were retained in the shooting-script.

A stronger possibility is that he acted here as a sort of "script doctor" for the picture, inserting some things in the script by Sam Hellman, Lamar Trotti, and Gladys Lehman that seem very much his own. He was once asked point-blank just what he had contributed to *Slave Ship,* and his answer suggests that his function was exactly that: "I'm a motion-picture doctor. When they run into a section they don't like, I rework it and continue to rework it until they do like it. In 'Slave Ship,' I reworked sections. I don't write scripts. I don't know enough about it."

Slave Ship was directed by Tay Garnett, a not especially distinguished director—*China Seas* and *The Postman Always Rings Twice* are perhaps his best-known films—but the only director other than Hawks to direct scripts on which Faulkner had worked. The result was an oddly entertaining film that became something of a minor hit and was included in the top-grossing films of 1937. It again starred Warner Baxter, along with Wallace Beery and Mickey Rooney. The story deals with the attempts of the captain (Baxter) of a "slaver" to give up the slave trade and retire to a new life ashore with his young bride. He is ruthlessly opposed by his crafty first mate (Beery), as well as by most of his crew. Only with the last-minute help of the bright young cabin boy (Rooney) does he succeed in either killing members of the crew or having them hanged by the British Navy. The "mood" of the film swings back and forth between the extremes of an early sort of "black humor" and bloody melodrama.

It is the atmosphere of the film that gives it whatever distinction it does have, and it is this atmosphere that Faulkner seems to have provided. The poet Delmore Schwartz wrote an essay on Faulkner in the early forties and noticed the unmistakable presence of Faulkner in the picture: "It was an astonishing and just experience five years ago to attend a film named 'Slave Ship,' be struck by the Faulkneresque quality of the way in which the story was presented and find later that Faulkner had written the scenario." Schwartz had not looked at the screen credits too carefully, but he probably was right about Faulkner's hand in "the way the story was presented."

A good deal of *Slave Ship* is seen through the wide-eyed gaze of Mickey Rooney as the very young cabin boy. He has painfully mixed feelings toward his rather lovable but absolutely murderous first mate, portrayed in Beery's usual style of simulated booziness. Although the first mate is not above tying the living bodies of his human cargo to the ship's anchor chain in order to destroy them as "evidence," he is also capable of extreme devotion to his canary. Eventually, the boy turns against the cruelty of his old friend and betrays him to the captain. The strange bond between the cabin boy and the first mate is rather moving, and their scenes together are about the best parts of the picture. With a single exception. My own strongest memory of this film is a series of extremely brief scenes that occur with slight variations throughout the entire length of the picture. They concern a ferociously silent Chinese cook who is planning the killing of the cat that has been raiding the ship's galley. The repeated image of this cook, constantly sharpening his cleaver in anticipation of the cat's next visit, serves the same function in *Slave Ship* as does the greenhouse scene in *The Big Sleep*—it exists independently of all the rest of the picture, but works wonderfully well in establishing the curious atmosphere of the film.

Without the helpful presence of Howard Hawks, Faulkner's screenwriting career soon ran into difficulties. He was assigned to writing still another war picture, *Splinter Fleet,* but there were again objections from his employers that his dialogue was not "right." After several weeks he was finally taken off the picture, and *Splinter Fleet* eventually became John Ford's *Submarine Patrol,* with none of Faulkner's collaborative screenplay ever being used. His employment at Twentieth Century-Fox soon became quite erratic, and he was loaned out wherever and whenever they could find employment for him. This situation brought him over to RKO Radio to work on the George Stevens production of *Gunga Din,* a project in which a large number of writers had been involved, including Ben Hecht, Charles MacArthur, Joel Sayre, and Fred Guiol. When the picture was finally released in 1939, Hecht and MacArthur received screen credit for the "story," with Sayre and Guiol listed as the authors of the actual screenplay. Faulkner received no credit of any kind, a situation that was rapidly becoming familiar to him.

He totally lacked self-assurance as a screenwriter, especially without Hawks, and never really felt comfortable in the performance of his job. In some ways he felt he was out there under false pretenses, working at a trade for which he sensed he lacked the kind of talent that could turn out "successful" screenplays. He kept on being surprised that his employers would go on paying him for what he was doing, so he was not too surprised when his pay was cut to $750 per week, beginning in August of 1936, not rising to $1,000 per week again until March of 1937.

He had also gotten bored with the work. Hawks could make almost anything interesting, but the daily fare at the studio became deadly dull for him; on projects such as *The Giant Swing* and *Four Men and a Prayer* he turned in not one single word. He was fighting a losing battle, but the money pressures remained as before, and he was forced to stay on in California for as long as he could.

Faulkner had a lot of difficulty in simply making the time pass in his nearly two years of work at Twentieth Century-Fox. He had invited his wife and young daughter out there on several extended visits and had even brought along a favorite black cook from Oxford to make things seem a little more like home; he now had hominy grits for breakfast. His social life was somewhat richer than it had been in his MGM days. He would occasionally go off with Nathanael West on long hunting trips to Catalina and Santa Cruz Island in quest of wild boar. West himself was just as much of an oddity in Hollywood as was Faulkner, and he spent nearly all his free time away from his work on "B" pictures at Republic Studios in hunting whatever wild game might flourish anywhere within 500 miles of Los Angeles. Faulkner had originally met West in New York in 1931 and was a great admirer of *Miss Lonelyhearts* at a time when there were very few people around who had actually read or even heard of his book. West deeply appreciated Faulkner's liking his work, and their hunting trips were especially pleasing to both of them, for the hunting expeditions seemed a lot closer to reality than did their daily routines at the studios. Faulkner always addressed West as "Mr. West" on these trips in a sort of parody etiquette they adopted.

West also introduced him to the world of Stanley Rose's bookstore on Hollywood Boulevard, a favorite meeting place for many of the writers living in and around Hollywood. Stanley Rose was a flamboyant self-styled "con man" from Texas with a passionate devotion to literature. This took the form of an enthusiastic, all-out patronage of the writers who came regularly to his avant-garde-style shop. He would actually pack up heavy briefcases filled with the latest books by these writers and would then peddle them from door to door in all the writers' buildings at the various Hollywood studios. He was always good for a quick loan or a sure thing at the track. He also had contact with the underside of Hollywood life—the world of call girls, small-time gangsters, and drug pushers. West got considerable help from Rose in the writing of *The Day of the Locust,* and West fondly used his name as a testimonial on the business card of his dwarf character, Honest Abe Kusich: ". . . *the Lloyds of Hollywood—Stanley Rose.*" He eventually became a literary agent, with William Saroyan as his major client.

Rose maintained a separate room in the back of his establishment where he was the genial host for a continuous seminar in contemporary literature that was held nearly every night. There Faulkner encountered, or rather listened to, the talk of such writers as John O'Hara, Erskine Caldwell, John Sanford, Dashiell Hammett, Gene Fowler, Horace McCoy, Meyer Levin, and even Budd Schulberg, who was a very young man at the time. Scott Fitzgerald, then working away unhappily at MGM, was still another regular visitor at Stanley Rose's, but there is no indication of his ever having encountered Faulkner there, or anywhere else in Hollywood. It was very much like a private club, and its facilities even included slot machines in the back of the store. It was all very sociable, but Faulkner remained just as much of a recluse in Hollywood as he was in Mississippi. If he spoke at all, it was mainly to

Nathanael West and concerned hunting matters. Many of his evenings, both at this time and later, were spent in long, lonely walks through Beverly Hills and the streets of downtown Los Angeles. He went on with his own work—his real work—as best he could, and drank quite a bit. The time passed.

Sometime in August of 1936, just after he had completed his final revisions on the galleys of *Absalom, Absalom!*, Faulkner wrote a letter to his literary agent, Morty Goldman, about his hopes for a movie sale on the book: "As you see, I am in California again up to my neck in moving pictures, where I shall be for about a year. . . . I am going to undertake to sell this book myself to the pictures, first. I am going to ask one hundred thousand dollars for it or nothing, as I do not need to sell it now since I have a job." There were no offers at this price, but he kept right on with his attempts to sell the book, gradually reducing the price as the weeks and months passed.

Faulkner's next assignment for Twentieth Century-Fox was a full-length treatment of Walter D. Edmonds's best-selling historical novel of 1936, *Drums Along the Mohawk,* a rather exacting job for any screenwriter, for the book is a long, discursive, loosely structured work with not very much of a cohesive plot. This treatment survives, and it clearly reveals some of Faulkner's real feelings about the kind of work he had been hired to perform. It isn't entirely bad as treatments generally go, but it all seems curiously detached, almost apathetic, as if he just couldn't maintain any real interest in the book. Only the Indian characters seem to have any genuine life in them, and his proposed basis for a screenplay is actually rather dull and plodding, reflecting a wearisome and time-consuming chore. On the very last page of it, as if completely bored and cynical about the entire project, Faulkner wrote these words: *"Lana tells Mary whatever sappy stuff we need here about love conquers all things, etc."*

He spent nearly three straight months of work on this, but his treatment was never used, and the project was reassigned to another writer. John Ford's production of *Drums Along the Mohawk,* with a screenplay by Lamar Trotti and Sonya Levien, was not released until 1939, perhaps indicating that other writers found it equally difficult. Zanuck and Johnson may well have detected Faulkner's extreme apathy at this time, for he received no further assignments from them, and things had clearly come to an end for him at Twentieth Century-Fox. He left California in August of 1937 for what he thought then was going to be the very last time. On his return to Oxford, he had this to say: "I don't like scenario writing because I don't know enough about it. I feel as though I can't do myself justice in that type of work, and I don't contemplate anymore of it in the near future." This was honest enough and should have marked the end of Faulkner's days in Hollywood, but it didn't.

[4]

"Was you ever bit by a dead bee?"
            —*Eddie in* To Have and Have Not, *1945*

I will take anything above $100.00
            —*Faulkner to Harold Ober, June 1942*

He took a dry, standoffish stance on Hywd, kept to himself, lived in a terrible motel kind of place just alongside the freeway (called in these days the Cahuenga Pass) . . .
            —*Daniel Fuchs to Tom Dardis, May 1975*

Faulkner always seemed to carry a part of California back to Mississippi with him. California forever remained an "alien" place to him, and it erupted oddly in the books he wrote just after returning home. This was true of *Pylon,*, written just after his year of work at MGM, and was equally true of *The Wild Palms,* completed during the year after he finished up at Twentieth Century-Fox. He often called it "that damned West Coast place," and he really seems to have had it in his mind when he wrote angrily and furiously about the "New Valois" of *Pylon,* or the actual New Orleans, Chicago, San Antonio, and Utah mountains of *The Wild Palms*—all of them equally "alien" and unpleasant in every way to him. To exorcise the actual California, he chose to write about "other" places, places he didn't really know very well. Sometimes he dropped the pretense, and openly invoked the sun-riddled realities of life in Southern California, as in *The Wild Palms:* ". . . the lunch rooms with broad strong Western girls got up out of Hollywood magazines (Hollywood which is no longer in Hollywood but is stippled by a billion feet of colored gas across the face of the American earth) to resemble Joan Crawford, asleep or not he could not tell."

In the years between 1938 and 1942, Faulkner published four more books, only one of which had anything approaching a reasonable sale. This was *The Wild Palms* of 1939, which actually reached the number eight slot on the *New York Times* Best Seller List and wound up selling about 15,000 copies. A sale of this size was somewhat freakish, for the next two books—*The Hamlet* and *Go Down, Moses*—sold less than half as well. His production of short stories had fallen off considerably, and he had difficulty in selling the few he did write at this time. His financial rock-bottom was probably reached when he received his royalty statement for the year 1942 from Random House—exactly $300 for all the books they still had in print. By the following year they were all out of print, with the sole exception of *Sanctuary* in the Modern Library Edition, and would remain that way until the end of the decade. Hollywood was now his only hope, and he began looking around for a contract.

There was not very much of a demand for either Faulkner or his books in the Hollywood of 1942. His first two series of visits had yielded him an actual total of only three screen credits—*Today We Live, The Road to Glory,* and *Slave Ship*—not very much by Hollywood standards. *Sanctuary* had been filmed by Paramount early in 1933 with a script written by Oliver H. P. Garrett and Maurice Watkins. It was released as *The Story of Temple Drake* and was not particularly successful. Not one of Faulkner's other novels was filmed until 1949, when MGM produced *Intruder in the Dust.* In the summer of 1942 he was a

writer who had never had a real best seller. He was scarcely a
hot property in that year, either in New York publishing circles or in Hollywood.

There are some details about Faulkner's finances during
this period that require an explanation of why he always
seemed on the verge of a total collapse, despite the quite large
amounts that occasionally came his way. In 1937, he had been
able to earn a total of $21,650 at Twentieth Century-Fox. The
following year was almost as good, for Bennett Cerf of Random House had been able to sell *The Unvanquished* to MGM
for $25,000; Faulkner's share of this was $19,000, but there
were also additional sums earned that year by the sale of short
stories. On the face of it, this seems to be a relatively high income for a writer whose books did not sell; the late-seventies
dollar equivalent to these sums would be about $80,000. The
answer to where all this money went is complicated, but the
main fact is that Faulkner was the sole support of three and
sometimes four families, starting with his own immediate one
of five people. He was also the sole support of his mother and,
for a great many years, the young widow and two small children of his youngest brother, Dean. The $19,000 from MGM
had gone largely to his purchase of a small farm as an investment, which he placed in the care of his brother John. Within
a few years, William had become the sole support of John's
family along with all the rest. The following letter, written in
May of 1940 to Robert Haas of Random House, can be understood only with this background in mind:

. . . I take these fits of sort of raging and impotent exasperation at
this really quite alarming paradox my life reveals: Beginning at the
age of thirty I . . . began to become the sole, principal and partial
support—food, shelter, heat, clothes, medicine, kotex, school fees,
toilet paper and picture shows—of my mother, an inept brother and
his wife and two sons, another brother's widow and child, a wife of
my own and two step children, my own child; I inherited my father's
debts and his dependents, white and black without inheriting anything yet from anyone one inch of land or one stick of furniture or
one cent of money. . . . Now and then, when pressed or worried

about money, I begin to seethe and rage over this. It does no good, and I waste time when I might and should be writing. I still hope some day to break myself of it. What I need is some East Indian process to attain to the nigger attitude about debt.

The simple truth was that he was finding it impossible to support all these people by his book and magazine earnings, and in many of these years the Hollywood money was often the main part of his income; by the late thirties it had become an absolute economic necessity to him. Nearly all the money he made in 1939 came through the book royalties on *The Wild Palms,* the quite respectable sum of $5,500, but scarcely the kind of money he required to pay all his bills. The year 1940 was even worse, and by the beginning of 1941 he was sending telegrams to Harold Ober, who had become his literary agent in 1938, that sounded very much like the ones Fitzgerald had been sending Ober in 1936 and 1937 and for years on end:

WIRE ME COLLECT WHAT POSSIBILITY OF ANY SUM WHATEVER AND WHEN FROM ANY MSS OF MINE YOU HAVE URGENTLY NEED ONE HUNDRED BY SATURDAY.

Ober sent him the hundred dollars immediately, for which Faulkner was grateful enough to send him a thank-you note that showed just how bad things really were:

Thank you for the money, I did not intend the wire to ask for a loan, but I have used the money and I thank you for it. . . . When I wired you I did not have $15.00 to pay electricity bill with, keep my lights burning.

By the early summer of 1942 it had become pretty clear that he must secure some sort of a contract in Hollywood, for he had begun to write letters like this one to the editor of *Story,* Whit Burnett:

I haven't even been able to pay a telephone bill in two months now and I owe the grocer $600.00 and no fuel for the winter yet. But if I can get to Cal. I believe I'll be all right in 6 mos. If you can think of any mag article job to pay my expenses to Cal. and keep me for a month, that will do it.

Faulkner's biographer, Joseph Blotner, reports that on the day after writing this letter, Faulkner wrote to Bennett Cerf filled with absolute desperation:

I have 60¢ in my pocket, and that is literally all. I finished a story and sent it in yesterday, but with no real hope it will sell. My local creditors bother me, but so far none has taken an action because I began last year to give them notes for debts. But the notes will come due soon and should I be sued, my whole house here will collapse: farm, property, everything . . . I have reached the point where I had better go to Cal. with just r.r. fare if I can do no better.

Harold Ober and H. N. Swanson, the Hollywood agent who had gotten Fitzgerald his job at MGM in 1937, did their best to get some sort of a contract for Faulkner, with Ober having to ask him at one point what exactly were his "credentials" as a screenwriter. His answer reveals how low he rated himself at the time as a money-making writer, especially as a Hollywood one:

I believe the agents who have tried . . . to sell me have talked about $1000 per week. I don't think I am or have been or will ever be worth that to movies. It just took them five years to find it out. I will take anything above $100.00 . . . I have cashed in my life insurance and if I were sued by anyone, all my property except my home would go and my daughter and mother and wife would have nothing. Once I get away from here where creditors cannot hound me all the time, I think I can write and sell again.

It took a considerable amount of time and effort to secure the contract he finally managed to get, $300 a week at Warner Brothers, with seven long years of options attached to it as part of the deal. To make matters still worse, he was forced (through various misunderstandings) to pay two different Hollywood agents their commissions for having set up this contract. It had actually been the joint efforts of Bennett Cerf of Random House and Harold Ober (Faulkner's New York agent) that had managed to create some interest in Faulkner at Warner Brothers, and without their influence there would have been no contract. If you write to Warner Brothers today about any of the facts concerning Faulkner's employment there, you may receive a letter from their legal department that will read something like this one:

He was employed by Warner Bros. Pictures Inc. under a so-called long term contract dated July 27, 1942. Under this contract Mr. Faulkner rendered services as a writer for the period July 27, 1942 to September 19, 1945. During Mr. Faulkner's period of employment he wrote or collaborated in the writing of approximately 17 screenplays, 11 of which were produced, and Mr. Faulkner received screenplay credit in connection with two productions.

This is a very neat bill of particulars, but it conceals the harsh reality of three long years of sustained and often painful effort.

These three years at Warner Brothers were the most difficult and humiliating Faulkner experienced in Hollywood. His rate of pay had now dropped nearly all the way to the bottom of the wage scale—even Nathanael West had made a good deal more that $300 a week at the time of his tragically early death in 1940. The truth was that Faulkner was actually now being paid the salary of a "junior writer" at Warner's. Alvah Bessie, one of the famous "Hollywood Ten" of the late forties and early fifties, was given a contract with exactly the same terms as Faulkner's in early 1943. At the time Bessie had published but a single novel, whereas Faulkner had published more than a dozen. It made absolutely no difference to Warner's—they were both "junior writers." If Faulkner had ever bothered to think of himself as having a "career" in Hollywood, it was clear that it had now assumed a steadily downward direction, with Warner Brothers as the last stop.

There were also the facts of his age and his talent: he was very nearly forty-five at the beginning of this contract and just forty-eight when he left Warner's for the last time. These were the years in which he may well have felt he was at the height of his creative powers, which in fact he was; they were years he could never recover. But the real despair came out of the sheer fact of his now complete and absolute bondage to film-writing in Hollywood. The public was simply not interested in his books and gave no indication that they would ever change their minds. As the months wore on, he would frequently curse both the place and the conditions that had brought him there.

These were the years of World War II, when food- and gasoline-rationing became a part of everyday life. Housing was especially tight in Hollywood, and Faulkner was often forced either to stay with friends or to live in cheap, second-rate hotels, never in the apartments of the now demolished Garden of Allah, the place Scott Fitzgerald had once lived in. A proud man under any circumstances, he frequently chose to walk all the way to work and back again. His feelings about this work ran hand in hand with his generally low regard for life in Hollywood. He became obsessively repetitious about it:

I'll be glad when I get back home. . . . Nobody here does anything. There's nobody here with any roots. Even the houses are built out of mud and chicken wire. Nothin' ever happens an' after a while a couple of leaves fall off a tree and then it'll be another year.

I don't like the climate, the people, their way of life. Nothing ever happens and then one morning you wake up and find that you are sixty-five. . . .

There is a series of photographs of Faulkner, taken at the Highland Hotel in Hollywood in 1944 by Alfred Eris. One of them shows Faulkner sitting outdoors in the full blaze of the California sun. He is sitting in a wicker chair on the patio outside his room, dressed only in shorts. His typewriter is placed squarely in front of him. His pipe is clenched firmly between his teeth. His eyes and whatever they contained cannot be seen, for they are completely covered by a large pair of sunglasses. His facial expression is tight and seems to be one of complete disdain for everything in his sight, an anguished disdain that asks the question *"What am I doing here?"*

He might well have asked. Many of the better-known American writers who went to Hollywood did so only when their talents were exhausted, Sinclair Lewis, for example, or when the writer had some cause to think they were—Fitzgerald. This was scarcely the case with Faulkner, although popular and critical esteem for his work had by then reached an all-time low. Although he had published "The Bear" (in *Go Down, Moses*), one of his greatest achievements in fiction, in the spring of 1942, it was dumped on the bookstore remainder tables within the very year of its publication, along with all the

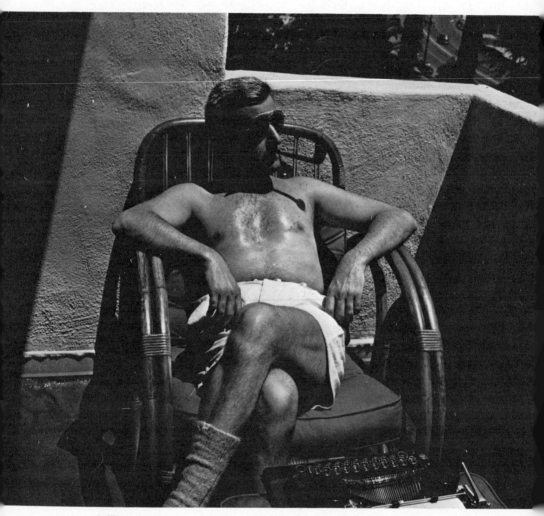

William Faulkner, taken at the Highland Hotel, Hollywood, 1944 (*Alfred Eris*)

rest of his books. So now he sat in the warm sun of California quietly wringing out just a few more words for Jack Warner and that weekly paycheck. There was not much else to do; he was trapped.

Warner Brothers had a definite style and temperament very much its own in the thirties and forties; a gaudily flamboyant yet somehow basically "serious" atmosphere prevailed in Burbank, which many of its writers found especially to their liking. While MGM was always *the* prestige studio for every other working group in pictures, the writers in Hollywood overwhelmingly chose (in a 1940 poll) Warner Brothers pictures above all others as "the ones they most admired." Their preference is easily understood, for there was a consistently higher content of what used to be called "social significance" in Warner Brothers films than in those of all their rivals combined. It was often the specific subject matter that gave them the image of an utterly fearless force in film-making, pictures like *I Am a Fugitive from a Chain Gang, They Won't Forget* (Southern lynch law), *Black Fury* (striking coal miners), *They Drive by Night* (sullen truck drivers), and *Black Legion* (American Nazis). It was no coincidence that out of the original "Hollywood Ten" (only eight were writers), no less than five were employed by Warner Brothers: Alvah Bessie, Albert Maltz, Dalton Trumbo, Lester Cole, and John Howard Lawson. They had all been hired to turn out films like those listed here, but they soon found themselves, as did Faulkner, working on entirely different projects.

Although in no sense genuine innovators at any time, Warner's was often the first major studio to succeed in making money on films in categories that had become unprofitable or unfashionable, or both. The fantastic success of both *42nd Street* and *Gold Diggers of 1933* was just as much of a surprise to Warner's as it was to anyone else, for the public had grown tired of "musicals" by the end of 1931. The same was also true of gangster films. The market had been glutted with them for years, and it was only the release of *Little Caesar* and *The Public*

Enemy a few months apart that brought them back into fashion again. In the late thirties, Warner's made a series of ponderously "dedicated" biographical films about such historical figures as Zola, Pasteur, Juarez, and Ehrlich that greatly enhanced the studio's public image at the time but which have dated very badly. Starting with *I Am a Fugitive from a Chain Gang* in 1932, Warner's had demonstrated that it could even make money on a "message" picture. In the summer of 1942 the message was patriotism, and they were a lot more adroit at delivering it than any of the other studios in Hollywood. Throughout the entire course of the war, Warner Brothers made an extremely wide range of patriotic films—*Mission to Moscow, Air Force, Yankee Doodle Dandy, Sahara, Destination Tokyo, Action in the North Atlantic*—by skillfully combining the most salable elements of their most successful films in the past. It was precisely this kind of picture that Faulkner was initially assigned to write for them, along with Maltz, Bessie, and Trumbo.

Not a single one of Faulkner's own patriotic efforts for Warner Brothers was ever produced. There were a number of reasons for this, the main one being that they were not very good screenplays. The first of them was *The DeGaulle Story*, an original screenplay about a rather stiff Brittany family divided against itself over the Vichy government of Marshal Pétain and the Resistance movement. A large part of this screenplay consists of talk about "the Cause," but there is very little in the way of action. In the story there is a girl called Emilie who is trying to talk her lover into joining the Underground. She talks about the ultimate vulnerability of the Nazis and of the need to resist them:

. . . It's like those little ants in the jungle that nothing can stand against—not the biggest and fiercest and the most powerful—nothing. You can kill them by the millions just by stepping on them, but they keep on coming because they are so little. That's the mistake they made. They tried to force the little people. And there are too many little people. There are so many of them because they are small. All they have to threaten us with is death. And little people are not afraid to die. The little people and the very great. Because there is something of the little people in the very great: as if all the little people had been trodden and crushed and condensed into one great one who knew and remembered all their suffering. And the little ones themselves are never afraid as long as they believe that the other little ants coming behind them will finally eat the elephant. . . .

There is a good deal more in this vein, another two full pages in fact, and Emilie sounds very much like Pearl in *Banjo on My Knee*. This passage shows pretty clearly what Faulkner would do as a screenwriter when left entirely on his own: he simply wrote as the novelist he actually was. What he wrote was often very good, even wonderful, but this dialogue is really close to a form of incantation, and although it might work in a film of the seventies, it was quite impossible in the Hollywood of the thirties and forties.

There is a deceptive similarity here to Fitzgerald's constant failure to get his material on the screen as he had actually written it. He also met considerable opposition from the producers he worked for, demonstrated by the frustrating difficulties he had with Joseph L. Mankiewicz over his script for *Three Comrades* in 1938. Fitzgerald's fantastic pride as a writer dictated his electing to play the game of screenwriting the way he thought Hollywood wanted it played, even going as far as "tailoring" his scripts for the talents of Shirley Temple and Joan Crawford. By desperately embracing the Hollywood "system," he wound up by severely compromising his talents and wrote some truly dreadful material that was clearly bad, even by Hollywood standards. He played it safe, so safe that he was often absurdly wrong, but he found that he simply couldn't accept the professional judgment of people he considered to be his literary inferiors, which they certainly were. Faulkner never claimed to know very much about screenwriting at any time and, with the exception of his work with Hawks, continued to turn out his "own" kind of material.

In the final pages of the unproduced *DeGaulle Story*, young Emilie succeeds in the political conversion of her lover, Jean, who is soon working as a secret agent for the Underground in a French munitions factory. The script concludes with a curious scene in which Jean has pinpointed the factory for an immediate attack by the Allied bombers. His fellow workers are perfectly aware of what he has done, and as the bombers begin the deadly raid, they all stand and sing the *Marseillaise* together. They were singing it down at Rick's Place in *Casablanca* that very same year, and this may have been just one of the reasons for the permanent shelving of the entire project.

Howard Hawks was himself working away at beating the patriotic drum for Warner Brothers. He had directed the immensely popular *Sergeant York* for them in 1941, with Gary Cooper in the title role, and his big project for 1942 was *Air Force*, a panoramic picture about the fate of a single B-17 bomber, the "Mary-Anne," and its crew in the days just before and after Pearl Harbor. The working screenplay was by Dudley Nichols, perhaps the most highly regarded screenwriter at the time. Nichols had written the scripts for a number of John Ford films (*The Informer, Stagecoach,* and *The Long Voyage Home*), as well as for Fritz Lang's *Man Hunt* and *Scarlet Street,* and Jean Renoir's *Swamp Water* and *This Land Is Mine.* Despite Nichols's impressive list of successful pictures (he had also written Hawks's own *Bringing Up Baby*), Hawks apparently felt there was something lacking in his script and decided to use Faulkner for the writing of several entirely new scenes.

One of these scenes in *Air Force* was the concluding one in which the dying Captain Quincannon thinks he is preparing his B-17 for takeoff. Lying on a hospital bed, surrounded by the surviving crew members, he runs through all the items on his flight checklist. Each crew member replies dutifully, until he finally asks the navigator for the direction to be taken. The film ends as the answer is given, "Due East—into the sunrise," followed by the final chords of Franz Waxman's score. Reduced to words on paper, the scene seems cheap and obvious enough, but Hawks and his cast (headed by John Garfield) managed to bring it off surprisingly well. It was the kind of scene that Hawks seemed to have felt he needed at the very end of a picture like this, and that Faulkner could supply on quick demand, which he did.

Air Force was a tremendously popular film, and although Faulkner received no official screen credit for his work, his contributions to it were generally known around Warner

Brothers. More importantly, it reestablished his contact with Hawks and served as his working credentials to go on working with him on a fairly regular basis, culminating in their two triumphs, *To Have and Have Not* and *The Big Sleep.* They worked together for several months in the spring and summer of 1943 on a project called *Battle Cry,* an extremely long and ambitious screenplay in the "Why We Fight" vein, filled with characters built around the talents of such actors as Henry Fonda, Charles Laughton, Paul Robeson, and even Ronald Reagan as a stupid sergeant. The writers at Warner Brothers had trouble finding roles suitable for Reagan, and he often wound up playing essentially stupid characters, *typage* with a vengeance. At about this time in his life, Faulkner seemed drawn to allegory as his favorite mode of expression, and *Battle Cry* contains quite a bit of it, especially the wounded black character called America. Faulkner's main contribution to the story was the central motif of Lincoln's funeral train, which carried the body of the murdered president from Washington to Springfield, an idea put to use by James Agee in his teleplay of the mid fifties. *Battle Cry* was to remain unproduced, largely because of the huge cost it would have entailed. There were definite cash limits to the patriotism of Warner Brothers.

Faulkner made one other effort on his own to write this kind of material, an original screen treatment for a project called *The Life and Death of a Bomber.* This was to be another inspirational film about the manufacture of a new type of military bomber deemed essential to the war effort. The story of the work on the plane is stymied by the effects of such disparate plot elements as a rather bloodless adultery story intermixed with a faceless battle between management and labor. It reads very badly; there is a portentously grim quality about much of it, as in these words, which Faulkner chose to introduce each of the story's three main parts: "IT IS GOING TO BE TOO LATE; IT IS TOO LATE; IT WAS TOO LATE." Whatever "it" was, it was clearly not for Warner Brothers, and he was soon shifted over to various adaptation jobs for the studio.

It is quite obvious that he didn't think very highly of some

of the properties he was given to adapt. One of them was Bel-
lamy Partridge's *Country Lawyer,* a best-selling, anecdotal biography of his father, who had practiced law in a small town in
upper New York State toward the end of the century. Warner's had owned the book for years; it was regularly assigned
to all new writers for the company, but it had successfully
resisted all efforts—including those of Alvah Bessie, among
many others—to be turned into a film. Faulkner coped with
the problem of *Country Lawyer* by the extreme solution of
throwing away everything but the title. He then went ahead
with his own completely original story (actually a fifty-two-
page treatment) of two warring families in his imaginary Jef-
ferson, Mississippi; it was a sort of Southern Montague-
Capulet story with a strong racial theme at the center. It
extended over three generations, contained dozens of characters, and was typically Faulknerian in its verbal complexities.
Here is a sample, in which a white boy of the second generation is writing home to his father during World War I:

I was assigned to this company because I was a Southerner, and
therefore I knew negroes. I told the Colonel: "Yes, sir, I know negroes, a few of them, that I was raised among and who knew me and
my fathers just as my fathers knew their fathers. I suppose what you
mean is, understand negroes." I told him I didn't know what there
was he wanted understood about them; that maybe any human
being was his own enigma which he would take with him to the
grave, but I didn't know how the color of his skin was going to make
that any clearer or more obscure.

Faulkner's *Country Lawyer* was not the kind of story that
Warner Brothers had in mind: Why play around that way
with a proven best seller? They immediately assigned the project to another writer, moving Faulkner on to two other jobs,
on neither of which did he get any screen credit: *Northern Pur-
suit* and *Deep Valley.* After working for over a year at Warner Brothers it began to look as if his days at Twentieth
Century-Fox were going to repeat themselves in the weeks
and months he spent on work that remained unproduced or
uncredited even if produced.

The racial theme was still very much on his mind when, at

about this time, he met the American film-maker Dudley Murphy. Murphy is a somewhat legendary figure who had done "pioneer" work in Paris, New York, Hollywood, and finally Mexico. In Paris he had been the photographer for Fernand Léger's famous 1924 short abstract film *Ballet Mécanique;* in New York he directed Bessie Smith in her only screen appearance, the *St. Louis Blues* short of 1929. In the early thirties he had made a short called *Black and Tan* with Duke Ellington, and in 1933 he produced and directed a feature-length film, *The Emperor Jones,* starring Paul Robeson, filmed entirely at the abandoned Paramount studios in Astoria, Queens. He was extremely adventuresome for the time, and now he and Faulkner embarked on a collaborative screen treatment of *Absalom, Absalom!* Faulkner had always thought there was a good movie in the book, and at the time of its original publication in 1936 he had offered it to Nunnally Johnson at Twentieth Century-Fox, with a little note attached to the galleys: "Nunnally—These are the proofs of my new book. The price is $50,000. It's about miscegenation. Bill."

They called their treatment *Revolt in the Earth,* with Murphy making the sales pitch. There were some nibbles, including a protracted one from Warner Brothers, but nothing came of it; 1943 was not the year for Hollywood to undertake a miscegenation film. It still isn't, and the film rights to the book have never been sold. Faulkner kept on with the daily tedium of his chores at the studio.

Howard Hawks was one of the few people in Hollywood well acquainted with both Faulkner and Hemingway. Hawks had done a lot of hunting and fishing with Hemingway in Key West and Sun Valley in the late thirties and early forties. After the publication of *For Whom the Bell Tolls* in 1940, there had been some talk between them about the possibility of Hawks directing the screen version of the book, but this fell through, and the film was given to Sam Wood. In the course of one of these talks, Hawks claimed that he could make a good film out of the very worst of Hemingway's books; they both agreed this was surely *To Have and Have Not*. Hemingway bet that he couldn't, but finally agreed to sell the film rights to the book to Warner Brothers if Hawks would direct it. This bet was the beginning of the most successful of all Hawks's collaborations with Faulkner, for Hawks chose him, along with Jules Furthman, to write the screenplay for *To Have and Have Not*.

A great deal has been written about both *To Have and Have Not* and *The Big Sleep*. Both films share a relentless pace and vitality, even a mad pace in *The Big Sleep*, that is constantly enlivened by the joy their makers obviously took in the work they were doing. This joy is still highly communicable; a quarter of a century after their release, both films continue to produce excited responses from the audiences viewing them. Without his contributions to these two films, film classics in every real sense of the word, Faulkner's time in Hollywood would have been largely wasted. It is in these two films that the working methods of Hawks and Faulkner can be seen most clearly.

Faulkner was being quite accurate in his own way when he said in 1937 that he didn't "know enough" about scenario writing. What he did know well enough was how to work with Howard Hawks. The precise nature of this work is somewhat vague, and the closest one can come to describing it is to call it a sort of improvisational teamwork. How did it actually work in practice? Faulkner once described it this way: "The moving picture work of my own which seemed best to me was done by the actors and the writer throwing the script away and inventing the scene in actual rehearsal just before the camera turned. . . ." This seems to be precisely the way a good deal of *To Have and Have Not* was made, with a number of the scenes being invented by the actors as the shooting on the picture progressed. A correspondent for *Time* reported that Lauren Bacall did some of the inventing: "After a highly charged few minutes with Bogart, late at night in a cheap hotel room, Marie played by Bacall reluctantly retires to her own quarters. At this point in the shooting, Miss Bacall complained: 'God, I'm dumb.' 'Why?' asked Hawks. 'Well, if I had any sense, I'd go back in after that guy.' She did." When *To*

Have and Have Not was released in 1944, James Agee noticed this "improvised" aspect of the picture: ". . . an unusually happy exhibition of teamwork, and concentrated on character and atmosphere rather than plot . . . still more, I enjoyed watching something that obviously involved relaxed, improvising fun for those who worked on it, instead of the customary tight-lipped and hammer-hearted professional anxiety."

This method of film-making, the work of a team, would do much to explain the wonderful pieces of pure invention that are found in so many of Hawks's films—things not so much written into a script as having *worked* their way in. The writer's job here was one of simply getting down on paper what he or she had just observed. The method is really not far from that of Brecht and his Berliner Ensemble or of Ingmar Bergman and his regular group of film workers. These inventive devices are found in nearly all of Hawks's best pictures: *Scarface, Twentieth Century, Ceiling Zero, Bringing Up Baby, Only Angels Have Wings, His Girl Friday, Red River,* and *Rio Bravo.* In interviews Hawks always says, "We did this," or "We did that," never using the "I" of other directors, constantly emphasizing the team system he developed in his forty years as a director.

Jules Furthman, Faulkner's collaborator on *To Have and Have Not,* was an extremely successful screenwriter—a real pro—who had been writing scripts in Hollywood for thirty years, among them those for Von Sternberg's *Morocco* and *Shanghai Express,* Frank Lloyd's *Mutiny on the Bounty,* and Hawks's own *Only Angels Have Wings.* In a career dating back to 1915, he had become sufficiently independent to pick his assignments as he pleased. He spent his final years in Hollywood working almost exclusively for Von Sternberg, Hawks, and Howard Hughes. Furthman had little regard for Faulkner's abilities as a screenwriter. There is little doubt that the main drift of the screenplay of *To Have and Have Not* was supplied by Furthman; not only was he in every way Faulkner's superior in the mechanics of screenwriting, but there are certain things in this film that link it convincingly with other films he had written previously. The heroine of *To Have and Have Not,* Marie Browning, is basically very much the same girl portrayed by Evelyn Brent in *Underworld,* by Dietrich in *Shanghai Express,* and by Angie Dickinson in *Rio Bravo.* These three films were released in 1927, 1932, and 1959, respectively, but it is the very same girl in all of them; she even has the same name in the first and last: "Feathers."

To Have and Have Not bears almost no resemblance to Hemingway's "socially conscious" novel of Cuba and Florida in the mid thirties; what it does resemble is the film *Casablanca* of 1943. Faulkner and Furthman changed the setting to Martinique during World War II, and the story line became concerned with Harry Morgan's attempts to resist the appeals made to him for the use of his fishing boat by the anti-Vichy forces on the island. In dramatic terms, it is pure melodrama and ultimately pure glorious hokum at the very end when Morgan, by then a convert to the Free French cause, is about to embark for Devil's Island to free a French prisoner held there by the Gestapo. Bogart was Harry Morgan in very much the same way he had been Rick in *Casablanca,* while the sex interest was supplied by Lauren Bacall as the tough-sweet young American girl named Marie Browning, or "Slim," the name of Hawks's wife at the time. The debt to *Casablanca* was further compounded by having Hoagy Carmichael singing and playing the piano "atmospherically," just as Dooley Wilson had done in the first film. Despite all these deliberate resemblances, *To Have and Have Not* never becomes a simple carbon copy of *Casablanca;* the Hawks film has a life very much of its own. It possesses a warmth of feeling and affection for the characters that is somewhat lacking in *Casablanca;* this is accomplished by an extremely shrewd and sensitive handling of the elements of sex and humor in the film.

Besides Harry Morgan, there is one other character in the picture taken over directly from Hemingway's novel. This is Eddie, brilliantly played by Walter Brennan, a shaky rummy who has seen better days but who now serves as Harry Morgan's not overly bright helper on his boat. Whenever Eddie encounters a stranger for the first time, he immediately asks him, "Was you ever bit by a dead bee?" If they simply ignore the question, or laugh at him, Eddie knows these people don't count—they aren't real. The girl "Slim" gives him a "serious" answer and wins his immediate respect. The question becomes a sort of talismanic offering by which Eddie lives. There is no mention of a dead bee in Hemingway, and I've always assumed that only Faulkner could have invented something like this, based on the simple logic that it *sounds* like Faulkner. But trying to establish who actually did precisely what in these old Hawks films, or any films for that matter, is difficult, with our having to settle for the uncertain testimonies of the survivors. Manny Farber has brought this question up a number of times: "One of the joys in movie going is worrying over the fact that what is referred to as Hawks might be Jules Furthman, that behind the Godard film is the looming shape of Raoul Coutard. . . ."

It is almost impossible to paraphrase Farber as a critic, but he has written better than anyone else about Hawks's methods of making films. In his famous essay of the late fifties on "Underground Films," he referred specifically to the opening scene of *The Big Sleep* as being typical of Hawks's main concerns as a director:

Easily the best part of underground films are the excavations of exciting-familiar scenery. The opening up of a scene is more concerted in these films than in other Hollywood efforts, but the most important thing is that the opening is done by road-mapped strategies that play movement against space in a cunning way, building the environment and event before your eyes. In every underground film, these vigorous ramifications within a sharply seen terrain are the big attraction, the main tent. No one does this anatomization of action and scene better than Hawks, who probably invented it . . . the shamus sweating in a greenhouse in *The Big Sleep*—the feeling is of a clever human tunneling just under the surface of terrain. *It is as though the film has a life of its own that goes on beneath the story action.**

Presumably, Faulkner undertook the writing assignments on both *To Have and Have Not* and *The Big Sleep* in order to provide Hawks with some of the material he needed to create that unique kind of "life" that pervades both films. Exactly how did Faulkner do this? There is absolutely no clear answer;

* *Italics added.*

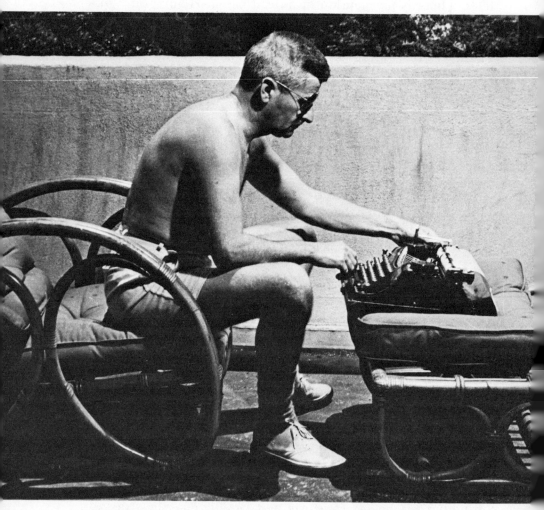

William Faulkner, taken at the Highland Hotel, Hollywood, 1944 (*Alfred Eris*)

Hawks has openly admitted that he simply liked having Faulkner *around* for some of his pictures—just having him *be* there. When finally pressed about Faulkner's specific contributions to these films, he summed up his need for him in this way: "He has inventiveness, taste, and great ability to characterize and the visual imagination to translate these qualities into the medium of the screen. He is intelligent and obliging—a master of his work who does it without fuss." He was probably all these things, but Hawks sounds here as if he were writing some sort of a trade testimonial for Faulkner. It doesn't convey any real sense of the talents of the man who may have created Eddie's dead bee.

Working on these two films with Hawks, the first in early 1944 and the second just a year later, must have given Faulkner a certain amount of relief from the frustrations he clearly felt at the time. Not only was he working with an old and trusted friend, but he was now actually getting screen credit for his work, something he had not received in his first two years at Warner Brothers. This was the case with the various other projects he was assigned during 1944: Robert C. Scott's *God Is My Co-Pilot* and Eric Ambler's spy novel *Background to Danger*. They were both filmed successfully by Warner Brothers, but without Faulkner's name on the credits for the collaborative screenplays he had written for them. He was then assigned a straight diet of remakes.

Warner Brothers held a rather extreme position on remakes; they remade more new versions of their pictures than did any other studio in Hollywood. These remakes were not always based on hits; when John Huston's *The Maltese Falcon* was produced in 1941, it was actually the third Warner Brothers version of Hammett's novel, for the first two had flopped. Conversely, they remade *To Have and Have Not* in the fifties after the great success of the Hawks version in 1944. Remakes were often assigned to writers on the payroll who had free time between assignments or for whom the studio could find nothing else to do. If the writer came up with a new script that was thought to be better than the old one, it might go into production; if the script wasn't considered an improvement, the project was then passed on to still another writer. Faulkner drew the assignment of preparing a completely new treatment of the 1938 success *The Amazing Dr. Clitterhouse,* an Edward G. Robinson film about a New York physician who becomes the leader of a gang of criminals in order to gain a working knowledge of the "criminal mind" in action. The original script by John Wexley and John Huston had been a rather gay, lighthearted comedy, and there was little hope of improving it by any new or radically different approach. In what he called *Fog over London,* Faulkner changed the entire concept of the original story by giving it a Jekyll and Hyde twist and made the doctor a brilliantly erratic psychiatrist plagued by the ravages of "schizophrenic amnesia." It was now deadly serious in tone, even painfully glum, as the doctor staggered from one disaster to another. It included a scene in which the doctor indulges in a little self-diagnosis:

CLITTERHOUSE (bitterly)
Who better than I? Amnesia, schizophrenia, the will-to-evil in man's subconscious which his conscious not only refuses to recognize but wills itself to oblivion rather than see. . . .

A good deal of time-consuming work went into *Fog over London,* showing that Faulkner was nearly always willing to do "just what the man said"; if they really wanted a brand-new *Dr. Clitterhouse,* he would be glad to oblige them. The entire project proved to be a complete waste of time for everybody, for it was soon passed along to Alvah Bessie, who was told to avoid Faulkner's approach and to stick as closely as he could to the original script. He did just that, producing what amounted to a carbon copy of that script. When this version was submitted, there were screams from the producer that Bessie had not done what he was told to do. Fortunately for Bessie, he was able to produce a copy of the directive memo he had received from the producer; at this point, all hopes for a remake were abandoned.

Something of the same sort happened with the plans for a

remake of Archie Mayo's *The Petrified Forest,* an extremely popular 1936 film starring Bette Davis, Bogart, and Leslie Howard in a version that had remained fairly close to Robert E. Sherwood's play. Any attempt at a new or improved rewrite of the material was almost certainly doomed to failure, but Faulkner spent weeks working on a totally new screenplay that was also finally shelved. For a writer of his energies, this steady diet of abortive remakes was truly demoralizing, for the sheer amount of time and energy he was forced to spend on them effectively prevented him from undertaking any new work of his own.

The weeks and months dragged on slowly for him in the perpetually sunny glitter of the writers' building in Burbank, as he slogged along on projects in which he often had little real interest. There were at that time six working days in each week, relieved mainly by the arrival of his paycheck. When asked in later years how he had been able to stand the grinding routine of what amounted to an office job, he replied: "I just kept saying to myself, they're gonna pay me Saturday, they're gonna pay me Saturday." At forty-seven, virtually his entire income consisted of this check; he simply could not afford to leave Hollywood.

Pretty much aloof from everything "social," Faulkner had taken no active part in the establishment of the Screenwriters' Guild in 1936 and seems to have had nothing to do with its affairs. He was occasionally invited to parties, but he usually just sat, silently, with a drink in his hand, until he felt it was permissible to leave. There were friends to be had at the studio if he wanted them badly enough, but he didn't for the most part. He was not taken with any of the left-wing group of writers, which had John Howard Lawson as its leader and which also included Bessie, Albert Maltz, and Dalton Trumbo among the faithful. Not all the writers at Warner Brothers were thus politically "engaged," for they also had under contract Daniel Fuchs, W. R. Burnett, James Hilton, Jo Pogano, Stephen Longstreet, and A. I. Bezzerides. Faulkner knew all of them, and they knew him, but he had never really cared for the company of writers as such, especially political ones, and

Hollywood was no exception. There were a few he did get along with quite well, especially Longstreet and Bezzerides, who both struck him as being a good deal less "literary" than most of the others at the studio. Longstreet had originally been a painter but had now turned popular novelist and screenwriter (*Decade* and *Stallion Road*), and Bezzerides had once actually driven a truck for a living—the source for his short novel *Long Haul* and the film *They Drive by Night*. As the months passed, they both served as regular listeners to Faulkner's bitter tirades about his life in Hollywood.

The kinds of friendships he made at this time were very much the same as those he had made in the past, his usual manner being that of quiet, distant reserve broken occasionally by sudden flashes of wit and humor, or equally sudden bursts of outrage and fury against everything in and about Hollywood. His heavy drinking continued as before, but the really serious drinking bouts intensified, occasionally requiring hospitalization and thus placing him in constant danger of losing his job at Warner Brothers. It was often only the strenuous work of his friends that saved him from doing so. But mostly he remained silent, smoking his pipe, drawn tightly into himself. Longstreet has recalled the distance he maintained from the people he worked with every day: "I was part of a car pool that picked him up every day outside his hotel, and he rode every day with four or five movie writers who were too scared to talk to him. It was at the end of one of these rides that one of the screenwriters said to me, 'He must like you, Steve, he said "Good morning" to you.' "

In addition to the fact of their own alcoholism, both Fitzgerald and Faulkner were married to women who also had severe difficulties with alcohol, creating intolerable sexual/marital problems for all four. Fitzgerald was perhaps extremely fortunate in his association with Sheilah Graham in his Hollywood years; the question of Faulkner's solution to his sexual problems is decidedly more problematic, this due in part to his ferocious defense of his own privacy. He did have what seems to have been an extremely passionate affair in 1943 and 1944 in Hollywood with a young woman associated with the film industry. She has recently written a full account, as yet unpublished, of her love affair with Faulkner.

At the very end of 1943 Faulkner became deeply involved in the plans of two men he met in Hollywood, an involvement that was to have far-reaching effects on his life there at the time and for a good many years after his final departure from California. These two men were both film-makers: William Bacher and Henry Hathaway. Faulkner's initial meeting with them led to many others and was to inaugurate the most sustained single writing effort of his entire life, the project that was to occupy him obsessively for nearly eleven years—the endless writing and rewriting of what became his longest, most ambitious, and perhaps worst novel, *A Fable.*

As a Hollywood producer, William Bacher was something in the way of a "visionary," as in Anthony Powell's sense of one who possesses "the Vision of Visions that heals the Blindness of Sight." In action, his flamboyant personality seems to have been an eerie combination of both Groucho Marx and General George S. Patton at their most extreme. His supreme gift was for salesmanship—the sort of salesmanship that enabled him to sell his visions, his highly "inspirational" film projects, to hard-bitten people like Darryl F. Zanuck among others, all of whom found it almost impossible to say no to this red-headed "visionary." Bacher's origins are obscure—he may or he may not have been born in Rumania—and most of the facts about him are vague or in dispute. In his earlier years he had, improbably enough, practiced careers in both dentistry and the law. His entry into motion-picture production in the early forties was based on his extremely successful career in the heyday of network radio in the late thirties. The pictures he produced for Twentieth Century-Fox in the forties were all of the superglossy schmaltz variety—*Leave Her to Heaven, The Foxes of Harrow,* and *A Wing and a Prayer*—all of them "visions" of one sort or another.

A number of Bacher's films had been directed by his friend
Henry Hathaway, a highly competent director who continued
to turn out a steady stream of pictures on into the late sixties,
films like *The Lives of a Bengal Lancer, The Trail of the Lonesome
Pine, The House on 92nd Street, Kiss of Death, Niagara,* and
Legend of the Lost. Starting off with the cheapest Westerns in
the early thirties, by 1944 Hathaway had risen to the professional level of directing films like Bacher's own production of
A Wing and a Prayer. Unlike Howard Hawks, Hathaway had no
style of his own; he was essentially a journeyman director
whose films were about as good or bad as the scripts they were
based upon. According to Stephen Longstreet, it was Hathaway who had first thought of the "germ" that eventually became the 200,000 words of *A Fable.* He had felt that an interesting film could be based on the popularity of the "Unknown
Soldier" legend of World War I. Urged on by the spur of
Bacher's grandiosity, this simple notion soon mushroomed
into monstrous proportions, including the moonlighting services of William Faulkner as scriptwriter. Stephen Longstreet
was present at the first story conference between Faulkner,
Bacher, and Hathaway. He recalls that Bacher soon ". . .
closed his eyes, seemed to go into a trance, then announced
the idea was the story of Christ and His Twelve Disciples returning to Earth as a Corporal and his Squad during World
War I to die again."

Faulkner, always notorious for his calm, was sufficiently
moved to say that it ". . . could be a pretty interesting thing."
He may have found it to be just that, for he immediately
began writing a 10,000-word screen treatment based on Bacher's vision of Hathaway's idea. The treatment bore the
rather ominous working title of "Who?" The three of them
had formed a partnership in which they would share equally
in the profits from the film, which Bacher planned to produce
independently. Hathaway was somewhat appalled when he
read Faulkner's treatment, for he later claimed, "I couldn't
find my story. I didn't recognize anything." Neither, apparently, could Bacher, for no screenplay was ever written on
the basis of this treatment, either by Faulkner or by anyone

else. A decade later, Faulkner was grateful to his old Hollywood friends, for when *A Fable* was finally published in 1954, it bore this note of thanks: "To William Bacher and Henry Hathaway of Beverly Hills, California, who had the basic idea from which this book grew into its present form. . . ." They had really given him more than they knew, for *A Fable* became Faulkner's own private albatross, which he was to carry around with him for the next decade.

Why would Faulkner have sprung so readily for such a supremely grandiose idea, a film idea that would have made even a Thalberg or a Zanuck blanch? The appeal it had seems to lie in Faulkner's absolute fascination with the events of World War I, along with almost everything associated with it. It had been the war of his time—*his* war, as it had been Fitzgerald's war. Although neither man had ever fought in that war, Faulkner liked to give the impression that he had. For years he gave passive credence to the myth that he had seen action with the RAF in France, and only when Malcolm Cowley was about to put this into print as an actuality did Faulkner refute the story once and for all.

It will be recalled that his first screenplay for Hawks in 1932 was *Today We Live,* a World War I story based on his own "Turn About." When he returned to Hollywood for the second time in 1935, his first task there was to write for Hawks the screenplay for *The Road to Glory,* still another story of the war. When *The Road to Glory* was reviewed in 1936, there were some critics who noticed a resemblance in the film to a novel by Humphrey Cobb, *Paths of Glory,* which had been published in the previous year. There is no doubt that Faulkner had read this war novel, liking it sufficiently to keep it in his library in Mississippi until the day of his death in 1962. He had signed his name and the date, October 1935, in the book, a thing he seems to have done only for those books he really liked. Nor is there very much doubt that some of the feelings about this book crept into his screenplay for *The Road to Glory,* which he began writing for Hawks in the following month at Twentieth Century-Fox.

Cobb's *Paths of Glory* takes place in the trenches of France in the spring of 1918, a story of men driven half-mad by the endless slaughter and poised on the brink of outright mutiny. When one regiment refuses to participate in a suicidal attack against the German lines, the rebellion is quickly suppressed by the brutal expedient of selecting three soldiers to die before the eyes of the entire regiment. The three have been chosen by lot, and Cobb's story was based on an actual event that took place in the French Army in 1918. Very much the same kind of mutiny, as well as the exact method of execution, take place in Faulkner's *A Fable,* with Faulkner's corporal now openly identified as Christ in the company of the Two Thieves. What Faulkner did was to combine the physical situation of Cobb's novel with all the religious "splendor" of Bacher and Hathaway's film idea about the reappearance of Christ on the Western Front in 1918. The result was the massive allegory, *A Fable.* The experience of having written the screenplay for *The Road to Glory* in late 1935 seems to have stuck in his head, for when Bacher made his "trancelike" pronouncement eight years later, Faulkner found himself on familiar ground and snapped at the idea.

So Faulkner got something from Hollywood he never thought he would have gotten: the subject of what he believed would be his masterpiece. Actually, he was to get something else from his obsession with *A Fable,* his final freedom from having to go on working in Hollywood, but this was to take more than another year.

. . . one day one leaf falls in a damn canyon up there, and they tell you it's winter.
　　　　　　　　　　　　　　　　　—Faulkner, 1945

Faulkner kept rocking in his office, he had a rocking chair put in there. . . .
　　　　　　　　　—Daniel Fuchs to Tom Dardis, May 1975

Hawks even enlisted Faulkner to work on a script about the building of the pyramids or some such nonsense, and engaged the late Harry Kurnitz to work with him on it. (Faulkner always had to have a collaborator or it was unlikely that he would have written anything at all.) That was a real saga, Faulkner and his bourbon and Harry Kurnitz and Egypt, but apparently Bill wrote no more in The Land of the Pharaohs than he did in Zanuckland.
　　　　　–Nunnally Johnson to Tom Dardis, November 1974

By the beginning of 1945 Faulkner was getting desperate about his prolonged and seemingly never-to-end stay in California. Most of the film projects he was assigned to were either permanently shelved or given over to other writers; the sheer waste of his time was terrifying. He had begun his stay in 1942 by strongly disliking the monotony of the weather; now, in 1945, he cursed it, day after beautiful day. He had also begun to fear Hollywood, a fear based on his firm belief that he was now doomed to stay out there for the rest of his creative life. He made various attempts to escape what he now regarded as a prison. By the end of 1944 he had established a new working relationship with Warner Brothers that required him to work for them only six months in each year and allowed him to spend the other six at home in Oxford. This was the only compromise he could afford to make with them at this time; his non-Hollywood income was still virtually nothing. His basic seven-year contract was still in full effect. There had been some small raises, but even at the very end he was still getting only $500 per week. He had been permanently typed as a low-salaried writer, and Warner Brothers was not eager to change this image. The writers he regularly collaborated with were often getting three and even five times this amount. Fitzgerald, who always considered himself underpaid, had received $1,250 a week from MGM in 1938.

Faulkner's various assignments at the studio went drearily on, just as they had in the past. These included James M. Cain's *Mildred Pierce* and Stephen Longstreet's *Stallion Road*. Both were eventually produced, but the final screen credits were not Faulkner's. His work on the script for *The Big Sleep* was completed early in 1945, and he was on hand daily for the production of the film, which involved constant changes during the actual shooting. This kind of work, with Hawks and Bogart, was fun, as opposed to the routine drudgery of his other assignments. Perhaps in part to escape from them, as well as hoping to make some more money, he soon became involved with still another film project that had nothing to do with Warner Brothers: Jean Renoir's independent production of *The Southerner*.

Jean Renoir had left France in 1940 as a refugee from the Nazis, at about the same time as had René Clair. Both directors started working in Hollywood in 1941, with neither finding any real measure of success there. Renoir's first American film had been *Swamp Water,* set and mostly shot in Louisiana. He was apparently fascinated with the American South, for he bought the film rights to a novel about young Southern tenant farmers, *Hold Autumn in Your Hand,* by George Sessions Perry. In France, Renoir had written many of his own scripts, but he soon ran into difficulties with this one, especially with the dialogue to be spoken by half-literate Southerners. Faulkner's specific Southern qualities were quite familiar to Renoir, for his books had been read widely in France in the late thirties. It may well have been Nunnally Johnson who first thought of using Faulkner on the script, for he and Renoir had known each other since the production of *Swamp Water* at Twentieth Century-Fox in 1941.

In later years Faulkner claimed that his work on Renoir's *The Southerner* had given him more genuine pleasure than just about anything else he had done in Hollywood. There is now some doubt about what kind of help, as well as how much, he actually gave Renoir. Leo Braudy's recent book on Renoir simply reiterates the fact that Faulkner was brought in to supply "authentic" Southern dialogue, and apparently nothing else. Zachary Scott, the star of the film, has gone so far as to claim that the whole script was entirely Faulkner's, and that only his contractual obligations to Warner Brothers had prevented Faulkner from receiving full credit for the work. There is also some indication that Nunnally Johnson himself had a hand in the final shooting-script, but the whole problem of who did what was neatly solved by Renoir's giving himself sole credit for the screenplay—the best way possible for an *auteur* director to label his films.

The Southerner has become something of a minor classic, deriving its status as much from being a Renoir film as from the supposed "honesty" it contains, a rare enough quality in films of the period. Since there is very little story or narrative content to the film, its appeal ultimately depends on the *quality* of its depiction of the daily life of tenant farmers, and this is precisely where it fails. It is just this honesty that is most open to question. Today the film seems curiously "stagy" and false in a way that contains a considerable amount of patronage to the tenant farmers whose lives it purports to be concerned with. It may very well be some of Faulkner's lines that we hear on the screen, but their effect on us is considerably weakened by the people speaking them. The author of *Let Us Now Praise Famous Men* found this aspect of the film particularly painful, for after admiring Renoir's intentions, James Agee could only say that

I don't so much mind that the dialect is very much thinned out, or even that it lacks uniformity. The thinning, to the point of general intelligibility, is a convention I would accept, though I'd put my money on handling it straight. The lack of uniformity, though far less defensible, I would accept if only the people were right in other

respects—which in that case would be unlikely. But most of the people were screechingly, unbearably wrong. They didn't walk right,
stand right, eat right, sound right, or look right. . . .

Working with Renoir was one way to pass the time in Hollywood, but there wasn't much of that time left, for Faulkner
was now absolutely sick of the place, and his only desire was to
leave it for the last time. There were some signs that it might
be now possible to do just that. Although it had been nearly
four years since he had published a new book, his name had
suddenly begun to be heard again. His reputation had increased enormously in Europe, mainly because of the strenuous efforts of people like Jean-Paul Sartre in Paris. Although
all his earlier books except *Sanctuary* were still out of print,
Faulkner managed to take eighth place among the "leading"
American novelists of the day in a poll conducted among the
contributors to the old *Saturday Review* in 1944.* Both his publisher (Cerf) and his agent (Ober) had been concerned for
some time over the long hiatus between books. These few indications of appreciation telling him that he was not totally
forgotten, combined with his hatred for his life in Hollywood,
convinced him that it was time to get back to his own writing.
But cutting the cord with Hollywood was not easy.

Some idea of just how depressed he had become with working at Warner's can be seen from part of a long letter he wrote
to Harold Ober in late August of 1945:

I think I have had about all of Hollywood I can stand. I feel bad,
depressed, dreadful sense of wasting time, I imagine most of the
symptoms of some kind of blow-up or collapse. I may be able to
come back later, but I think I will finish this present job and return
home. Feeling as I do, I am actually afraid to stay here much longer.

By the late summer of 1945 he had attempted to terminate
his original seven-year contract with Warner Brothers and obtain some sort of a new one, preferably a considerably shorter
one with improved financial terms. At this point, the Bacher-
Hathaway film project for *A Fable* came back to plague Faulkner, for Warner Brothers had become aware of it. They now
wished him to sign a document entitling him to work on the

---

* He tied for eighth place with Kenneth Roberts and Marjorie Kinnan Rawlings.

novel version of *A Fable* at home for six months, with the clear understanding that they, and they alone, would own the screen rights. Since these rights were already in the possession of Bacher and Hathaway, he obviously could not sign the Warner document, and the whole affair reached a complete stalemate, with Faulkner returning sullenly to Mississippi at the end of that summer with every intention of never returning to Hollywood.

Neither Jack Warner nor anyone else at his studio was interested in losing Faulkner's services at this time. Both *To Have and Have Not* and *The Big Sleep* had been extremely successful pictures for them, and at $500 a week, Faulkner may well have been the best bargain in town. His contract was fully enforceable from a legal point of view, and in September of 1945 it still had nearly four years to run. When he left the studio he was told to report back in Burbank in March of 1946.

At home again in Oxford he continued his futile efforts to extricate himself from the Warner contract. He was reminded, not so gently, it would appear, that a contract was a contract. His letters to Malcolm Cowley at this time indicate that by January he had fully resigned himself to returning to California. There were now serious threats if he didn't comply: ". . . I'll have to go back to Warner by 15 Mar. or have his legal dogs on me. He has already made vague though dire threats about warning any editor to buy my stuff at his peril, if I don't come back."

In the middle of October 1945, a month or so after his return to Oxford, he wrote a long and curious letter to Jack Warner, the purpose of which was simply to convince him that he should be set free from the contract that still bound him so tightly. He set out to inform Warner that since he wasn't really any good at what he'd been doing for them, why continue any further?

I feel that I have made a bust at moving picture writing and therefore have mis-spent and will continue to mis-spend time which at my age I cannot afford. During my three years (including my leave-suspensions) at Warner's, I did the best work I knew how on 5 or 6 scripts. Only two were made and I feel that I received credit on these not on the value of the work I did but partly through the friendship of Director Howard Hawks. So I have spent three years

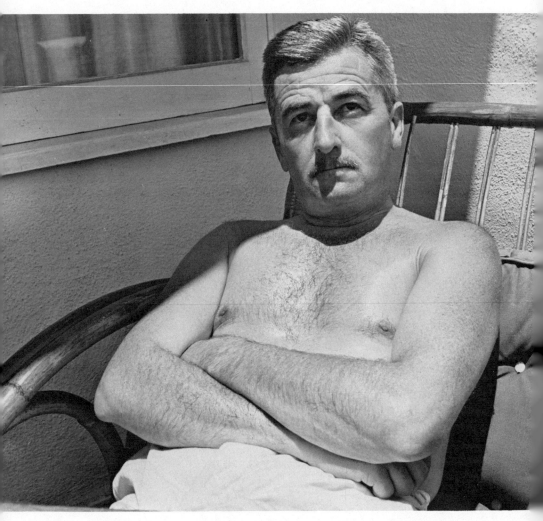

William Faulkner, taken at the Highland Hotel, Hollywood, 1944 (*Alfred Eris*)

doing work (trying to do it) which was not my forte and which I was not equipped to do, and therefore I have mis-spent time which as a 47 year old novelist I could not afford to spend. And I don't dare mis-spend any more of it. . . . So I repeat my request that the studio release me from my contract. . . .

Warner turned the letter over to his legal department, which simply informed Faulkner that the answer was no. But very soon after this he got what seemed to be a reprieve of sorts: "Random House and Ober lit a fire under Warner, I don't know how, and I am here until September anyway, on a dole from Random House, working at what seems now to be my magnum o."

The "magnum o" was, of course, *A Fable,* which he continued to work on during the rest of 1946. In December he wrote Cowley again to say that he was ". . . on Random House's cuff, to write a book, won't go back to Cal. until Random House gets tired and money ceases. I shall get back to work on it. . . ." He did get back to it, keeping it up, on and off again, for most of the next seven years. The writing of *A Fable* had become in a very real sense his passport to freedom, for only Random House's financial faith in the project could have bought his release from Warner Brothers. In the course of the next few years Faulkner's books began to sell sufficiently well so that he was never again forced to rely on Hollywood for his income.

The concluding of his contract with Warner Brothers nearly brings the story of Faulkner's career in Hollywood to an end, although not quite yet. Twice again, both in the early and mid fifties, he agreed to work for Howard Hawks, seemingly as much in gratitude to him for his past kindnesses as perhaps simply as an escape from the difficulties he found in finishing *A Fable.* There was also the question of money. On these last two occasions, the fees he received for his services were commensurate with his having won the Nobel Prize for Literature—his bargain days were over at last. Hawks engaged him to write the screenplay for William E. Barrett's religious novel, *The Left Hand of God,* which he thought would be fine for Humphrey Bogart. Faulkner returned to Hollywood early in 1951 to write the entire script himself, at $2,000 per week for

eight weeks, but the production deal fell through. His screenplay was never used, nor did Hawks direct the film. This work
secured his formal release from Warner Brothers.

Faulkner's final picture for Hawks was *Land of the Pharaohs*,
a film about ancient Egypt for which he wrote the screenplay
during 1953 and 1954, along with Harry Kurnitz and Harold
Jack Bloom. This was a writing task that took place all over the
world, in Cairo and Paris as well as in Italy and Switzerland.
Faulkner drank quite a bit in all these places, as was his habit,
especially when far from home. These were the years in which
he was frequently hospitalized for detoxification, both in New
York and in Mississippi. This was also the time when stories
about Faulkner's legendary drinking habits proliferated to the
point where they began to resemble those concerning W. C.
Fields a decade earlier, even down to the one about the necessity of his having to hire a male nurse to follow him around at
a distance of ten feet, fully armed with the liquid necessities.
These stories stopped being funny, if they ever really were,
after Faulkner's sudden death at Wright's Sanitorium, located
in the backwoods at Byhalia, Mississippi, at the end of his last
drunk in 1962. His problems with alcohol were severe enough
by 1954, but they still weren't that bad. He managed to get
through most of his work on the picture but was forced to return to New York before the script was completed.

It is difficult to see Faulkner's hand in the picture, for *Land
of the Pharaohs* turned out to be a "spectacular" film of "epic"
proportions, shot mostly in a Cinemascope Egypt in the old
DeMille tradition. It had scenes requiring ten thousand extras
building the pyramids, wickedly beautiful princesses being en-
tombed alive in them, and almost anything else the three
writers and Hawks could think of to keep it all moving. It was
all hokum, almost *pure* hokum, and Faulkner seemed happily
aware of this when he later said that the picture was ". . . the
same movie Howard has been making for 35 years. It's *Red
River* all over again. The Pharaoh is the cattle baron, his jewels
are the cattle, and the Nile is the Red River. But the thing
about Howard is, he knows it's the same movie, and he knows
how to make it." Maybe he did, but Hawks later admitted that
he thought it was really a pretty bad film and explained to his

interviewer that the trouble with *Land of the Pharaohs* lay in the fact that he "didn't know how Pharaohs talked." Neither did Faulkner, who liked to think of these Pharaohs as Confederate generals, or so he claimed.

The formal ending of Faulkner's career as a screenwriter might best date from the spring of 1955, when he declined to accept the job of writing the screenplays for some of his own novels. Jerry Wald, then at Twentieth Century-Fox, had obtained options on several of the novels, but Faulkner refused the job, telling Wald: "I have never learned how to write movies, nor even to take them very seriously. I don't think I need the money at present, and that is the only reason I would have to try the job, or any movie job. . . ." Three and a half years later, in September of 1958, the story was very much the same. This time MGM wanted him to write the screenplay for *The Unvanquished,* which they had bought from Random House twenty years earlier but had never produced. Their price for the work was supposed to be between $50,000 and $75,000, but Faulkner declined it, telling Harold Ober, "I am no good at picture scripts, and I had better leave this alone and stick to my own work."

This was the truth as he saw it, for he had done little to advance himself in this line of work, fleeing as he did in mock horror from the MGM projection rooms and sleeping his way through the story conferences at Twentieth Century-Fox. He had never really cared very much about becoming a "successful" screenwriter, and it was only when it looked as if he might actually make the grade, after the success of *To Have and Have Not* and *The Big Sleep,* that he began to leave for good. He always regarded screenwriting as a job to be done like any other job. If his employers wanted stories about the pharaohs of Egypt, they got them; if they wanted sexy, punchy dialogue for Humphrey Bogart, they got that too. The only thing that Faulkner had wanted from Hollywood was to get enough money together to pay his bills and keep on writing his own books. He got the money—never all that much of it—and he managed to write the books.

Hollywood, 1936

Nathanael West

The Scavenger of the Back Lots

[1]

. . . I did not want to take a chance on seeing anything that might have made me wish I had stayed home, and this is why I waited for the darkness, for the night-time. That is when Hollywood is really glamorous and mysterious and you are glad you are here, where miracles are happening all around you. . . .
—Horace McCoy, I Should Have Stayed Home, *1938*

The climate out here makes me feel peculiar. I get very sleepy about 9 o'clock and must go to bed by 11. The sun gave me a frightful headache and I have to wear smoked glasses all the time. In other words, phooey on Cal. . . .
—West to Josephine Herbst, *1933*

Nearly everyone who has written about Nathanael West with any personal knowledge of the man made much of the complexities they found in his life. They have managed to produce an oddly secretive, *hidden* Nathanael West, whose identity often seems a bit clouded, as when William Carlos Williams discovered, only a decade after West's death, that he could not actually recall his old friend's face. Many of the mysteries about West arose from the curiously "made-up" or counterfeit things about him, including not only his simple change of name from Weinstein to West but also the whole complicated process by which he did so. The names of his parents had obsessed him; at school he had written, over and over again, the words *Nathaniel Von Wallenstein Weinstein* on all his papers, an elegantly aristocratic blending of his mother's and father's names.

This is also the West who altered his own high school transcript in order to gain admission to Tufts College in Boston; he followed up this deception the following year by forging

152

his Tufts records (they were terrible) in order to transfer to Brown University as a member of the junior class. This habit of inventing his own kind of reality continued after he began to write, for his first published book bore the imprint "Paris" on its title page, but *The Dream Life of Balso Snell* was printed entirely in New York City.

The novelist Josephine Herbst was one of West's closest friends in the early thirties; she once said of him that he was "a labyrinth who concealed things, even from himself." He may have been, for he was a man who wore Brooks Brothers clothing, was an enraptured hunter of wildlife, and who wrote "surrealistic" novels that didn't sell. Although very much a private person, he became a union organizer for the Screenwriters' Guild; he despised sentiment in any form, but he wrote *Miss Lonelyhearts*.

Some of the more outwardly contrary aspects of West's actual appearance in the early thirties, just before he left for Hollywood for the first time, have perhaps been described best by Miss Herbst, looking back twenty years after West's death in 1940:

In the early fall of 1932, when William Carlos Williams urged John Hermann and myself to "look up young West," we drove straight from Rutherford to the Hotel Sutton to find him. This tall slim young man with the warm handclasp was the author of *Balso Snell,* and it was no surprise. His composure, his quick repartee, his sudden silences, resounding like a pebble dropped into a well, suggested the complexities, the contraries to be found in the work. He could hand you a drink with the grace of someone offering you a rose; could stand at ease, listening, with the aristocratic air of detached attachment. He could flash and blaze; then, suddenly, you were looking at the opaque figure of a man gone dumpy, thick, who might be brooding behind a cash register in a small shop on a dull day.

West worked almost continuously at screenwriting from the beginning of 1936 until very nearly the end of his life. In a real sense, Hollywood became West's permanent home, just as it did for Aldous Huxley and Christopher Isherwood. Unlike the other writers considered here, West spent a great deal of his time in Hollywood working at the smaller and poorer studios like Republic, the largest organization on what used to be called "Poverty Row," and whose reputation was partially based on the fiction that it had never made a decent picture. Fitzgerald, Faulkner, and Huxley all spent their time working in Hollywood in the relatively lavish surroundings of places like MGM and Twentieth Century-Fox, while the best that West could ever attain were RKO and Universal, and these only at the very end of his life. For a man of West's temperament, working daily in an atmosphere of absolute and continuous cheapness seemed to delight him in ways that would never have appealed to Fitzgerald. For it was West who got more out of his Hollywood experiences—the *schlock* side of picture-making—than any of the others here; the result was *The Day of the Locust.*

The main reason for West's going to work in Hollywood in the summer of 1933 was very nearly the same as Faulkner's had been in the previous year. Both men had published novels considered sufficiently sensational at the time to warrant the kind of reviews that stirred interest in Hollywood; both *Sanctuary* and *Miss Lonelyhearts* were purchased for film production shortly after their publication. Neither of the two writers had a hand in the resulting films, but both managed to obtain short-term contracts that ultimately led them to longer ones. Just as Faulkner had shoveled coal on the night shift at the Oxford, Mississippi, power plant to earn a living, so too had West taken up a line of business that might have seemed foreign to someone who considered himself an artist: hotel management. All through the late twenties and early thirties, West had supported himself by managing two hotels on the East Side of Manhattan, first the Kenmore Hall on Twenty-third Street, and then the Sutton on Fifty-seventh Street. The construction work on both of these establishments had been done by West's father's bankrupt construction firm; both hotels had then been legally attached by the family, and only because of this situation did West manage to get these jobs in the first place.

It was a fine job for a writer, for the hours were good and West got to meet a lot of writers he might not otherwise have encountered. In time West became well-known in New York literary circles in the early thirties by his putting up without charge a number of his writing friends who simply could not afford to pay their hotel bills; they included Dashiell Hammett, Lillian Hellman, Robert M. Coates, Erskine Caldwell, James T. Farrell, and Leane Zugsmith. As the depression worsened, West found that even the hotel business was in danger, for he wrote to his friend William Carlos Williams that "business is lousy and my company is close to bankruptcy. . . . I guess I'll have to go to Hollywood or start a brook farm experiment and wait for THE REVOLUTION. . . ."

Unlike *Sanctuary,* which actually received at least some sort of a sale despite the bankruptcy of its publisher, Harrison Smith, *Miss Lonelyhearts* had almost no sale whatever. The publishing firm of Liveright, Inc., went into its own complicated bankruptcy proceedings only one month after the book's publication in April of 1933, just a month after all the banks in the United States were closed by presidential order. No important American novel of this century was published at a worse moment in the economy of the nation, but the truth is that the time of publication is of very little importance here, for *Miss Lonelyhearts* would have been hard to sell at any time. Startlingly original books almost never sell at first—*The Sound and the Fury, Wise Blood, Call It Sleep,* and *Let Us Now Praise Famous Men* are the first titles that come to mind—and *Miss Lonelyhearts* was no exception. West himself never had any illusions about the book's ever becoming anything of a best seller; a sale of 5,000 copies would have delighted him.

Although the book was a total commercial failure, the reviews were nearly all good, so good that the film rights were sold almost immediately, to West's great joy. It was Joseph M. Schenck and Darryl F. Zanuck's brand-new firm, Twentieth

Century Pictures, that bought the film rights to *Miss Lonely-hearts*. They produced it in the summer of 1933 as *Advice to the Lovelorn*, starring Lee Tracy. The price for the book was only $4,000, not very much, but all they were buying in the long run was West's highly original story idea about the private life of a newspaperman assigned the task of answering letters addressed to the "Lovelorn Editor." West's most recent biographer, Jay Martin, thinks that Twentieth Century may have been frightened by a vicious attack on the book from one of the industry's chief trade papers of the time, *Harrison's Reports,* and that their fear altered the kind of film eventually made by the studio. Here is what the paper had to say:

> . . . I have never read anything to compare in vileness and vulgarity with Nathanael West's "Miss Lonelyhearts" announced by Twentieth Century Pictures. I am surprised that its publication should have been permitted, particularly because of its implications of degeneracy. It cannot be defended on the grounds of art; it has none; it is just low and vulgar, put out undoubtedly to appeal to moronic natures.

It is quite possible that Zanuck may have thought of *Miss Lonelyhearts* in just this way, but it is useless to conjecture what kind of film his firm might have produced in 1933, either with or without the influence of *Harrison's Reports.* This was the very last year in which Hollywood films were made in relative freedom from censorship, for the following year brought in the industry's self-regulating Hays Office, which would have taken just as dim a view of the proposed film as had the publisher of *Harrison's Reports.* The picture they *did* make, *Advice to the Lovelorn,* is a "comedy-melodrama" with a murder subplot, and it is now seen mainly for the personal charm of Lee Tracy.

Like Faulkner, West had sold his book to one studio but obtained his screenwriting contract at another, and in West's case this was Harry Cohn's Columbia Pictures. At the time, Columbia and Universal were regarded as the "Little Two," as compared to the "Big Five," or the majors.* With the exception of

---

* *The majors at this time included Metro-Goldwyn-Mayer, Paramount, RKO, Fox, and Warner Brothers.*

the relatively expensive Frank Capra productions like *The Bitter Tea of General Yen* (1932) and *Broadway Bill* (1933), most of Columbia's output at this time was of the grade "B" variety, the films shown at the bottom half of a double-bill. West was not starting at the bottom in Hollywood, but he was close to it.

Columbia hired West as a junior writer on a week-to-week basis, essentially a trial period, at a salary of $350 per week. He lasted exactly seven weeks there. During this time he produced two complete screenplays for Columbia, *Beauty Parlor* and *Return to the Soil,* which seems like quite a lot of work, even for a cost-conscious studio. He wrote about his working conditions at Columbia to Josephine Herbst:

. . . this stuff about easy work is all wrong. My hours are from ten in the morning to six at night with a full day on Saturday. They gave me a job to do five minutes after I sat down in my office—a scenario about a beauty parlor—and I'm expected to turn out pages and pages a day. There's no fooling here. All the writers sit in cells in a row and the minute a typewriter stops someone pokes his head in the door to see if you are thinking. Otherwise, it's like the hotel business.

The first of his two Columbia projects, *Beauty Parlor,* was a type of genre movie made frequently in the thirties—essentially a pulp love story set against the background of a particular kind of occupation, the type of picture that Warner Brothers made better than any other studio in Hollywood. West's first effort at this kind of work was typical enough, but Columbia did not choose to produce it. They felt the same about his second project, *Return to the Soil,* which appears to be an out-and-out travesty of all the "Soil" movies ever made in Hollywood. Parts of it oddly resemble F. W. Murnau's last film for Fox, his "Soil" film, *City Girl* (1930), for it includes dialogue like this:

SON
Nature will always provide for those who love her. Soon she will give us potatoes, corn, sweet butter, eggs. Not slimy stuff from cans, but rich, beautiful vegetables and fruits that are loaded with life.

There is a great deal more of such dialogue, pages and pages of it, giving one cause to think that this script was one of

Nathanael West and John Sanford, Viele Pond, New York, 1931 (*John Sanford*)

West's private "jokes" carried out to the limit of an actual shooting-script. It is possible that Harry Cohn himself may have actually read *Return to the Soil* and concluded that they didn't really need S. J. Perelman's brother-in-law on his payroll, at least not in the year 1933. West was let go at the end of August, but he remained in Hollywood for several months before returning to New York. Although he had no job in sight, or even much hope of ever getting another one, he nevertheless became a member of the newly created Screenwriters' Guild. Although he had failed at his first attempt at screenwriting, perhaps he knew it wouldn't be the last.

[2]
_____

To the memory of Monogram Pictures.
—Jean-Luc Godard's dedication of Breathless

. . . he was no fool, and he knew the possibilities of the medium. He did much of his screenwriting for Republic, an outfit with the rep of never having made a good film but even so West took his work quite seriously.
—John Sanford to Tom Dardis, April 1975

Throughout most of his life West was known as "Pep" to his friends, a name derived from the fact that he seemed to have none and that he was very slow in most physical activities and extremely awkward at nearly everything he did. His boyhood friend, the novelist John Sanford, has recalled this aspect of West, the hidden grace behind the awkwardness:

. . . his way of walking, which was a sort of shamble, awkward and out of sync, or his way of putting on a coat, which made you think he was trying to climb down the arm-hole and come out of the cuff, or his way of picking up change, which couldn't have been harder for him if the coins were made of water. He was always tripping, always fumbling, always ill-related to still objects, and he was like

that in everything you'd ever seen him put his hand to—everything
but writing, and there alone he seemed to be at home, moving language with such ease and grace as he could never master in so little a
thing as lighting a cigarette.

Almost immediately upon his return to his farm at Erwinna,
Pennsylvania, West went back to his first love, the ordered
movement of language; he began his new novel, *A Cool Million,* which was to deal with a subject always of interest to him:
success, or in this case the complete lack of it. The book was
the Horatio Alger story of American success turned completely around, the hero winding up totally dismembered. It
was published in June of 1934 by West's third publisher, the
new firm of Covici-Friede, whose editorial staff at the time included Mary McCarthy. Despite the personal enthusiasm of
Donald Friede, the book managed to sell just as badly as did
all the rest of West's books; *A Cool Million* was on the bookstore remainder tables by the beginning of 1935. West liked to
tell his friends that his total earnings from his first three books
amounted to exactly $780, which was probably the truth. With
the hotel business a thing of the past, the problems of earning
a living began to concern him acutely.

When he came in to New York, which was often, he usually
stayed at the Hotel Brevoort on lower Fifth Avenue, spending
a good deal of his time in the company of writers like Tess
Slesinger, Edward Newhouse, John Sanford, Leane Zugsmith,
and James T. Farrell, all of them politically left wing. Most of
these people were either writing strike novels, or at least books
dealing with what they believed to be the intellectual and cultural crisis they were all a part of. But this was not for West.
He became quite depresssd about what to do with his talents
at this time; he seemed doomed to write books that didn't sell,
and that even some of his literary friends held in low esteem.
By the early spring of 1935 he had begun to think about writing still another novel, perhaps one that would *sell* this time,
and break the pattern of doom he had begun to think was his
special fate as a writer.

He had found no solutions to his money problems. The Modern Library (Random House) reprinted *The Great Gatsby* in the summer of 1934, mainly because of the publicity generated by *Tender Is the Night,* and they commissioned Fitzgerald to write a new preface for it. He did so, offering a few comments on the literary scene as he saw it in that year of his own great depression. He singled out Vincent McHugh (*Sing Before Breakfast*) and West for special attention as talents to be watched. Fitzgerald's push for West did not succeed in advancing his status as a professional writer any more than had his strong recommendation that West be given a Guggenheim Fellowship that very same year. West had written Fitzgerald in September of 1934, requesting the use of his name as a reference in order to convince the Guggenheim Committee that he deserved the fellowship:

You have been kind enough to say that you liked my novel, Miss Lonelyhearts. . . . As you know, the committee will probably submit my plan for future work to you if you give me permission to use your name as a reference. This will be a nuisance, of course, but the plan is a very brief one and you are only obliged to say whether you think it is good or not.

If you can see your way to do this, it will make me very happy.

Despite the fact that West had edited two different literary magazines, he now found that he could not place a single one of his own short stories. The only good news about his work at this time was that Columbia decided to buy the movie rights to *A Cool Million* for reasons that remain mysterious to this day, for they never seem to have had any intention of actually producing it, either then or later. The studio's reader's report summed up the contents pretty fairly by saying, "Honesty and hard work will buy you pain, disgrace, and death."

As noted earlier, the early years of sound were a good time for writers in Hollywood, for they were then very much in demand. After about 1934 this demand slowed down considerably, along with everything else, and when West returned to California in April of 1935 he found he could not get a job anywhere in Hollywood. This is the same year that Faulkner was desperately seeking a contract there, *any* kind of contract, and that Harold Ober thought Fitzgerald's only hope lay in his getting one. When West had begun to think about writing another novel his thoughts had kept returning to the Hollywood he had known briefly in 1933, and it was this factor plus the urgent need for a job that brought him back to California.

He remained unemployed for nearly all of 1935 and was eventually forced to live on the money he borrowed from his brother-in-law, S. J. Perelman, a role he hated. To save money he moved into a cheap hotel called the Pa-Va-Sed, on North Ivar Street, near Hollywood Boulevard. This hotel was inhabited by precisely the kind of people West was to depict in *The Day of the Locust,* and the hotel itself became in part the model for the San Bernardino Arms. Living a jobless life in this atmosphere may have contributed mightily to his store of knowledge about the lower depths of Los Angeles, but it also depressed him terribly. Here is part of a letter he wrote to Perelman at this time:

I spend my time thinking of how much money I owe you, and how it seems to be impossible for me to ever get on my feet again. My new book will be a failure. I can't possibly get a job. I have deteriorated mentally. I have nothing to say, and no talent for writing, then I get up and take two more tablets of morphine, against the doctor's orders. I fall asleep for half an hour—then wake up and find myself laughing quietly.

This letter is typical of many letters West wrote at this time; it is half-funny and yet deadly serious, and at the very end it seems on the verge of hysteria. In addition to his economic problems, West was also suffering terribly from a whole series of extremely painful venereal problems that plagued him all that summer of 1935 and that did not leave him completely for a number of years—hence his use of morphine to alleviate the pain.

There was little for him to do as the days passed but simply observe the life around him, this life of the Hollywood extras, the stuntmen, the grips, and all of those he came to call "The Cheated." He was a fascinated onlooker at the world of the gamblers, the pushers, the madams and their callgirls—the whole underside of life in Los Angeles. Before leaving New

York, West had vaguely thought of writing a novel with a "Ship of Fools" motif; now he began to add to it these new characters and situations he had encountered—all were to appear in the pages of *The Day of the Locust.* West habitually told his friends long and complicated stories about these people. The stories were a curious blend of the truth and totally made-up details, very much as had been the case with his high school and college records. Jay Martin mentions a woman who knew West well in the thirties and who told him this story:

He said he was coming home about three or four in the morning, walking down the dim corridor leading to his apartment, when he heard screaming and yelling and cursing in a woman's voice. Suddenly the door opposite opened and one of the prostitutes whom he happened to know was a prostitute, said something like "You goddam son of a bitch, get out of here," and kicked something out the door that looked like a dirty bundle of laundry. It started rolling down the hall and suddenly it got up and walked off.

West may or may not have seen this, but something like it gave him the *idea* for Abe Kusich, the unforgettable dwarf in *The Day of the Locust,* whose actual character—his speech patterns and all the wonderful details about him—were derived directly from a well-known dwarf who sold newspapers on a street corner off Hollywood Boulevard.

West found no relief from his financial worries until January of 1936, when he signed his first contract with Republic, the beginning of a two-year-long association with that studio. His starting salary was $200 a week, which was soon increased to $250 a week only four months later, in May of 1936. In earning power he was getting $100 less than he had at Columbia in 1933; he was now close to the very bottom of all the screenwriters working in Hollywood—but he was working.

All through the thirties and forties there were quite a number of small, independently owned production firms operating in Hollywood on tiny budgets, most of them located on or near Gower Gulch, or what was called "Poverty Row." These included such organizations as Tiffany, Liberty, Mascot, Majestic, PRC, Chesterfield and Monogram. They specialized almost entirely in action pictures: Westerns, adventure serials for boys, detective mysteries, or what we would call today "category" films. In 1935 four of these firms—Liberty, Mascot, Majestic, and Monogram—were taken over by a fifth, Republic Studios, whose president, Herbert Yates, was also the owner of Consolidated Film Laboratories, an organization that had been advancing credit to the four small firms. Yates hoped that the amalgamation of the five would someday rival one of the larger and affluent companies. To this end he purchased the old Hal Roach Studios in North Hollywood; the newly created firm, Republic Productions, Inc., was known familiarly in the trade as "Repulsive Productions."

Few people born after about 1940 are apt to have seen more than one or two of the films made at Republic; Welles's *Macbeth* and John Ford's *The Quiet Man* are the only two I can think of, and these were made at the very end of the firm's existence. Almost no one is likely to have seen much more than these, for nearly all of Republic's films possess a special kind of badness that has made them unattractive to even the cheapest forms of television syndication. The old Republic films of the thirties are quite unlike most of the other old films of the time—they are *really* bad, for they were made as cheaply as was humanly possible. They were often made under bone-cracking shooting schedules from dawn to dusk, utilizing economies that have been long forgotten in the industry. They probably looked cheap enough at the time they were made, but today they seem only grotesque.

There were few American film houses in the thirties that were eager to book any of Republic's pictures; they would do so only if they couldn't afford the output of the larger studios. The rental fees were incredibly low by today's standards; it was possible to rent a feature film for as low as $10 a day, and short subjects went for $1 or so. With prices as low as this it became an absolute necessity for Republic, as well as all the other "Poverty Row" producers, to turn out a product utilizing the cheapest methods of film-making. If an actress or an actor muffed their lines badly enough, the scene would probably be reshot if there were time for it; if the director thought it wasn't *too* bad, the scene went right into the film can.

These films were shown at what used to be called "selected neighborhood playhouses," a phrase that covered all the theaters that thought they could make a buck showing them, and there were quite a few. The economies were often bizarre, for it was not uncommon for the products turned out by the "cheapies" occasionally to utilize the same footage more than once, *even in the very same picture.*

This was particularly true of their serial offerings, those episodic films of the thirties and forties that were made up of a dozen or more separate parts shown at weekly intervals. I still recall seeing, on successive Saturday afternoons, the individual chapters of an action serial entitled *The Black Coin,* which took nearly four months to run its course. There would come a time in each of the fifteen episodes, always at dusk, when the young teenage hero of the film would find himself all alone on the docks of what seemed to be some abandoned piers in what may have been San Pedro, California. Suddenly the young hero, wearing a white sweater as I recall it, was suddenly attacked by three or four burly men dressed in dark clothing who appeared to be set on beating him to death with whatever they could lay their hands on. As the weeks passed I began to look forward to seeing *The Black Coin* each Saturday. Would this favorite scene of mine be included, the one at dusk in which the very same things happened over and over again?

The beginning of this sequence of the film was always signaled by "danger music" on the sound track, and the young audience would scream their approval. The fight would continue, with the young hero getting the worst of it until he was suddenly rescued from certain death by the arrival of two or three of his friends, appropriately dressed in *light* clothing. The footage was identical each week, for the producers had actually shot only *one* fight sequence, which was then regularly spliced into each of the episodes of the complete film whenever it was felt it might speed up the action, which was admittedly on the slow side. So it was with *The Black Coin.* I imagine that I must have been amazed at the audacity of the film's makers in offering this duplicated footage, week after week. The theater managers were resentful of such practices, for they resented Mascot's or Monogram's cheapness being shown up in a such a bare-faced way, for they felt they too were being victimized, along with the audience.

The prevailing economies at Republic were extended to the people who appeared in their films, for the salaries there were not large by industry standards. The actors and actresses starring in Republic's pictures were quite often people on their way *down* professionally—Kay Francis, Bela Lugosi, Jackie Cooper, and Mae Clarke—but who still possessed at least some remaining box-office appeal, even if faint. There were actually a few people on the payroll who were on their way up, such as Rita Hayworth and John Wayne, but they were extremely rare. The great majority of the performers were the "regulars," such as Gene Autry and Roy Rogers, who were used in scores of their Western films, and Judy Canova, who was used for their "hillbilly" comedies. They also had a small stable of straight dramatic players, people like Wendy Barrie and Roger Pryor who had never really made it at the larger studios.

It has been frequently assumed that West spent a great deal of his time at Republic working on their Westerns, but he actually never wrote a single Western. All his work there was concerned with the preparation of shooting-scripts for the basically simple "problem" pictures that the studio turned out on a regular basis. Besides being made as cheaply as possible, these films had one thing in common: a totally simplistic approach to human character, which resulted in pictures of an almost unrelieved dullness. At the outset, the characters were quickly established as either totally good or bad, and everything about them was reduced to these polarities. There were never any doubts about much of anything in a Republic picture, even their mysteries, for you always knew what was happening from the opening shot.

Several commentators on West's film-writing career have stressed the high degree of fantasy they feel characterized so many of the films he worked on at this time, but this element was the mainstay of a great many of the films made at MGM, Paramount, Warner Brothers, as well as all the other studios,

although on a much more lavish scale. These films of the thirties in which the fantasy elements dominated were often tiresome and boring and were relieved only occasionally by films
into which a great deal of taste, intelligence, and care had
gone, films like Lubitsch's *Trouble in Paradise* and Hawks's
Scarface, both released in 1932. There were as many films
made then of this quality as there were good books published:
not very many. Without a first-rate director, and sometimes
even with one, a great many films of this period are now only
bearable because of the sheer charm and vitality of the principal performers; the Hepburn and Cagney films show this
pretty clearly. Neither at Republic nor at any of the other studios West worked for did he have the luck to encounter either
directors or performers of this quality; he was in the world of
"Cheapsville."

[3]

---

*It's easy to call his old studio Cheapsville, but that's not how
any Hollywood writer ever saw it. Those who were simply
making a living by writing scripts were much more respect-
ful; those, like West, who were buying time for other things,
were rightly grateful for the chance that Cheapsville gave
them.*
                              —John Sanford to Tom Dardis, April 1975

*I don't know how seriously he took movie writing—I believe
he worked at Republic and the motto there was, as you
wrote, Never Look Back—and he bad mouthed Hywd, you
could say, but you can't go by what people say in these
things. Every writer I know about here knocked his brains
out when he worked on movie scripts, although some times
he said he didn't.*
                              —Daniel Fuchs to Tom Dardis, May 1975

Horace McCoy, the author of *They Shoot Horses, Don't They?*
and *I Should Have Stayed Home,* was probably the best-known
writer on the Republic payroll when West joined the firm at

the beginning of 1936. Lester Cole and Samuel Ornitz, later famous for their "Hollywood Ten" connection, were also at Republic and glad to be there, despite the firm's reputation. Their common task was to turn out a product that was not dissimiliar in theme and content from that of the major producers of "B" movies, and to do this as quickly and as economically as possible. West did just this, some of it very much in his own way, for he took this work seriously enough to do his very best with it. He was quite successful; if he hadn't been able to supply what his employers wanted, his contracts with them would not have been regularly extended as they actually were.

As for the money he received from Republic, Leo C. Rosten's survey of the film industry, *Hollywood: The Movie Colony, the Movie Makers,* reveals that although West was at the very bottom of the scale in earning power he was not entirely alone there. Rosten's figures show that 40.8 percent of the screenwriters, all employed by the majors, earned under $250 per week. By the end of his second year at Republic, in 1937, West had been raised to $350 per week, one step further up in the hierarchy (22.8 percent), but this was still a long way from the $1,250 per week earned by Fitzgerald at MGM in 1938, or even the $1,000 per week that Faulkner got from Twentieth Century-Fox for a brief period in 1935–36.

Two of West's films for Republic have been singled out for particular attention, and even praise, by his biographers because they contained what used to be called "liberal thought," a mild enough concoction. The first of these, *The President's Mystery,* was an outgrowth of a *Liberty Magazine* series of stories that had been presumably "inspired" by President Franklin D. Roosevelt but that was actually a sales gimmick to push the faltering weekly. West's film dealt with the doings of a wealthy but crooked Washington lobbyist who is inspired to abandon both his way of life and his money to become the head of a strike-ridden canning factory in New England. The mere mention of the word "strike" in a film was considered quite daring in 1936, and a number of the critics were taken with *The President's Mystery;* the *New York Times* found the picture "interesting." West's second venture into the making of liberal films for Republic was called *It Could Happen to You,* which dealt with the rise of Nazism in the streets of a small American town, a sort of *It Can't Happen Here* picture. I've seen only the first of these films, *The President's Mystery,* and it is woodenly earnest from beginning to end; there is simply no life in it, and it failed for the same reasons that so much of the "socially conscious" fiction of the thirties failed just as badly: there is a complete lack of entertainment value.

In his full two years at Republic, West turned out nearly a dozen complete screenplays. A large number of these were actually filmed; they bore titles like *Jim Hanvey—Detective* (Guy Kibbee), *Follow Your Heart* (Marion Talley), *Ticket to Paradise* (Pryor and Barrie), *Born to Be Wild, Rhythm in the Clouds, Stormy Weather,* and *Orphans of the Street.* He could likely have gone on doing these for the next decade, but he may have realized that he could probably better himself elsewhere. He quit his job at Republic in January of 1938, worked briefly at Columbia again, and then was without work for four months. His risk paid off, however, for he was finally hired on a short-term basis by RKO Radio Pictures, the smallest of all the majors, but still a major.

[4]

Sometimes it is better to die on your feet than live on your knees!
— *West,* The Spirit of Culver, *A Universal Production, 1939*

Of course he was more deeply committed to books than pictures, and it's true too that he used what he made in pictures to buy him time for books. But the fact is, he never drew a top salary and was never able to buy complete freedom for himself, assuming that he wanted it. On what he earned, he never could've salted away enough to quit. . . .
— *John Sanford to Tom Dardis, April 1975*

West had already finished the writing of *The Day of the Locust* by the time he began working for RKO in June of 1938, although the book was not published until May of 1939. The money he had been receiving from Republic had, in effect, underwritten the time necessary to write the novel. His contract with Random House provided that he was to receive an advance of $500 against royalties. Bennett Cerf concluded his telegram to West offering to buy the book by saying, "Here's hoping that you will be a Random House author for the rest of your natural life." This was very nice, but the total of this advance amounted to less than two weeks' pay at RKO. As to the amount of the advance, Random House was not being niggardly with its money; for a writer with West's track record, $500 was about right. It was exactly the same amount of money advanced to William Faulkner on all his books up to 1940, when it was increased to $1,000. Since *The Day of the Locust* finally sold just under 1,500 copies, it produced royalties in the amount of about $300, with West being overpaid by $200. The Random House advance was quite realistic.

Working for RKO was a big upward step professionally, but West's weekly paycheck remained the same, for his salary there was his "established" one of $350 per week, the exact amount he had been getting at Republic. In order to break out of this established salary bracket it was necessary at that time either to get sufficiently important solo credit on pictures or else to share the billing on pictures that were real hits. West's very first job for RKO started off with the possibility of getting a solo credit, but he shared equal billing with Dalton Trumbo on *Five Came Back,* released in 1939.

When West started work at RKO in June 1938, he found that it was a typically uncertain time for that studio, a firm that from the time of its creation in 1921 until its final demise under the direction of Howard Hughes in 1955 had always seemed on the brink of coming apart or going under for good. Although it regularly kept coming up with smash hits— *King Kong, Little Women,* the Astaire and Rogers films like *Top Hat* and *Roberta*—disaster always seemed close, for what must have been considered mysterious reasons. Besides owning hundreds of its own first-rate theaters throughout the United States, one of RKO's major strengths was its distribution arm, which resulted in its being the releasing organization for all the Walt Disney, Sam Goldwyn, and David Selznick productions of the thirties and forties.

All through the thirties RKO had the reputation of having the best technology of any of the major studios, supposedly one of the major reasons for Orson Welles's accepting their offer in 1939 rather than one of the other, richer organizations. Their parent company of the early thirties was RCA, who had developed the RCA Photophone System, which along with Western Electric became the standard sound systems for the entire industry, supplanting the short-lived Warner's Vitaphone System. Although RKO had its own stars like Katharine Hepburn, Astaire and Rogers, and Ann Harding, it never really had enough of them for the company ever to show a profit. If there was a relatively good year, the next one would surely be bad. Many of the troubles were compounded by the rapidly changing patterns of ownership the firm endured from year to year. At one time or another Sarnoff's RCA, the Rockefellers, the Chase Bank, Howard Odlum, and finally Howard Hughes owned major shares of the company. As this ownership changed, so too did the management and the direction of the firm. In many ways it was an exciting place to work, but the turnover was faster than at any of the other major studios.

West was quite far down in the hierarchy of RKO and was assigned to write scripts for their "B" pictures, largely because of his background at Columbia and Republic. His first of these was *Five Came Back,* which proved to be a "sleeper" that somehow turned out to be a lot better than was anticipated, both with the critics and at the box office. This film and one other, *I Stole a Million,* are the two films that created West's reputation as a professional screenwriter in Hollywood. West's script, based on a short story by Richard Carroll, concerned a young American pilot's desperate attempt to repair his damaged aircraft that has crashed down in the jungles of the Amazon, leaving only five survivors. The plot of this film, whether in its entirety or in parts, has been one of the mainstays of American television entertainment for the past two decades, as it was of Hollywood movies, both "A" and "B," for the two decades preceding these. The pilot was played by Chester Morris, the girl by Wendy Barrie, and the heroic anarchist by John Carradine. The big moment in the film, the one that people talked about, was the *cessation* of the jungle drums, which had been playing without much letup from the moment the surviving passengers found themselves trapped in the shattered plane. Everyone knew that the moment the drums stopped the Indians (head-hunters?) would attack for the final kill. After nearly twenty minutes of the drums, the effect of the silence was astonishing.

The film attracted a certain amount of attention in the industry, mainly as an example of what could be done with a "B" picture. As for West, he was advancing professionally, but he again must have realized that if he didn't watch out he might be spending the rest of his life writing "B" pictures for RKO. He was much too ambitious for that and turned to a project he thought would advance him in another area, the stage.

While still finishing *The Day of the Locust,* West had been collaborating on an antiwar play with Joseph Shrank, which they called *Good Hunting,* a work that is a World War I equivalent of Richard Lester's *How I Won the War.* West spent the summer of 1938 busily making the final revisions in *The Day of the Locust* for Random House, as well as working on the play for Broadway production in the fall of the year. West's whole notion of writing the play had been to make enough money to enable him to quit his job at RKO and then, he hoped, write another novel. But there were risks involved, for if he came East for the play he would endanger his work status at RKO. He wrote a letter to the play's producer, Jerome Mayer, about his hopes for the play's success:

I would hate to go to New York City and just hang around waiting when I am sure I can continue to work out here and make some money. It has always been my contention that money is a very valuable commodity, and that those who scoff at it or its power will someday have their fingers burnt or their snook cocked. Money is really a wonderful thing. I can't say too much in praise of money. I adore it. Good old money. Good young money, too. Folding money and hard money alike transcend the common distinctions which make of our life one continuous round of humiliation.

His hopes were in vain, for the play opened shortly after the Munich Crisis, the beginnings of the pogroms in Germany, and a general feeling that war was not very far away. It was precisely the wrong time for an antiwar comedy; it did not please anyone, including one of its authors, who had been forced at the last possible moment to invest his own hard-earned RKO money in the play in order to guarantee the opening. It closed after two performances.

West was now left virtually bankrupt again and with no job at RKO to return to in California. He was lucky, however, for some very fast work on his part landed him a new job at Uni-

versal, the fourth Hollywood studio to employ him. Just before returning to California, by car as usual, he visited his old
friend, Josephine Herbst, who asked him if he thought he
could still write in Hollywood, that is, really write the kind of
things he wanted to write. He answered her this way: "I'll be
writing, but a writer needs to lead a writer's life. It isn't just a
sitting down—it's the whole business of thinking and reverie
and walking and reading, and you can't do that in Hollywood,
so I don't know what my future will be. But I'm going to be
working."

[5]

*Why don't you get out of that ghastly place? You're an art-
ist and really have no business there. . . .*
        —*Edmund Wilson to West, 1939*

*I once tried to work seriously at my craft but was absolutely
unable to make even the beginning of a living. At the end
of three years and two books I had made a total of $780.00
gross. So it wasn't a matter of making a sacrifice, which I
was willing enough to make and will still be willing, but
just a clear cut impossibility.*
        —*West to Edmund Wilson, 1939*

When West began working for Universal at the very end of
1938, it had become a totally different kind of company than
the somewhat paternalistic one founded by old Carl Laemmle
in 1912. Both of the Laemmles, junior and senior, had been
forced out of their business by irate stockholders, for Universal's operating deficits were running over $1 million a year all
through the period of 1935–38. The firm was completely
reorganized in 1938 by Nathan J. Blumberg, who placed all of
Universal's production in the hands of people reared and
trained in the *exhibition* of films, people who presumably knew
what would fill theaters. As had been the case with Republic,

all unnecessary costs were cut to the bone, but things were really a lot better off at Universal, for they had actual stars of their own under contract—Deanna Durbin and Abbott and Costello.

The type of pictures that West was hired to write for Universal were of the prefabricated kind, designed for highly specific markets, with very little left to chance, series pictures like the endless *Ma and Pa Kettle* films of the forties and fifties. Some of Universal's innovations in film-making were portents of things to come, for the studio was able to convince a number of stars to invest their own money in the films they were to appear in, while getting them to agree to working for a lot less than they were accustomed to receive. The W. C. Fields pictures *The Bank Dick* and *My Little Chickadee* came out of such cooperative ventures, as did Bing Crosby's *If I Had My Way* and *East Side of Heaven*. A lot of Universal's pictures at this time were simply built around titles that sounded "popular," and the films were then created to cash in on them: *Frankenstein's Daughter* and *The Tower of London*. They managed to rerelease every picture in their vaults they thought might still have some potential; they were right about films like *Dracula* and *Frankenstein,* for they made more money in 1938 than they did in 1931. All these activities produced a complete financial turnabout, so that in 1939 the studio showed a net profit of $1.5 million, the first profit picture of any sort in years, and by 1940 profits had reached nearly $2.5 million.

What all this meant to West was that he was now doing at Universal essentially the same thing he had been doing at Republic in 1936 and 1937, and for exactly the same money. His salary was still $350 a week, his old "established" rate of pay, which still clung to him. He began earning it by collaborating with Whitney Bolton in writing *The Spirit of Culver,* a film "tribute" to the famous military academy. For a man of West's political sensibilities—he was a member of the Hollywood Anti-Nazi League, the studio chairman of the Screenwriters' Guild, a member of the Hollywood Committee of the League of American Writers—this must have required

a special sort of effort, for the picture was to be an endorse-
ment of a good many things he found distasteful. But this first
script for Universal just had to be "good" if he wanted to go
on working there. It was, for his superiors at the studio apparently loved it, and West himself was unusually kind to his
own efforts at this type of work, as shown by his description of
the job to a friend as "an over-sweet, over-foolish sob story
with here and there a fairly decent moment." One of these
moments may be the one in which the upper-class boy named
Bobby (played by Freddie Bartholomew), while expounding
on the virtues of patriotism to the boy without roots (Jackie
Cooper), states that "sometimes it is better to die on your feet
than live on your knees." It has been pointed out by one of
West's biographers that his speech is an almost word-for-word
rendition of La Pasionaria's most famous remark about Fas-
cism, which she made in the early days of the Spanish Civil
War. This switching of what some would have called seditious
material into an ostensibly patriotic picture is typical of West's
sense of humor.

West's next job for Universal, *I Stole a Million,* was probably
his best-known film script except for *Five Came Back.* It starred
Claire Trevor and George Raft, and West based his script on
an original story "idea" by his friend Lester Cole. Raft played
the same kind of character he always played in his Warner
Brothers films; this time the film was about a crook who really
wanted to go straight but needed to "pull off just one more
little job" before doing so, and there was lots of shooting at the
end. The reviewers liked this film, and it made money. By
pure chance, it opened up in New York only three weeks after
Five Came Back, and the joint success of these two pictures did
a lot for West's reputation in the industry.

Reports of West's social life in Hollywood are contradictory,
for there are those who have described him as very much a
recluse, withdrawn and solitary, another Faulkner whose main
"talk" interest lay in hunting. Others have described him as
extremely outgoing, very sociable, a hard-working union func-

tionary for the Screenwriters' Guild. There can be little doubt about his passion for hunting wild game, on which he spent large amounts of both time and money. Dove shooting was his special delight—Josephine Herbst called her short novel about West *A Hunter of Doves*—but quail, geese, and duck were also his joy as he followed them throughout the seasons in both California and Mexico. There were times when his friends thought that hunting had become a mania for him, as he immersed himself in the world of decoys, imported shotguns, and endless lore. At one time he wrote a script (in collaboration) called *Flight South,* which concerned the slaughter of wild birds by illegal hunters; this was sold to MGM but never produced. In his early days at Republic, in 1936 and early 1937, West hunted on several occasions with Faulkner, including legendary trips in quest of wild boar on Santa Cruz Island, but this may well be pure invention on the part of either or both of the two writers.

Nearly all the writers discussed in this book seem to have spent a good deal of their time eating and drinking with their friends at the Musso & Frank Grill, or as it was known to all, Musso Frank's, a place that reminded many Easterners of a New York chop house, such as Keen's. West was also a regular at Stanley Rose's bookstore, where the man known as "Pep" addressed the owner of the place as "Jeeter," after Caldwell's character in *Tobacco Road,* for he was said to move even more slowly than did West.

West was also quite friendly with Fitzgerald in Hollywood, but nearly all the time they spent together was at the very end of both their lives. West had been in Hollywood for two full years before Fitzgerald arrived in the summer of 1937, but their few meetings seem to have taken place almost entirely in 1939 and 1940. At the beginning of April 1939 West sent Fitzgerald a set of galleys of *The Day of the Locust,* accompanied by a letter:

I'm taking the liberty again of sending you a set of proofs of a new novel.

It took a long time to write while working on westerns and cops and robbers, but reading the proofs I wish it had taken longer. I never thanked you for your kindness to me in the preface to the Modern Library edition of "The Great Gatsby." When I read it, I got a great lift just at a time when I needed one badly, if I was to go on writing. . . .

Here the friendship was almost entirely literary, and perhaps just a little political. Fitzgerald would appear to have had an almost proprietary interest in the career of the younger man whom he may, perhaps wrongly, have regarded as a disciple of his. It may be that Fitzgerald simply regarded himself as one of the first, along with Edmund Wilson, to recognize West's supreme talents. As is generally known, they died less than twenty-four hours apart, both of them with Hollywood still very much on their minds.

West stayed on at Universal for most of 1939, terminating his employment there with an enforced hospitalization for urethritis, related to the same trouble that had been so painful to him in 1935. After leaving the hospital he decided to see if he could write an original screenplay for one of the studios, rather than just going back on salary to one of them again. This occurred in the fall of 1939, just after the complete failure of *The Day of the Locust,* which had been demoralizing enough, but not bad enough to prevent him from wanting to write still another book. He wrote to S. J. Perelman about his intention to write a slam-bang winner of a script, one that would be sure to bring in the money he needed to write the novel: ". . . a real guzma about aviators, lost cities, jungles, and such guzmarie. Right now, my agent tells me, escape literature is the thing and so the one I am concocting touches the earth nowhere and is spun out of pure, unadulterated bubameiser."

It may have been all these things, but there were no buyers for it, and West was finally forced to go back on a contract basis to RKO at the end of 1939. It was at this time that he became associated with Boris Ingster, with whom he formed a working partnership that lasted until the end of West's life. Ingster had been born in Russia and is equally known as a writer, director, and producer. He had originally come to America at the end of 1930 in the company of Eisenstein and his team of coworkers, Tissé and Alexandrov, who had all come to Hollywood to fulfill their ill-fated Paramount contract. Ingster quickly disassociated himself from that group, or, as is more than likely, they may have wanted to get rid of this man who quickly struck out for himself. By 1935 he was working at RKO; he then went to Fox where he wrote the screenplays for the Sonja Henie ice-skating films, *Thin Ice* and *Happy Landing*. His story in Hollywood was a success story of the first magnitude, for he ultimately became the producer of one of the most popular television shows of the 1960s: *The Man from UNCLE*. In 1939 Ingster's greatest problem was still how to write good English dialogue, and this is why he teamed himself with a man whose latest book had sold just under 1,500 copies.

Their first assignment together at RKO was their joint script for *Before the Fact,* a then little-known English suspense story written by the mystery writer Francis Iles. The West-Ingster script was to star Laurence Olivier as the murderous Johnnie. At the very last minute, however, Alfred Hitchcock is supposed to have "discovered" this project, liking it well enough to obtain the rights to it for himself. The result was his *Suspicion* of 1941, starring Joan Fontaine and Cary Grant. In a number of interviews Hitchcock has described the West-Ingster script as "being absolutely beautiful," but he has never been able to convince anyone why he had to have an entirely different script written for him by Samuel Raphaelson, Joan Harrison, and his wife, Alma Reville, the one he actually used.

In the spring of 1940 West received another solo credit for his *Men Against the Sky,* a film about a formerly alcoholic airplane designer who is attempting a comeback, with Wendy Barrie as the girl, her third time in one of West's pictures. This film also received extremely good reviews, and RKO finally raised West to $400 a week, thus allowing him to escape from the $350 bracket in which he had been placed at the end of 1937 at Republic. In April he married Eileen McKenney, the "Eileen" of the well-known "My Sister Eileen" stories written by her sister, Ruth, which eventually became the basis of a Broadway musical and two films. The marriage was a surprise to some of his friends, but everyone who knew West agrees that it was a complete success.

When West returned from his honeymoon with Eileen in Oregon, which became an extended hunting and fishing trip, he was virtually broke. Ingster and he quickly cooked up a rough sort of adaptation of *A Cool Million* and were able to sell it to Columbia for $10,000. It had been Columbia that had bought the film rights to the book when it was first published in 1934; this time they bought a comic treatment of the book's theme, which involved a young man's being falsely accused of having embezzled $1 million from his bank. Everyone then worships the young man who acts as if he *had* embezzled the money; by the time the mistake is cleared up he has made many thousands on the stock market with the credit his "theft" had given him. There seems to be no rational explanation of why Columbia bought this property, unless it is simply that Ingster and West were an excellent team of consters.

Almost immediately after the Columbia sale they were able to sell still another treatment they called *Bird in Hand,* this time to RKO, for the sum of $25,000. This was a farcical mystery plot about a stockbroker who, in a raffle, wins a turkey that eventually turns out to have the American secret bombsight formula engraved on its back. There are three murders, and it all sounds strangely like a precursor of Graham Greene's *The Ministry of Fear.* As West might have said, this was a real "guzma," maybe even a "bubameiser guzma," but this time it sold.

In the last few months of his life West had begun to work on a novel for which he signed a Random House contract in the spring of 1940. The advance for the new book was for $250, for Bennett Cerf had not forgotten the sales of *The Day of the Locust.* This new book, for which only a few chapters were ever written, concerned the operation of a network of what he described as "Friendship Clubs," but which, as had *Miss Lonelyhearts,* promised something much wider in its implications.

The year 1940 was the best that West had financially in his entire time in Hollywood. In addition to being able to sell his original scripts to RKO and Columbia, his weekly rate of pay had suddenly risen to $600. He was now making it in a way quite unlike his old recurrent dreams of absolute and total failure, his Faye Greener world of "any dream was better than no dream and beggars couldn't be choosers," but he was also not forgetting that "no dream ever entirely disappears."

West was perhaps more at home than some in grinding out the rather stupefying plots that his employers at Republic, Universal, and RKO demanded of him, for his usual attitude toward the work was one of amusement, even sustained, gleeful amusement. It was junk all the way, but it supplied him with the money to keep on with his writing when nothing else would, the writing that in *The Day of the Locust* finally turned into an examination of the entire junk world of which he was now at the very center. No American writer got as much out of Hollywood as did West; the creation of the curious atmosphere of that book is a triumph. No writer was ever as successful as was West in simultaneously destroying the old romantic myth of Hollywood glamour and replacing it immediately with a brand-new one—the one of sinister decay in blazing sunlight.

Aldous Huxley in Los Angeles in 1938 (*Wide World*)

Aldous Huxley

The Man Who
Knew Too Much
Goes West

[1]

"Bob," he said, "in this studio, at this time, not even Jesus Christ himself could get a raise."
—*Huxley,* Ape and Essence

I remember him leafing through a copy of transition, *reading a poem in it, looking again at the title of the magazine, reflecting for a moment, then saying, "backwards it spells NO IT ISN(T) ART."*
—*Igor Stravinsky and Robert Craft,*
Dialogues and a Diary

At no time did Aldous Huxley's screenwriting activities ever take on the quality of absolute desperation that so strongly marked those of Faulkner and Fitzgerald, both of whom were finally forced to depend upon Hollywood as the major source of nearly all their income derived from writing. Unlike Faulkner's books, Huxley's began selling quite well very early in his career, and for the most part they kept right on selling, particularly in England, but he was often afflicted with worries about the occasional slumps in his sales that would occur between the publication of his major novels. It was at times such as these that he turned to movie-writing, as any truly professional writer might, for the sheer money to be made doing it, in very much the same spirit in which he had regularly turned out his brilliantly literate magazine articles on every conceivable subject, month after month, for *Vanity Fair* in the late twenties and early thirties and for *Esquire* in the fifties. It was much the same case with the Huxley screenplays of the forties—perhaps the most literate ones ever to be written in Hollywood by anyone at any time.

There are those who find something almost grotesque in the

mere fact of Aldous Huxley working in Hollywood at *any* time: "Did Aldous Huxley *really* write *A Woman's Vengeance?*" The tone of a question like this seems to contain more than just incredulity. In actual fact, Huxley spent quite a good bit of his time in California—twenty-five years in all—writing a wide variety of screenplays. While it is perfectly true that he almost never found himself in the position of really *having* to write for the movies, as did so many other writers of the time, his feelings about Hollywood and films in general were not as casual as some of the foregoing might suggest. The effects of Hollywood on his sensibilities were both profound and lasting, often showing up in his fiction of these years. His novel of Los Angeles as it might be in the year 2013, *Ape and Essence* (1948), appeared in the actual format of a "lost" screenplay rescued from a speeding truck bound for the flames of a film studio's incinerator.

The little story about Christ asking for a raise at the studio, quoted at the beginning of this chapter, is one that obsessed Huxley and that he loved telling people. He had actually heard these words at Universal in 1947, at the time he was present for the shooting of *A Woman's Vengeance*. He loved to make up ever more elaborate versions of this story; here is the Breughel one:

And then there would be Breughel's version of the subject. A great synoptic view of the entire Studio; a three-million dollar musical in full production, with every technical detail faithfully reproduced; two or three thousand figures, all perfectly characterized; and in the bottom right-hand corner long search would finally reveal a Lublin, the producer no bigger than a grasshopper, heaping contumely upon an even tinier Jesus.

There is poetry of a sort in *Ape and Essence,* and here are some lines about Los Angeles:

> And in the midst of them the City of the Angels,
> Half a million houses,
> Five thousand miles of streets,
> Fifteen hundred thousand motor vehicles,
> And more rubber goods than Akron,
> More celluloid than the Soviets,
> More Nylons than New Rochelle,

> More brassieres than Buffalo,
> More deodorants than Denver,
> More oranges than anywhere,
> With bigger and better girls—
> The great Metrollopis of the West.

In addition to its having been partially written in the form of an actual screenplay, *Ape and Essence* resembles a great many old movies, and one in particular. The plot of the book concerns a Dr. Poole from New Zealand, a member of an exploration party in the year 2013 engaged in finding out what traces of life are still to be found on the American mainland. Most of civilization had been wiped out by an atomic holocaust, and Los Angeles is now a huge necropolis whose cemeteries are being systematically looted by the survivors of the blast. Dr. Poole's native New Zealand has remained intact from the effects of the global disaster, but he has decided to attempt contact with an America he hoped would be free of radioactivity. After Poole has been placed ashore by his party and has proceeded to what seems to be left of Forest Lawn Cemetery, he is captured by some of the looters and dragged into the presence of "The Chief," a local strong man who holds absolute sway by his sheer brutality. He questions Dr. Poole closely about the conditions of life in New Zealand:

"Then you've still got trains?" he questions.
"Yes, we've still got trains," Dr. Poole answers a little irritably. "But, as I was saying . . ."
"And the engines really work?"
"Of course they work. As I was saying . . ."
Startlingly the chief lets out a whoop of delight and claps him on the shoulder.
"Then you can help us to get it all going again. Like in the good old days before . . . We'll have trains, real trains." And in an ecstasy of joyous anticipation, he draws Dr. Poole toward him. . . .

Almost everything in this scene is a very close approximation of a similiar situation in William Cameron Menzies's *Things to Come,* the 1936 British film version of H. G. Wells's tract about the immediate holocaustal future of Europe. A character in that film, played by Raymond Massey, like Dr. Poole in *Ape and Essence,* has also been sent to find out how the "survivors" are doing after the cataclysm. He lands his futuristic aircraft in the midst of a totally broken-down society ruled by "The Chief" (Ralph Richardson), who attempts to bully Massey into supplying him with the technical know-how to fly his smashed planes and "get things moving again!" Huxley saw this film in London at the time of its much heralded premiere and recalled it strongly enough to reproduce it *in toto* twelve years later in *Ape and Essence.*

Some of the oddities of life in California appeared in the very first novel Huxley wrote in America, *After Many a Summer Dies the Swan* (1939), which featured certain aspects, mostly sexual, of the private lives of the host and hostess of San Simeon/Xanadu—Hearst and his beloved Marion Davies, or Charles and Susan Alexander Kane as Welles chose to call them in *Citizen Kane.* Quite a bit of Huxley's fiction written after his arrival in California contains a number of obsessive images and themes not found in his work previously, and which arise from his prolonged "exposure" to the life in California. This includes the impact of an actual weekend he once spent with his wife at San Simeon, and which later became a part of *After Many a Summer:*

. . . The Rumpus Room, for example, with frescoes of elephants by Sert. The library with its woodwork by Grinling Gibbons, but with no books, because Mr. Stoyte [Hearst] had not brought himself to buy any. The small dining room, with its Fra Angelico and its furniture from Brighton Pavilion. The large dining room, modelled on the interior of the mosque at Fetehpur Sikri. The ballroom with its mirrors and coffered ceiling. The thirteenth-century stained-glass in the eleventh-floor W.C. . . . The chapel, imported in fragments from Goa, with the walnut confessional used by St. Francis de Sales at Annecy. . . .

A full decade after he had written *After Many a Summer,* Huxley encountered for the first time a woman who had worked for *Vanity Fair* in the twenties and who was noted for her sharp tongue. She informed Huxley that he had really been guilty of minimizing the oddities of Hearst and Marion Davies in his novel. In a letter written to his son Matthew in 1949, Huxley attempted to convey what this old friend of Hearst had witnessed on a long visit to San Simeon:

. . . the old man, who is dying, emaciated almost to the vanishing point, but desperately clinging to life (he won't lie down, for fear of not being able to get up again, but spends all his time sitting bolt upright); Marion Davies permanently drunk, dressed only in a dressing gown which constantly flies open at the front, expressing genuine adoration for Hearst, but meanwhile sleeping with the young Jewish ——— and announcing to all the world that she does so and saying what a stinker he is, both in bed and out; in the next breath confiding triumphantly to fellow-Catholic ——— that she has persuaded the old man to leave two million dollars to the convents of Southern California. The reality sounds infinitely more grue-some, and also more improbable, than the fictions of *After Many a Summer*.

Huxley began writing screenplays almost immediately upon his arrival in California in 1937, and he was still actively dick-ering with George Cukor in the very last few months of his life (March of 1963) over a possible film project about two eccen-tric spiritualists. Although it could scarcely be called a screenwriting "career," Huxley's active interest in writing for films spanned over a quarter of a century.

[2]

There is no substitute for talent. Industry and all the other virtues are of no avail.
—*Huxley,* Point Counter Point

When Huxley and his first wife, Maria, came to the United States in April of 1937, their stay was projected to be one of perhaps a year at most, but America became their new home-land for good, and the Huxleys lived nearly all the rest of their lives in Southern California. He was initially drawn to visit this country because of his close association with the writer Gerald Heard, with whom he was scheduled to conduct a series of joint lecture-discussion appearances throughout the United States on the subject of world peace, with Los Angeles as their starting point. Both Huxley and Heard were convinced that a worldwide cataclysm was something inescapable for the immediate future, and that Americans should know about it. The Huxleys spent that summer of 1937 at Frieda Lawrence's ranch at San Cristobal, New Mexico, and Heard and he began their tour of the United States in the early winter. The Huxleys fully expected to return to Europe at the beginning of 1938, perhaps a bit reluctantly. They did not return there, however, for at about this time Hollywood began to be a real possibility for Huxley, although his interest in working there dated back to the previous summer.

In June of 1937 the Los Angeles rare-book-seller Jacob Zeitlin had written to Huxley in New Mexico with regard to his acting as an agent in the matter of selling some of Huxley's stories and novels to one of the Hollywood studios. Huxley had replied to him in July:

. . . I am prepared to authorize you to take up the matter with film studios for the remainder of the present year. [He then listed those novels and stories of his he believed best for filming, among them *Antic Hay,* "The Gioconda Smile," *Point Counter Point,* and *Eyeless in Gaza.*]

About the possibility of my working in Hollywood—it is probable that I shall be staying in California for a time after the New Year. . . . I might perhaps make that stay an occasion for doing work for the films, if something satisfactory could be found. Will you, as you suggest, make tactful enquiries, without, please, in any way committing me definitely? I hope we may see you here in the course of the summer.

Zeitlin did visit San Cristobal that summer and strongly urged Huxley to try his luck in writing for Hollywood while he himself went on with his attempts to sell the film rights to the older properties. This visit seems to have been instrumental in making Huxley write an original screenplay that he called "Success," but which was never sold.* Zeitlin's inqui-

---

* *Now lost, this scenario was destroyed in the 1961 fire that consumed the Huxley home in California.*

ries in Hollywood produced no concrete offers for any of the older Huxley properties, but they apparently did produce at least one serious writing offer, which did not in any way appeal to him. He wrote to his brother Julian from the East about it in December of 1937:

The best they cd do in Hollywood was to ask me to adapt *The Forsyte Saga* for the screen: but even the lure of enormous lucre cd not reconcile me to remaining closed for months with the ghost of the late John Galsworthy. I couldn't face it! However, there is just a chance they may take an interest in something of mine [i.e., "Success"]; in which case I might go back to the West Coast for a short time to see what was happening.

While the fate of his "Success" was still in the balance, Huxley wrote again to Zeitlin from Rhinebeck, New York, in January of 1938: ". . . we shall aim at Los Angeles. Whether the stay there is to be short or long depends on the fate of the scenario, partly on other matters, not yet fully decided." Eventually, it was the fate of this scenario that drove the Huxleys all the way back to Los Angeles, where they finally arrived in February of 1938. Huxley then became quite ill with acute bronchial pneumonia, and he needed three weeks of hospitalization before beginning the long convalescence that occupied a good part of that year. It was at about this time that he renewed his friendship with Anita Loos, whom he and his wife had originally met in New York on their first trip to America in 1926, just a year after the publication of *Gentlemen Prefer Blondes*. That summer he had written about Miss Loos to his brother Julian in a letter that contains a much quoted phrase about her:

I had a very pleasant evening on Friday last with Anita Loos, who is ravishing. One would like to keep her as a pet. She is the doyenne of Hollywood, having started to write for the movies when she was seven. Now, at the age of, I suppose, about twenty-eight, she feels that she can retire with a good conscience, to live in cultured ease on the fruits of her labours. What she really likes doing, it appears, is plain sewing; spends all her holidays in making underclothes which nobody can wear.

This "doyenne" of Hollywood has never really retired and was, from the early 1930s onward, employed at MGM where

she wrote the screenplays for such well-known films as *Riffraff,
San Francisco,* and *The Women.* Miss Loos is unique in the his-
tory of film for having been present at so many pivotal mo-
ments in the careers of such diverse figures as D. W. Griffith,
Wilson Mizener, Buster Keaton's first wife, Natalie Talmadge,
F. Scott Fitzgerald, and Irving Thalberg among many others.
Huxley's friendship with her proved to be lifelong, and it was
finally through her efforts that he began writing for MGM.

At the time when Anita Loos decided to act as the go-
between on behalf of MGM to hire Aldous Huxley as a
scriptwriter, she was largely motivated by her close friendship
with him, but it should be emphasized that Huxley was very
much a marketable commodity in 1938, for his *Eyeless in Gaza*
had been one of the four or five best-selling novels of 1936.
Although he may have been quite properly regarded by many
in Hollywood as a "highbrow" writer, he was also very much
of a best-selling, "Full-Book-Club-Selection" kind of writer. As
early as 1930 W. Somerset Maugham, himself no mean judge
of the current literary competition in England, had his character Alroy Kear say of Huxley in *Cakes and Ale,* "Of course
there's Aldous; he is a good deal younger than me, but he's
not very strong and I don't believe he takes great care of himself. . . ."

Maugham was totally wrong about Huxley's not taking care
of his health, for both Huxley and his wife kept trying out
new doctors and their various remedies until the end of their
days. It was in the area of money matters that Maugham
might have been right about Huxley's lack of knowledge, for
he was quite naive about what he might be able to earn as a
screenwriter. His initial hopes were for $1,000 a month, out of
which he hoped to save at least half. This hoped-for amount,
$250 per week, must be contrasted with, for example, the ac-
tual $1,250 per week that F. Scott Fitzgerald was receiving that
same year at MGM.

It was in May of 1938 that Miss Loos phoned Huxley to see
if he would be willing to undertake the job of writing the
screenplay for what was to be the Bernard Hyman production
of *Madame Curie,* a film to be based on Eve Curie's best-selling
biography of her mother. It may now all sound irresistible, for

in addition to Huxley writing the script, the film was to star Greta Garbo in the title role and was to have been directed by George Cukor. Strangely enough, Huxley was at first unsure of himself, thinking it would be quite impossible to please the MGM executives with the rather "special" kind of material he'd be expected to come up with.

He then had a very quick change of heart, the entire project fully catching his imagination, and he began to take it very seriously indeed. As was usual, the people at MGM were slow in making up their minds, and Maria Huxley wrote to her sister Jeanne about Aldous's impatience to get started on the job: "Aldous wants it to be done properly and nobly . . . the great advantage of having Garbo is that she passionately wants to play that part; she admires Aldous and would do a bit more under his direction. . . ."

It was not until July that MGM finally made its decision, and only then did Huxley sign his first Hollywood contract. He was to receive $15,000 for eight weeks' work, or just under $2,000 per week. Both of the Huxleys were stunned, for this seemed to be an enormous sum to them, something unimaginable. But there it all was, in American dollars. He reported for work at MGM at Culver City at the beginning of August, with Maria driving him to and from the studio each day, as was her usual custom; she had once stated her occupation in a hotel register as "chauffeur." Huxley was now a professional screenwriter with an air-conditioned office and windows he could not open; he began to work on *Madame Curie*.

As indicated in the chapter on Fitzgerald, *Madame Curie* was always something of a problem picture at MGM, particularly with regard to the way the "science" should be handled. In a very long letter written to his brother Julian many months later, Huxley summed up his thoughts about the problems involved in writing it:

. . . I've done a fair amount of work: a "treatment," as they call it in the jargon of the films, of the life of Mme Curie for Garbo. Rather an amusing job—tho' I shdn't like too many of the kind, since this telling a story in purely pictorial terms doesn't allow any of the experimentation with words in their relation to things, events and ideas, which is, *au fond,* my business. They gave me 8 weeks to do the job and I turned in what is, I think, quite a good script in which the scientific processes used by the Curies and the trains of reasoning they pursued are rendered in pictorial terms (all within the space of about 5 minutes, which is about all the public will tolerate of this kind of thing!) It now remains to be seen whether the studio will preserve anything of what I've done. They have followed their usual procedure and handed my treatment over to several other people to make a screen-play out of. By the time they are ready to shoot it may have been through twenty pairs of hands. What will be left? One shudders to think. Meanwhile they have paid me a lot of money. . . .

Huxley was quite right about his prediction about what might happen to his work, as well as perhaps feeling the need to shudder about it. His original treatment was given to a great many of the writers at MGM over the course of the next few years. One of them was F. Scott Fitzgerald, who spent the last two months of his MGM contract, in November and December of 1938, attempting to come up with something that would please Bernard Hyman, but with no more success than Huxley. While it is quite likely that the Huxley treatment did contain a little too much "science," the real trouble with the *Curie* project, perhaps right from the very start, may have been the frightening prospect of Greta Garbo besmocked in a laboratory coat, toiling messily with test tubes and Bunsen burners—*not* MGM's Garbo of *Anna Karenina, Camille,* and *Conquest.* The filming of *Madame Curie* was finally achieved in 1943 as a Sidney Franklin production, with Greer Garson and Walter Pidgeon as Marie and Pierre Curie, and with Mervyn LeRoy directing a script credited to Paul Osborne and Paul Rameau. It is possible to trace tiny pieces of Huxley's original material in the finished picture, but it is rather like looking for dust motes; his entire approach to the subject was totally abandoned for what now seems to be "Mr. and Mrs. Miniver Discover Radium."

Huxley's contract was not extended by MGM, and his film-writing career might very well have ended at this point if it had not been for the presence of Anita Loos. Like Faulkner six years before him at MGM, Huxley's first attempt at writing for the movies had produced rather negative feelings in his employers. It was mainly Howard Hawks's continuing faith in Faulkner that got him virtually all the work in Hollywood he did there, and it was now only the persistence of Anita Loos that got Huxley back into the good graces of MGM, although this was still another year away.

[3]

. . . this time he is doing some sort of nonsense for Fox, and Fox is nice. They don't expect him to go there and sit there every day. . . .
—Maria Huxley to Sybille Bedford, July 1941

The natural rhythm of human life is routine punctuated by orgies.
—Huxley, Beyond the Mexique Bay

From quite early in his life until very nearly the end, Aldous Huxley created an astonishing first impression on people he met. He must have done so at MGM in August of 1938 when he first reported for his work on *Madame Curie,* for here in the flesh was this literal giant of a man, this prodigy of learning and culture who seemed to be always fully informed on every conceivable subject known and unknown to man. For this was the truly legendary Huxley who had his special luggage so constructed that he could easily carry the eleventh edition of the *Encyclopaedia Britannica* with him wherever he went on his travels—volumes that he read over and over again. This was the Huxley who had become one of the most influential minds of his generation in several areas of thought. This was Huxley, now forty-four years old and nearly blind, for he did not begin to employ the Bates Method of "rediscovering" his vision until the next year, 1939. This was the man that MGM had hired to write *Madame Curie.*

There were those who found him truly frightening and overpowering in his knowledge, and perhaps even terrifying in his manner, but there were many who found him to be the gentlest man they had ever met. As was usually the case wherever he went, he made many long-lasting friendships in the Los Angeles area, and the spectrum of these friendships is truly astonishing: Charlie Chaplin and his wife at the time, Paulette Goddard; Igor Stravinsky and his wife, Vera; Christopher Isherwood; Garbo; the astonomer Edwin Hubble; and the psychologist Dr. Humphry Osmond. Despite his staggering work output, Huxley was very much a social being and really liked entertaining people as well as being entertained.

Christopher Isherwood arrived in Hollywood for the first time in June of 1939, and he and Huxley began a close friendship that lasted until Huxley's death in 1963. Isherwood's first impressions of Huxley, although not actually written until 1964, give what seems to be the most vivid picture of Aldous Huxley in the summer of his forty-fifth year:

Aldous's physical appearance took me by surprise. I had expected somebody resembling the skinny, thickly bespectacled, spider-like intellectual of the early photographs. . . . In any case, the Aldous in his middle forties whom I now met in the flesh was slender but not at all skinny, and the insect-look I had discovered in his photographs now seemed to me to be more of a bird-look, benevolent and quick with interest in his surroundings. He no longer wore spectacles. When he talked, his beautifully sensitive features seemed literally to shine with enthusiasm. He was interested in so many subjects that he could take to anybody—anybody, that is, who was also interested. Thus he could thoroughly enjoy the company of children and teenagers, scientists, ranchers, actresses, priests and professors. . . .

When Huxley had finished his MGM job on *Madame Curie* in October of 1938, he almost immediately began work on what he called a "short phantasy novel in the manner, more or less, of *Brave New World.*" This was *After Many a Summer Dies the Swan,* the first of his books to be entirely set and written in the United States. The locale of the novel is the vast palatial California estate of Joe Stoyte, the book's Hearst-like millionaire who lives with his young blonde mistress, Virginia Maunciple. In his first draft of the book, Huxley had called her Virginia Dowlas, which resulted in his having to make some last-minute changes. He wrote to his English publisher, Harold Raymond of Chatto & Windus, in August of 1939:

. . . I am sending you on a separate page a series of corrections relating mainly to the finer shades of the American language, on which I have been taking expert opinion.* The name Dowlas, I am afraid, has got be changed, owing to its fortuitous resemblance to that of a notorious lady in this neighborhood.† I think that Maunciple should prove a sufficiently euphonious and safe substitute. Please have a careful eye kept on the proofs to see that every mention of the name is corrected.

He had completed *After Many a Summer* in July of 1939, and in the following month he again began negotiations with MGM, this time in connection with their forthcoming version of Jane Austen's *Pride and Prejudice,* to be produced by Hunt Stromberg. Once again, it was Anita Loos who acted as the go-between, but this time there were some difficulties. Miss Loos has written this account of what happened by relating a three-way phone conversation between herself and Huxley and his wife, Maria:

"I'm sorry," Aldous said, "but I can't take that movie job."
I wanted to know why not.
"Because it pays twenty-five hundred dollars a week," he answered in deep distress. "I simply cannot accept all that money to work in a pleasant studio while my family and friends are starving and being bombed in England."
"But Aldous," I asked, "why can't you accept that twenty-five hundred and send the larger part of it to England?"
There was a long silence at the other end of the line, and then Maria spoke up.
"Anita," she said, "what would we ever do without you?"
"The trouble with Aldous," I told her, "is that he's a genius who just once in a while isn't very smart."

This is a pleasant story, but there are a number of inaccuracies in it that should be corrected. Huxley's dealings with MGM over *Pride and Prejudice* took place in August of 1939,

---

* *From Anita Loos.*
† *Marion Davies, whose real name was, in fact, Douras.*

while the conversation related here seems to have taken place at the height of the Battle of Britain, a year later, in the summer of 1940. The amount of Huxley's weekly salary is incorrect; it was $1,500 a week, not $2,500 a week. But Miss Loos has more good stories to tell about Hollywood than almost anybody; one should perhaps not complain.

Unlike his work on *Madame Curie,* there was to be no specific time limit on *Pride and Prejudice,* and this may explain the slight drop in Huxley's weekly rate of pay down to $1,500 from nearly $2,000. In actual fact, the job lasted nearly six months, for this was a Hunt Stromberg production, with Huxley having as much trouble getting to see him as Fitzgerald had the year before. There were a great many delays, and by January 14, 1940, he wrote about them to his brother Julian:

No news here. Pee and Pee (as Jane Austen's masterpiece is called at M.G.M.) drags on—not through any fault of writers and director, but because we cannot get to see our producer without whom nothing further can be done. If he does get round to seeing us, it will all be finished in a few days: if not, God knows.

It is quite conceivable that Huxley and his wife might have returned to Europe at about this time, but the outbreak of World War II effectively kept them in Southern California for its duration. The longer they remained in the United States the better the reasons seemed to be for their never returning to Europe. It now seems tragic that the Huxleys were denied the American citizenship they so strongly desired. It was denied because a Los Angeles judge found Huxley's pacifism unacceptable to him because it had nothing to do with Huxley's religious beliefs.

The work on "Pee and Pee" continued. His main reason for undertaking the job was the usual one, for he was again between books. He took up the task of transforming Jane Austen into film with all his typical enthusiasm but with some worries about what might happen to the spirit of the author's book. After two months of working on the job, he wrote to his American publisher, Eugene Saxton of Harper's:

. . . I work away at the adaptation of *Pride and Prejudice* for the moment—an odd, cross-word puzzle job. One tries to do one's best for Jane Austen; but actually the very fact of transforming the book into a picture must necessarily alter its whole quality in a profound way. In any picture or play, the story is essential and primary. In Jane Austen's books, it is a matter of secondary importance (every dramatic event in *Pride and Prejudice* is recorded in a couple of lines, generally in a letter) and serves merely as a receptacle for the dilute irony in which the characters are bathed. Any other kind of receptacle would have served the purpose equally well; and the insistence upon the story as opposed to the dilute irony which the story is designed to contain, is a major falsification of Miss Austen.

Despite all these fears about violating the spirit of Jane Austen, Huxley and the various people he worked with at MGM produced a first-rate film. The extreme excellence of MGM's *Pride and Prejudice* (1940) is not really attributable to any particularly faithful adherence to the novel on which it was based, for Huxley and Jane Murfin simplified the plot considerably and actually advanced the time of the story by some forty years in order to show the ladies and gentlemen of the cast in more "pleasing" costumes. But the script is perhaps a model of what a screenplay based on a play or a novel ought to be: just right. Robert Z. Leonard's direction was professional to the point of being scarcely noticeable. The two principal actors, Greer Garson as Elizabeth and Laurence Olivier as Darcy, were both superb, as was practically the entire supporting cast. Almost everyone was English, with the notable exception of Mary Boland as Elizabeth's mother. The film still possesses a great deal of its original charm and freshness, and although it has been officially identified as a certified "classic," it is just exactly that.

Huxley had completed his first version of *Pride and Prejudice* just after the beginning of the year, but the studio then recalled him for revisions, this time at only half-pay, or $750 a week. Even half of his old salary was extremely welcome, for two unpleasant things of a financial nature were to happen in that year. Quite early in the year he took the time to read his semiannual royalty statement from Harper's, a thing he didn't usually do, expecting to see good news about the sales of *After Many a Summer*. He found the sales to be reasonably good, but he was deeply shocked to see that he had been overpaid by

Harper's in the previous year by $9,000. This situation had come about because of his having set up with Harper's an arrangement similar to the one he had always had with Chatto & Windus in London—essentially a regular drawing account against which were accrued the royalties actually earned on the sale of his books. In England his older titles continued to sell quite well, but in America, as he ruefully discovered, they did not.

The other bad news about money matters came later in the year. His British literary agent, Ralph Pinker, had been secretly embezzling his author's royalty accounts for some years; he was caught doing it and the firm was liquidated, with Pinker being imprisoned in Wormwood Scrubs. Huxley's loss was only £500, but coming after the shocking news from Harper's earlier in the year, even MGM's reduced monies were all the more welcome.

A good deal of the money Huxley earned in Hollywood was simply given away, for both he and his wife were always extremely generous. Although they never lived in a particularly lavish manner, they would often find their funds seriously depleted because of Aldous's contributions to various "needy" causes, especially among the members of Maria's family during the war. There were in fact times when he was supporting more than one household. Both Huxleys had always felt that mounting bank balances were much less preferable to seeing and doing things with the money; travel and the cars required for it had always been their major luxury.

Everyone at MGM seems to have been pleased with Huxley's script for *Pride and Prejudice,* so pleased that he was told there would be work for him at the studio whenever he desired it. This offer was apparently genuine, for Maria Huxley wrote to her sister Jeanne about it:

Which by the way is not just niceness on their part. It's because Aldous has learned to do their kind of thing extremely well, as he does anything he really wants to. The only thing he still has to learn is to pay some attention to his own finances; the kind of surprise we just had simply shouldn't have happened. It proves that he doesn't even look at his accounts. . . .

She is referring here to the Harper's overpayment, which had left them both shaken. Despite these worries about money, Huxley began working on his biography of Cardinal Richelieu's Père Joseph, *Grey Eminence,* which he completed in May of 1941. This was not the kind of book that could be counted on to sell particularly well, and he again began to think about possible movie work to improve his finances. His agent, Leland Hayward, managed to get him the job of adapting Charlotte Brontë's *Jane Eyre* for Twentieth Century-Fox. He did this with the collaboration of both John Houseman, and Robert Stevenson, who also directed the film, which was not released until the very end of 1943, after a great many delays. This time Huxley was allowed to do a good part of the work at home, which he greatly preferred to what he felt was the *coldness* of the studio. His wife wrote to Sybille Bedford at this time about his working activities:

Aldous, poor Aldous is making a little urgently needed money at the Fox studios . . . he is correcting proofs which come in like punishment. And that combined with the movie work is a lot for him. But this time he is doing some sort of nonsense for Fox and Fox is nice. They don't expect him to go there and sit every day, so our life is much as ever.

The producer of *Jane Eyre* was William Goetz who had been associated with Darryl F. Zanuck's Twentieth Century Pictures from the very beginning of the firm in 1933, two years before the merger with Fox. In later years he produced independently for both Universal and Zanuck films as diverse as *Sayonara, They Came to Cordura,* and *The Man from Laramie.* Huxley had become acquainted with Goetz in part through some long and tortuous negotiations concerning the dramatization of D. H. Lawrence's *Lady Chatterley's Lover,* which eventually involved W. H. Auden, Christopher Isherwood, Samuel Beckett, and the Hungarian dramatist Melchior Lengyel.

Frieda Lawrence, the novelist's widow, had given the Hungarian playwright Lengyel the right to dramatize *Lady Chat-*

terley, with perhaps some faint hope of turning the play into a film. Lengyel's chief claim to fame in Hollywood was as the author of the original story on which Ernst Lubitsch's *Ninotchka* was based. Lengyel completed a draft of *Lady Chatterley,* and it was then given to Goetz for a professional reaction, which was quite negative. Frieda Lawrence was equally disappointed with the play, and she then turned to her old friend Aldous Huxley for help. Huxley agreed at least to read the play, and he did so, telling Frieda that what it really needed was some good modern dialogue, and that Isherwood and Auden were just the people to write it, with his own assistance if that proved necessary. She appears to have agreed to this but quite suddenly informed Huxley that she had been in touch with Samuel Beckett, who was also willing to revise Lengyel's text. This news caused Huxley to remonstrate with her strongly, attempting to discourage her from proceeding any further with Beckett. Frieda's reaction at this point was to attempt to get rid of Lengyel, but both Goetz and Huxley warned her that she could not do so, either legally or morally. A good deal of heated correspondence ensued before everything came to a complete standstill, with Huxley finally writing what amounted to a sort of an apology to Frieda:

Work was held up because Isherwood, who had undertaken to do the recomposition, was tied up at Metro-Goldwyn-Mayer. I saw Isherwood yesterday, for the first time in several weeks, and it seems they are keeping him on for another month or two at Metro and are then lending him (he being under contract to them) to Twentieth Century-Fox. This means, I'm afraid, that his collaboration is ruled out. Meanwhile there is absolutely no news of Auden, who has changed his address in New York and has not written to anyone here since he came to California in August. Another disappointment has been that John van Druten has declined to take on the job . . . This leaves us for the moment high and dry. I have told Goetz that the only hope seems to be to find some good and experienced dramatist who is prepared to try his hand at the job. . . .

That dramatist was never found, but Huxley managed in the course of his letter to extricate himself gracefully from the picture, pleading the pressures of his book work, in addition to his MGM work on *Pride and Prejudice.* His dealings with

Frieda Lawrence in this ill-fated project had at least produced a working relationship with Goetz and contributed to his being willing to undertake the writing of *Jane Eyre* for Fox.

Orson Welles is present in *Jane Eyre* in a double sense. In his portrayal of Rochester, he gave one of his most stupefyingly bravura performances, but the film is actually quite good enough to withstand even this, as in his own *Lady from Shanghai*. A good part of the physical look of this picture can be traced directly to Welles, who was present at the studio during much of the shooting, giving Robert Stevenson (the nominal director) a great deal of help in achieving a film that pictorially bore a strong resemblance to his own *The Magnificent Ambersons*. The mood of all the Gothic scenes involving Rochester's mad wife from Jamaica are extremely Wellesian in almost every detail, as are a great many of the other scenes. John Houseman's presence undoubtedly helped in achieving the beautifully somber tone of so much of this film, as in the scene in which Jane goes to visit her dying aunt, while the sound track carries Rochester's cry of "Jane, Jane!"

There were some differences of opinion between the collaborators, with Stevenson being brought in as a writer fairly late in the production schedule. The script itself seems to follow the same basic principles Huxley had utilized in writing *Pride and Prejudice,* and *Jane Eyre* has gone down as a "classic" in film history, as did the first film.

The work on *Jane Eyre* dragged on all through the fall and winter of 1941; Huxley was still working on it at the beginning of 1942 and did not finish until the late spring of that year. He discussed several aspects of this job with an old friend: ". . . have been working at the adaptation of a story for the movies—tiresome work, but unavoidable, since books at the moment don't keep wolves very far from doors, and the movie work is on the whole preferable to the continual shallow improvising of articles and stories, which is the practical alternative to it."

By the end of 1941 it would seem that Huxley preferred to

earn money from screenwriting rather than grinding out magazine articles, but this feeling did not last very long. In the long run, writing his books, particularly *successful* books, pleased him most of all. The two books he did publish in 1942 and 1944—*The Art of Seeing* and *Time Must Have a Stop*—were precisely that. The first of these, a basic introduction to the Bates Method of "reeducating" the eye, was enormously popular in both England and America and is still in print thirty years after its original publication. The subject and his treatment of it were "controversial" in 1942 and still are today. Christopher Isherwood's brief comment best conveys how strongly some people can feel about it: "I have neither the authority nor the inclination to express a personal opinion on this subject; I merely record that I have seen people who were discussing it become enraged to the point of incoherence and I can well believe that it has sometimes been the cause of fistfights." There has been considerable controversy about just how well and how much Huxley could actually "see" after embracing the Bates Method; there are no very definite answers to such questions except to state that he was absolutely convinced of a tremendous improvement in his vision.

The second of these two successful books, *Time Must Have a Stop,* was Huxley's own favorite of all his novels, and it sold over 40,000 copies within the first few months of publication in the very last days of the war. As had become customary with him, he managed to do some screenwriting in between the publication of these two books, this time under rather different circumstances.

In the early spring of 1944 Huxley collaborated for the first of a number of times with Christopher Isherwood on an original screenplay about a faith healer, which they called *Jacob's Hands.* He wrote about it to Frieda Lawrence, saying, "I hope that we shall be able to sell it, as it will help solve a lot of economic problems, and will make it unnecessary to go into temporary slavery at one of the studios."

This attempt to go it on his own with Isherwood as an independent screenwriter was doomed to failure, for *Jacob's Hands* proved to be unsalable to any of the studios in 1944, although for reasons not immediately obvious to either Huxley or Isherwood. In July of that year, Huxley wrote to his collaborator:

. . . I have just had a rather gloomy account of our story. It appears that the reason for the hitherto universal rejection of it is fear of the doctors. . . . I have written at length to Hyde [of MCA] exposing all the reasons why the doctors have no grounds for complaint—the healer's biggest medical success is a moral failure, his biggest moral success is a medical failure, he retires from all but veterinary business because he feels he can't use his gift rightly. . . .

The "doctors" won, for the script of *Jacob's Hands* was never filmed, but was only heard as an adapted radio drama.

[4]

But, *Aldous needs to work for the movies to make a living—he says so in so many words.*
                              —*Maria Huxley to Matthew Huxley, 1947*

However much Huxley may have been pleased by the huge success of *Time Must Have a Stop* in late 1944 and early 1945, he soon became worried enough about money to be caught up in several movie projects. Walt Disney had come up with the notion that an interesting film could be made about the life of the creator of *Alice in Wonderland,* Charles Dodgson. Huxley wrote to his South American friend, Victoria Ocampo, about his part in the proposal:

I have been asked by Disney to help in the production of *Alice in Wonderland.* The phantasy will be embedded in real-life episodes of the life of Charles Dodgson, the Oxford don who wrote under the name of Lewis Carroll. Dodgson is a fascinating mid-Victorian eccentric, and I had hoped to bring in something of the old, unreformed Oxford of the eighteen-sixties—but, as usual it turns out to be impossible to make any of the documentary points which would be so amusing (at any rate for me) to elaborate . . . But, alas, there is no time in an hour of film—and even if there were time, how few of the millions who see the film would take the smallest interest in the reconstruction of this odd fragment of the forgotten past! So I have to be content with bringing out as many of the oddities of Dodgson as possible, and with preventing producer and director from putting in too many anachronisms and impossibilities for the sake of the story.

He wrote to many of his friends at this time, wishing them to share his enthusiasm for the *Alice* film, which Maria Huxley told her friends was "the first movie he likes doing." He wrote to Anita Loos about it in October:

I think something rather nice might be made out of this—the unutterably odd, repressed and ridiculous Oxford lecturer on logic and mathematics, seeking refuge in the company of little girls and his own phantasy. There is plenty of comic material in Dodgson's life, and I think it will be legitimate to invent some such absurd climax as a visit of Queen Victoria to Oxford and her insistence on having the author of *Alice* presented to her, in preference to all the big wigs—the scene dissolving, in Carroll's fancy, to the end of *Alice:* "They're nothing but a pack of cards"—and the Queen and her retinue become ridiculous cartoon figures and are scattered to the four winds.

Although Huxley spent several months working on the Disney *Alice,* none of his material was utilized, and the film that finally emerged was simply a rather flat Disney version of the John Tenniel illustrations for the Carroll text. This was sad, for he had derived more pleasure from this work than in anything else he had done in Hollywood.

The other 1945 project that occupied quite a lot of his time was the film *Brave New World.* The producers of the film were to be his friends Paulette Goddard and her new husband, the actor Burgess Meredith. The exploding of the first nuclear weapon had made a film version of Huxley's 1932 novel especially timely, or so it was thought, but there proved to be a series of apparently insurmountable obstacles in the way of ever getting it produced. At first Huxley was worried about the censorship problems of the screenplay they wanted him to write, especially about the insemination techniques of the future he had set forth in his book. He turned to Anita Loos for advice: "One practical point worries me: what will the Hays

Office say about babies in bottles? We must have them, since no other symbol of the triumph of science over nature is anything like as effective as this. But will they allow it? This and other problems will need a lot of discussion later on. . . ."

In his concern about the difficulties in getting *Brave New World* filmed, Huxley was forced to face some plain truths about the very nature of the film medium in the mid forties, as he did in this letter to Victoria Ocampo:

There are possibilities that my book *Brave New World* may be turned into a film . . . if the negotiations with the present owners of the rights go through, I shall probably do the screenplay. It will be interesting to see how much can be said in that medium—and how much one will be allowed to say. The fact that films cannot pay their expenses unless they are seen by twenty or thirty million people, imposes the most enormous intellectual and conventional limitations. There can be no change in the present situation until arrangements are made for exhibiting special films to a limited public, as is done with plays. But this can't be done unless the cost of making films is enormously reduced.

The problems concerned with the rights on *Brave New World* dragged on into the spring of 1946. The trouble had all begun back in 1932, at the time of the book's original publication, when Pinker, Huxley's reckless agent, had sold *all* the dramatic rights in the property to RKO Radio Pictures, which had never done anything with them and apparently had no intention of doing anything with them in 1946. However, they also refused to let anyone else do the film. He explained the mess to his brother Julian:

Although he has no rights in the movie . . . the producers and their financial backers won't embark on the thing until he signs a release. Meanwhile the situation has been made more complex by the fact that the Pinker brothers . . . were inexcusably inefficient—so much so that no trace of the original contract with Mr. ———— can be discovered. So there we are, in the midst of a first-class mess, which is a pity. . . .

It was indeed a mess, for in the following decade all Huxley's efforts to make RKO part with these rights were in vain. At one point, in 1957, RKO offered to sell the rights back to

Huxley and his friends for the sum of $50,000, a figure they all judged excessive. In 1963 the new owners of what was left of RKO sold the rights to Samuel Bronston. Huxley had been promised a share in the proceeds of such a sale, but he received absolutely nothing; *Brave New World* has yet to be filmed.

In the winter of 1946 the English literary critic Cyril Connolly came to visit Huxley at his home in Wrightwood, California. They had not seen each other in a decade. Connolly was amazed to find how well his old friend had adapted to life in Los Angeles, something he knew he could not himself do:

The California climate and food creates giants but not genius, but Huxley has filled out into a kind of Apollonian majesty; he radiates both intelligence and serene goodness, and is the best possible testimony to the simple life he leads and the faith he believes in, the only English writer, I think, to have wholly benefited by his transplantation and whom one feels exquisitely refreshed by meeting.

Huxley's biographer Sybille Bedford relates a story in which Connolly had a dream in which he had seen Huxley in a blue light and from which he had awakened feeling extremely serene. On being told about the dream, Huxley's comment was, "Yes, I thought about you a good deal. I felt you were unhappy."

After the defeats with *Alice* and *Brave New World,* Huxley began to write a screenplay based on his own short story "The Gioconda Smile," which was eventually filmed in 1947, bearing the title *A Woman's Vengeance.* He hoped to be able to utilize the film's dialogue for a possible stage version if the necessary financing could be obtained. He wrote to Anita Loos about this:

I have finished my screen play of "The Gioconda Smile," and I think it should make a very likely movie. . . . So I am at present working on this stage adaptation. It raises some rather tough problems. I wish you were here, so that I could get the benefit of your experience. Working on the script with Zoltan Korda was very pleasant. He is a nice, intelligent fellow and we were able to co-ordinate our respective specialities of writer and director without the interference of a producer. Consequently the work was done quickly and efficiently, without being held up by retired button-manufacturers using the Divine Right of Money to obstruct the activities of those who do the actual work.

While the screenplay of "The Gioconda Smile" was being read by its potential producers, Huxley finished a draft of the play version. But he ran into serious trouble with it, serious enough to ask the well-known playright John Van Druten for assistance. He got it, but in the course of their work together it became quite evident to Van Druten that Huxley had absolutely no visual imagination—he simply couldn't see what he wished to portray on either stage or screen and desperately needed the help of someone who could see for him. Early in 1947 Huxley wrote his old friend E. McKnight Kauffer about his twin projects:

. . . my old short story, "The Gioconda Smile," which was bought last year by Zoltan Korda, the brother of Sir Alexander, who is much nicer than his brother and a good director. There will be revisions to do on the screenplay, and I am now near the end of the second version of the drama. It is rather maddening work, resembling jig saw puzzles rather than literature. . . .

Zoltan Korda was able to sell the Huxley script to Universal, who then scheduled it for production in the summer of 1947. Zoltan Korda, the director, had been born in Hungary and was, along with his older brother, Sir Alexander, one of the prime movers of the British film industry in the early thirties. While still working in England he had codirected *Elephant Boy* with Robert Flaherty. He was active in Hollywood from 1940 through 1948, directing such films as *The Jungle Book, Sahara,* and *The McComber Affair*—entertainment with a certain class. He had a liking for writers and writing and liked the notion of transforming Huxley's cynical story of jealousy and murder into a film as much as he did the possibility of working with its author.

Huxley was placed on Universal's payroll in May of 1947 at $1,560 per week; his presence was required for the great number of revisions Korda wished him to make in his original script. There then proved to be problems with the Johnson Office, the forties equivalent of the old Hays and Breen Office, which demanded further changes regarding the taboo aspects of adultery. Huxley was on hand for the actual shooting of *A Woman's Vengeance,* which began in July and ended in September. He wrote to Anita Loos about the progress of the picture in a letter that gives the circumstances of his Christ story:

We failed to get Claude Raines, as he wanted a salary raise and the Studio casting manager was adamant. "In this Studio," he told Korda, "not even Jesus Christ could get a raise in salary." (it would make a splendid subject for a religious painting—the Saviour before Mannix, Katz, and Mayer, pleading for a hike in his wages, and being turned down cold.) . . . Meanwhile there is talk of the Korda brothers, Alex and Zoltan, doing *Point Counter Point,* if I make the script. Which I wouldn't mind doing under the same conditions as I have done this one—that is, with no interference from producers, only consultation with the director.

He was quite pleased with the way Korda had respected his screenplay, and he genuinely liked the results. There was only one unpleasant aspect to the whole affair, and this was the title. At the very last moment some of the people at Universal became frightened by it, claiming that scarcely anyone in America had ever heard of the "Gioconda" and that Huxley and Korda must come up with a "better" title. Huxley's suggestion was to use the title of one of his early collections of short stories, *Mortal Coils,* but Universal had its own ideas, and Huxley wrote to his cousin Gervas about them:

We saw the finally cut version of the "Gioconda Smile" movie before leaving—very satisfactory, I think, except for the fact that the all-powerful Jewish gentlemen in charge of distribution have elected to call the thing *A Woman's Vengeance,* and there is nothing to be done about it. The consolation is that the title is seen for only thirty seconds, and that the picture, thanks to the untiring resourcefulness of Zoltan Korda, came through the cutting rooms without losing anything from any of the essential scenes.

A Woman's Vengeance was as literate a film as *Pride and Prejudice* and *Jane Eyre* had been, but it somehow lacks their glitter and polish; Olivier and Welles are hard to top. James Agee gave the picture a capsule review in *The Nation,* stating that it was "a rather literary movie, but most movies aren't even that; much less are they real movies. Sensitively directed by Zoltan Korda, generally well played, above all by Jessica Tandy." The film was simply not exciting enough to generate much business at the box office; it was not terribly successful upon its release, despite the presence of Charles Boyer, whom Korda thought could "float" the picture.

Nothing ever came of the plan for the Kordas to produce *Point Counter Point,* but in the summer of 1948 they were both sufficiently taken with Huxley to entrust him with the writing of a screenplay based on another of his short stories written in the twenties, "The Rest Cure." The proposed film was to star Michele Morgan and was to be produced entirely in Italy. The method of payment was a curious one; the Huxleys were to have an "all expenses paid" Italian luxury vacation in exchange for Aldous's work—all this because the Italian currency available to the Kordas was blocked. Huxley spent most of the month of July in Italy working on "The Rest Cure," but the film was never made.

The Huxleys spent the entire summer of 1948 in Europe; it was their first visit there since their arrival in the United States in 1937. They found their villa at Sanary in France, which they had never sold, virtually unchanged after eleven years, or as Maria Huxley told her friends, "as if we had never left." The Huxleys finally returned to America in October of that year by way of London. Cyril Connolly interviewed Aldous at Claridge's, giving a glimpse of Huxley in his fifty-sixth year:

He dressed like an Argentine dandy who moves between Oxford and Rome, and he is adored by Chaplin and other Hollywood magnates, often inaccessible to them. He eats fish, but not meat, will drink wine, but not spirits; goes to bed early, studies painting corner by corner through a magnifying glass, enjoys seeing his old friends. Yet I know no-one more desperately concerned about the state of the world.

Connolly was particularly taken by Huxley's serenity: ". . . almost peculiar to him is the radiance of serenity . . . one no longer feels 'what a clever man' but 'what a good man,' a man at peace with himself."

[5]

The eye with which we see God is the same as the eye with which God sees us.
—Meister Eckhart

[Huxley] cannot resist new gadgets, whether spiritual ones like LSD or physical ones such as the vibrating chair in his study which relaxes me about as much as would a raft ride in the English Channel.
—Igor Stravinsky and Robert Craft,
Dialogues and a Diary

Huxley obtained no further screen credits after *A Woman's Vengeance* and spent comparatively little of his time working on screenplays. However, he never totally disengaged himself from the possibility of doing further movie work and kept getting himself involved in quite a few more film projects. His central activity during these last years was the writing of his books, which included his three final novels: *Ape and Essence, The Genius and the Goddess,* and *Island.* The ratio of his nonfiction to his fiction remained consistent, and *The Devils of Loudun* and *The Doors of Perception* were perhaps the most successful of his nonfiction works. He did an enormous amount of lecturing in these last years, in the East at Cambridge (MIT) and at Santa Barbara College in California, on a very wide spectrum of topics. Huxley was almost never idle at any time of his life, and the last part was no exception.

But Hollywood was always there, for in the spring of 1950 he and Christopher Isherwood again embarked on the writing of an original screenplay they finally called *Below the Equator,* which seems to have been concerned with revolutionary violence in South America. It was never sold, and Huxley may

Aldous Huxley in New York in the early fifties (*Fred Stein*)

have despaired of any further movie work, for he wrote to Anita Loos that winter, just after the New York failure of his play *The Gioconda Smile:* "Now I must settle down to some honest work—and perhaps some dishonest work in the movies, if I can find it, which isn't so easy nowadays."

Apparently it wasn't easy, for it was not until the spring of 1952 that the possibilities of writing still another screenplay became even halfway real. He began negotiating with Gabriel Pascal in February of that year to write a screenplay for him on the life of Gandhi, a subject for which he had the greatest enthusiasm. The film was to be shot entirely in India, and Huxley was to spend some months there researching the life and times of the Mahatma. It all sounded wonderful until the delays began.

Gabriel Pascal, still another Hungarian, had come to England in the thirties, as had the Korda brothers. He had managed to secure the friendship of G. B. Shaw, who gave him the film rights to a number of his plays—something he had never done for anyone, regardless of the price. Pascal produced three of the Shaw plays as films: *Pygmalion, Major Barbara,* and *Caesar and Cleopatra.* Several months passed as the negotiating continued, dragging on until May, when Huxley wrote to his brother Julian about it:

. . . waiting to see if my agents can get a satisfactory contract out of Gabriel Pascal in regard to the Gandhi film. There is something simpatico about Pascal—he is a kind of Central European Baron Munchausen, boastful in an altogether childish way, mildly paranoic, but well-meaning, I believe, with those he likes, and when he can afford it. But he has the bohemian's horror of being pinned down in black and white, of having to commit himself to anything . . . the haggling has been going on since February . . . so the Lord knows what will happen. . . .

Sadly enough, nothing ever did happen, for Pascal simply could not stand being pinned down with the Gandhi project, and the film was never made.

Still another abortive project of Huxley's in these later years was agreeing in 1957 to write a "basic outline" for a UPA animated cartoon version of *Don Quixote,* which was to utilize the voice of old Mr. Magoo as the Don. No more came of this than of the Gandhi film.

Huxley was in his sixty-ninth year when he found that old habits die hard. In the spring of 1963 he and the director George Cukor discussed the possibility of Huxley's writing a script about Sir William Crookes and the Cook family, a true story about murder and spiritualism in Victorian England. Huxley wrote to his friend Eileen Garrett of the Parapsychology Foundation, requesting her help in supplying him with documentation concerning the facts of the case with a view to using them in his screenplay. This was another unrealized project.

Throughout his entire life as a writer Huxley had no illusions about the nature and scope of his talent. He wrote to his son Matthew in August of 1959, telling him of the troubles he was having with his novel *Island:*

But meanwhile I am always haunted by the feeling that, if I had only had enough talent, I could somehow poetize and dramatize all the intellectual material and create a work which would be simultaneously funny, tragic, lyrical, and profound. Alas, I don't possess the necessary talent, and so shall have to be content with something that falls short of the impossible ideal.

From the very beginning of his literary career Huxley's main interest as a novelist was always the communication of what he simply and accurately called the Idea. In a letter to me in June of 1963, four months before his death, Huxley mentioned this goal in connection with what he then regarded as his best book: ". . . *Time Must Have a Stop* is the novel in which I have been most successful in fusing ideas with story . . . the book 'comes off' more harmoniously than the others."

At no time did Huxley ever come close to getting his ideas as such into films; he was quite aware that he was working in a medium that tended, quite rightly, to distrust not ideas as such but the intrusion of the overly verbal. Despite all this, he left a small legacy of two absolutely first-rate screenplays that have never been surpassed for what they attempted and succeeded in doing so well.

As indicated at the beginning of this chapter, Huxley never had that quality of desperate urgency that was so painfully apparent in both Faulkner and Fitzgerald in Hollywood. Huxley's last years were relatively serene ones; he loved to repeat the quotation from Meister Eckhart that appears at the beginning of this section. The spiritual serenity of these last years had very little to do with his being a proselytizer of LSD or any of the other hallucinogenic drugs.

He performed his screenwriting tasks when he wanted to and with people and on terms that he found agreeable. Despite his chronic bad health, near-blindness, and own avowed lack of dramatic sense, his high degree of success as a screenwriter was astonishing.

Mia and James Agee, taken at Bleecker Street, New York City, 1945 (*Helen Levitt*)

James
Agee

*The Man
Who Loved
the Movies*

To me, the great thing about the movies is that it's a brand new field. I don't see how much more can be done with writing or with the stage. . . . as for the movies, however, their possibilities are infinite. . . .
                                   —Agee to Dwight MacDonald, July 1927

Since the time of his death in 1955, James Agee has become another modern cultural hero, an artist who possessed many of the qualities often found in that breed—immense prodigality of talents; self-inflicted bad health; a sudden, early death. Although he tried his hand at nearly every literary form known to him, often with astounding success, his longest and most sustained aesthetic interest was always film, "*the* great, new twentieth-century art form." In a way that clearly distinguishes him from all the other writers in this book, Agee had an absolute passion for film that he acquired very early in life and that never left him. He was able to express this passion in two very different ways: as both a widely read, "influential" film critic, really the first of these, and as a writer of screenplays that were actually produced. There is a causal link between the two activities, for it is unlikely that he would have been given the chance to write commercial films without the evidence of his violent enthusiasm for the medium displayed in his reviews.

Along with Otis Ferguson and Manny Farber, Agee has become a venerable figure in the history of American film criticism, by now indeed one of the "Sacred Three," the founders, so to speak, of all serious, "engaged" film criticism. As a working screenwriter Agee's scripts were a strangely mixed lot, with his own commercial films frequently violating many of the principles he seemed to hold most dear in his critical reviews of other people's films. His noncommercial efforts seemed oddly enough to have about them things he had himself found arty and/or self-conscious in the work of others. Behind all these contradictions was the continuing presence of a man who wanted to be a film-maker from the very start, a man with a total commitment to film. Agee's career in film is like no one else's in the history of the movies.

As a small child, he was taken to the movies regularly by his father, later recalling them with the affectionate warmth that is found in his unfinished novel *A Death in the Family*. He remembered with particular fondness the early Chaplin comedies of World War I. One of Agee's most attractive qualities as a critic was his uncanny ability to recall the exact details of a Keaton or Chaplin sequence he had seen thirty years previously with apparent total recall. His friend Robert Fitzgerald, the poet and translator, has brought to mind Agee's fantastic ability to relive the films he had most enjoyed:

He loved movies more than anyone I ever knew; he also lived them and thought them. To see and hear him describe a movie that he liked—shot by shot, almost frame by frame—was unquestionably better in many cases than to see the movie itself. Once when I was driving him across the Brooklyn Bridge in an open Model-A, he put on beside me such a rendering of Jimmy Cagney that I had to take my eyes off the road. . . .

As older children, he and his sister Emma would see as many as four films in four different theaters in one busy Saturday. All through his four years at Phillips Exeter he saw every film he possibly could, and by the time he was seventeen he was writing to his friend Dwight MacDonald (then at Yale) about his favorite directors, his likes and dislikes among them, and his firm belief that film was really the great new art form of this century:

. . . so far as I can see, all that's been done so far is to show that art is really possible on the screen. We've barely begun to stir the fringes of their possibilities, though. . . . Can writing or drama hope to rub your nose in realism as the movies do? Could *Potemkin* have been staged or described to even approximate the realism of the movie itself? I don't see how.

But the screen needn't stop at realism. The moving picture can catch the beauty of swaying, blending lights and shadows, and by its own movement impart to it as definite a rhythm as poetry or music ever had.

In still another of these long letters to MacDonald, also written in his seventeenth year, Agee shows clearly his overwhelming desire to direct films himself:

I saw both *Variety* and *Potemkin* and know of nothing to beat *Variety* for realism except Stroheim's *Greed.* Have you seen it? . . . I have a wild desire to direct *Ethan Frome,* and the first thing I thought of was my first and final shots. . . . Have you ever thought of trying to direct in the movies? I'd give anything if I had the guts to try it—to go within a year or so, too. . . .

His wish to work in Hollywood at such an early age was not as fanciful as it might now sound, for Howard Hawks began working for Famous Players–Lasky (now Paramount) during his summer vacations from Cornell in 1916 and 1917 and began directing scenes for them in 1917, when he was still only twenty. Irving Thalberg was running Universal at the age of only twenty-one. Agee elected to enter Harvard in the fall of 1928, and by the spring of 1929 he had carried his dreams of directing films one step further:

A fellow at my dormitory owns a movie camera . . . and has done some interesting work with it. . . . It's possible we'll do two movies, a documentary on Boston and a film version of a short story he had written. The idea is that I'll devise shots, angles, camera work, etc., and stories; he'll take care of the photography and lighting.

Eventually all these campus film activities proved to be in direct conflict with his desire to write, for by the winter of 1930 he was telling his childhood friend, Father James Harold Flye, that he dropped all his early film-making efforts of his own volition. He still regretted that he had not put his earlier desire to drop out of school into action and tried his luck on the West Coast: ". . . last spring I was all but ready to quit college and bum to California and trust to luck for the rest."

In the course of this very long and by now quite famous letter to Father Flye, Agee told his friend that he wanted to become "a really great writer" more than anything else in the world, a task he thought he must attempt against all the odds—the perfecting of a full-blooded epic writing style in a "prose that would run into poetry." This is just what he attempted to do in the following decade, despite, or perhaps more accurately *because of,* the various job assignments that came his way through journalism. Working for *Fortune* and *Time* meant taking a good look at things, and this is just what the author of *Let Us Now Praise Famous Men* learned as a journalist.

Immediately upon his graduation from Harvard in the hot, dismal depression summer of 1932, Agee obtained his first job writing for the Luce publications, the first long-term assignment being for *Fortune,* the business magazine. In the next few years the magazine published some of the best prose to appear regularly in any American periodical, mass circulation or otherwise, and Agee devoted as much care and precision to writing about the manufacture of steel rails as he did to writing about the working lives of Southern tenant farmers. For several years his interest in films was largely confined to being a constant viewer.

In the late thirties Agee wrote two very different film scripts, *The House* and *Man's Fate,* both probably for the sheer fun of doing them, exercises to get some things down on paper. The first of these, *The House,* is the kind of screenplay that could probably have been written only in the thirties, for it is actually a sort of homage to avant-garde films, the very genre itself of the films produced, mostly in Paris, at the beginning of the decade. It may now be difficult to understand the shock effects produced at the time by films like Cocteau's *Le Sang d'un Poète,* the Buñuel-Dali collaborations *Un Chien Andalou* and *L'Age d'Or,* and Carl Dryer's *Vampyr,* all four of which were released between 1929 and 1932. These films, as well as others like them, convinced a great many people that there might well be a chance of there being a truly poetic cinema, the cinema of those "infinite possibilities" that had stirred Agee so strongly back in 1927. *The House* was very much in this tradition of film-making.

The full title of Agee's first published screenplay was actually *Notes for a Moving Picture: The House*. It is obviously something to be read, for both the ear as well as the eye, and there was never any idea of having it "produced" in any real sense of the word. It was common practice among the younger and experimental writers of the thirties to write in the scenario form. The quality of the writing in *The House* is so good that a reader might well enjoy reading it a lot more than "seeing it." The following excerpt may give some idea of what Agee would have liked to see on a screen in 1936:

In a series of shots to be somewhat detailed in a minute, these people come out through the screen door across the porch and down the steps. They are and are dressed as follows: A strong iron-like man of sixty-five, his face somewhat like those of the crueller photos of Harding late in his life; looking like and dressed like a slick portrait of a hybrid big-business and society man and moving that way; his face made up chalk white, his eyebrows very black; costumed as for a political funeral; wearing a silk hat on his bent left arm. . . .

A scalpel-like, chalk-white young man, thirty, wearing a checked sports coat and otherwise a Tuxedo; everything about him like a barely restrained explosion, intensely quiet and strict in his movements. He is carrying a cocktail glass brimful of lightly fuming acid, and of this he must not spill a drop. A beautiful, petrified young woman in an extreme bathing suit and an evening wrap. Her skull is closed in a pessary. She carries a clear globe in whose center, sustained in alcohol, hangs a miniature foetus in a baby bonnet. . . .

This entire scenario of nearly 10,000 words is actually a catalog of often startling images, linked together in much the same way as they are in the Buñuel and Cocteau films, but Agee is so prodigiously *generous* with his endless stream of images that the resemblance here is actually closer to Eisenstein's *October*. There is some sort of a "story line" to *The House,* but it resists being paraphrased. The presence of sound is indicated throughout the text, but there is no dialogue whatever, for Agee had strong reservations about the advent of the talkies, as did most of the film-makers he most admired, Keaton and Chaplin in America and Eisenstein and Dovzhenko in the USSR.

There is a kind of ultimate "home movie" quality to much of *The House*, a sort of felt ecstasy about the conjuring up of these hundreds of images, with the camera itself a joyful participant:

. . . the camera settles gently to rest in the dark front hallway before an ornate hatrack and looks at itself close and hard in the mirror, beginning very softly to purr (the reduced dry sound of its motor); swings back to center of hall, beneath center of stairwell, and delicately takes flight, swinging slowly round. . . .

There is an occasional complete slowing down of everything in *The House,* as if Agee wanted to make sure that his readers would truly know what was at hand or, taken in another way, that a possible director would know precisely what must be done. This early working habit of "taking a really close look at things" persisted all the way through Agee's later Hollywood scripts.

His other major film interests in the mid and late thirties included the work of all three of the great Russians, Pudovkin, Eisenstein, and Dovzhenko, with Dovzhenko becoming his favorite director for a number of years. The maker of *Arsenal, Earth, Ivan,* and *Frontier* seemed to combine intellectual excitement, pictorial splendor, and a strong feeling for the Ukrainian peasantry that impressed Agee as did the work of no other director of those years.

There were individual scenes in Dovzhenko's films that he found so beautiful that he would see them again and again, sometimes taking his friends along in order to share the experience. One of his particular favorites deserves mention. In Dovzhenko's 1935 film *Aerograd* (released in America as *Frontier*) there is an episode in which a Bolshevik partisan leader must execute his life-long friend for espionage. After the brief "trial," the two men walk into deep woods for the scene that follows. As the condemned man faces his executioner in a clearing, he nervously touches the lapels of his jacket, accompanied by vague, fluttery motions of his hands. There is a complete silence in the woods, broken only by the soughing of the wind. The condemned man finally stops moving his hands and looks all around him for a moment, then he begins to make a series of high-pitched HO, HO, HO! sounds, as if testing the power of his vocal cords. He then resumes the fingering of his lapels, staring shyly all the while at the man who is about to kill him. When the shot finally rings out, the man collapses like a paper bag, uttering only a single whimpered word: MAMA!

Agee never forgot this scene of nearly unbearable poetic beauty, in which everything has been slowed down to an almost complete cessation of movement. The aesthetic principles behind its deeply felt emotion appear again and again in all of his film scripts, especially in his handling of the death of the Swede in *The Blue Hotel.*

He found very little to interest him in the American films of this period, except for Chaplin's only two films of the entire decade, *City Lights* and *Modern Times,* Lubitsch's *Trouble in Paradise,* and all the bravura appearances of Cagney. There was little else.

In 1939 he published in Jay Leyda's *Film* a partial screenplay or treatment based on the final chapters of André Malraux's novel *Man's Fate,* the section of the book dealing with Chiang Kai-shek's betrayal of the Communist forces in Shanghai during the great insurrection of 1927. Agee's treatment dealt with the execution of these Communist leaders, who were thrown alive into the boilers of the locomotives that were to have taken them into the capital. All the shots in this script were set down with extreme precision in a way that no other screenwriter had ever set things down before, for Agee had apparently decided to take no chances about having his work or his vision misunderstood or somehow changed by those others who might have to work with it. By 1939 he had combined the functions of both writer and director, a singularity he never totally abandoned in his more commercial ventures.

The *Man's Fate* script was again meant to be read, and read carefully, rather than to be taken as any sort of seriously intended script for a director to follow. Agee attached some general notes at the very end of the published material which give some further idea of just what he would have liked to see and hear on the screen:

By taking its resonance from that of the bell I mean that that should be the rhythm of the grain in the film, as if produced of the sound. All the film should be grainy, hard black and white, flat focus, the stock and tone of film in war newsreels, etc., prior to the invention of panchromatic. No smoothness and never luminous. It should not seem to be fiction.

There is a very strong reliance on the maximum use of sound to enhance the dramatic effects of this scene (shrieking loco-motive whistles and clanging bells), for Agee had always felt that "natural sounds" had been sorely neglected in nearly all the early American sound films.

The writing of scripts like *The House* and *Man's Fate* might be thought of as Agee's cinematic "closet dramas," but they do indicate the kind of reality he would have liked to see on the screen. They also indicate that as late as 1939 his talents as a film-maker were pretty much those of an avant-gardist who relied heavily upon existing models from Europe. He was able to break out of this extremely confining position by the conse-quences of taking up the duties of regular film critic for *Time* and, amazingly enough, the same job for *The Nation* a year later. These two jobs and the individuals he encountered in the course of them permitted him to write screenplays not just for himself but for an entirely different audience—one that paid.

[2]

The whole business has been dying here, ten years or more. Last year, it seems to me, was the all-time low—so far.
        —*Agee,* The Nation, *December 25, 1943*

. . . I think you will find the work of this last or any recent year, and the chance of any sufficiently radical improve-ment within the tragically short future, enough to shrivel the heart.
        —*Agee,* The Nation, *January 20, 1945*

Agee became the regular film reviewer for *Time* in November of 1941 and for *The Nation* at the very end of 1942, not breaking off from either of these jobs until late in 1948. A good deal of surmise has gone into what has seemed to some the insurmountable difficulties of writing for two such radically different publications, week after week. There actually proved to be few real problems in Agee's being able to perform this work at the very high level at which he did all the other things he did so well.

Agee brought an overwhelmingly powerful literary personality to his regular film reviewing, something absolutely new to film criticism, and something we have not really seen the likes of since. In his weekly pieces for *The Nation* he spoke out in the voice of a man *talking seriously about film,* a journalistic novelty at which he was almost alone in America. It has been often noted that the sheer power of Agee's personal style was quite enough to make him nearly always fascinating reading even when you totally disagreed with him; Auden didn't care much for the movies, but he never missed reading Agee.

As a working critic he was often contradictory and even quite perverse in some of his likes and dislikes. His list of personal favorites, his "touchstones" of what he regarded as the best films of the forties, have been systematically downgraded by a great deal of contemporary criticism. He especially loved *Monsieur Verdoux, The Best Years of Our Lives,* and *The Treasure of the Sierra Madre.* These films, particularly the first two, have fared rather badly at the hands of the critics in recent years, but it is doubtful if Agee would ever have changed his mind about them, for they all possessed certain qualities that he regarded as the dead center of film art.

Besides his strong likes, Agee also had violent antipathies for certain kinds of films, particularly those he considered demonstrably "arty" or that in any way drew special attention to themselves as artifacts. He wanted a film to attain the quality of straight realistic documentary, unencumbered by any traffic with "Art." It was for this very reason that he belittled the films of Orson Welles. Knowing as much about the history of film as he did, Agee was able to spot all the various "influences" that lay behind Welles's *Citizen Kane;* he then proceeded to find the film entirely derivative and therefore "arty." When Welles's *Journey into Fear* was released early in 1943 Agee did not conceal his feelings about the nature of its maker's art: "It is good to see so likable an entertainer as Welles making an unpretentious pleasure-picture; but to make a good one you need to be something of an artist, and Welles has little if any artistry."

Quite properly suspecting the presence of Welles in the 1944 John Houseman–Robert Stevenson production of *Jane Eyre,* Agee found Welles's contribution to be the only worthwhile part of the film:

Those first twenty minutes, however, which are devoted to Jane's schooling and her first meeting with Rochester, are a lush beetle-browed, unusually compelling piece of highly romantic screen rhetoric. I suspect Orson Welles had a hand in this stretch—for good and for bad; it has a good deal of his black-chenille-and-rhinestones manner.

By 1946 Welles was virtually unemployable in Hollywood, partially but not entirely because of the relative failure of his first three films. He agreed to direct *The Stranger* under restrictive conditions that most directors would have refused to accept, but he had no choice. The film got a very mixed press, with many of the reviewers stooping to the level of personal attacks on Welles. With that quality of total honesty that was habitual to him, Agee wrote a favorable review of the picture that included both a defense of Welles and an apology for having attacked him: "In any case, many people who overrated him and many others who, knowing better and annoyed by all the talk, stupidly blamed Welles for it and underrated him—as I did for a while—are now so eager to think ill of him that they will hardly bother to look at what is before them." Although willing to give the devil his due, Agee maintained his reserve about Welles, concluding his review of *The Stranger* by saying, "So far as I can make out, Welles never was and never will be a genius, but he is just as gifted as he ever was."

Agee could often be very funny at the expense of absolutely rotten pictures, as in his capsule review of *I Walk Alone,* which concluded with these words: "Otherwise the picture deserves, like four out of five other movies, to walk alone, tinkle a little bell, and cry 'Unclean, unclean.' " But it was Agee's *enthusiasms* for certain films and their directors that distinguished him from all the other reviewers of the time. There were times when his passion for a film-maker's work would take on a quality of personal anguish, especially if he felt that the film in question was despised by his fellow critics or neglected by its potential audience. He would actually become quite angry with these hostile critics, as he did in the case of Jean Vigo's two films *Zéro de Conduite* and *L'Atalante* when they were both shown here for the first time in 1947. After advising his readers not to bother going to see the films if they didn't care for experimentation in art, he went on railing at his audience:

. . . go on back to sleep, lucky Pierre, between the baker's wife and the well-digger's daughter, if you can squeeze in among the re-viewers who have written so contemptuously of Vigo's work. If you regard all experiment as ducky, and all bewilderment as an opportu-nity to sneer at those who confess their bewilderment, and if you ask of art only that it be outré, I can't silence your shrill hermetic cries, or prevent your rush to the Fifth Avenue Playhouse; I can only hope to God I don't meet you there.

Affronting his audience this way seems to have worked, for Vigo's present reputation owes quite a bit to Agee's persever-ance in finally getting these films established as the first-rate works they are.

With the exception of the Chaplin comedies, there were very few silent films shown publicly in the United States in the thirties and forties, and by 1950 Buster Keaton had been al-most totally forgotten as a great film-maker. Although Keaton was still a name of sorts in the Hollywood of 1950, he was by then chiefly recognized as a pathetic survivor of the twenties, just the right face to appear in bit parts in pictures like Wil-der's *Sunset Boulevard,* along with still another survivor, Erich von Stroheim. All the enchanting magic and mysterious po-etry contained in films like *Our Hospitality* and *The Navigator* had been almost totally unavailable for over twenty years, but Agee had remembered them as had apparently few in his generation. While working in Hollywood in 1949, Keaton was approached by Agee in the guise of someone coming to see a great living artist, not some freak held over from a dim and distant past who might have some "interesting" tales to tell. Keaton is said to have told Agee that no one had approached him as any kind of serious artist in at least a decade. It was his meetings with both Keaton and Chaplin that partially prompted him to write his famous essay "Comedy's Greatest Era," which did so much to "rehabilitate" the lost art of all four of the great silent comedians, including Harry Langdon and Harold Lloyd.

Even with all the joys of his discoveries and rediscoveries, the weekly reviewing of films in the years 1942–48 remained pretty much a task of fighting one's way out of a dismal swamp. There were no foreign films to be seen for a good deal of the period, and the Hollywood product was scarcely encouraging to a man who regarded film as an art. On a number of occasions Agee became deeply distressed over what he saw as the total failure of Hollywood to produce anything except the routine junk it kept turning out. He responded immediately to anything that promised even a flicker of life, once joining his praise with that of Orson Welles and Manny Farber for a now forgotten film called *When Strangers Meet:* ". . . but taking it as a whole I have seldom, for years now, seen one hour so energetically and sensibly used in a film. . . . Thanks to that, I can no longer feel by any means so hopeless as I have, lately, that it is possible to make pictures in Hollywood that are worth making."

At the time when Agee wrote this, in 1945, the only Hollywood film-makers he really liked besides Chaplin were Val Lewton, who made cheap RKO horror films, and Preston Sturges. It was indeed a bleak period, and though Agee seemed to know it better than anyone else, he kept on hoping: "I know there are enough people out there of real ability to turn the whole place upside down. I doubt they will ever do it, partly because I doubt it could be done without a great deal of gunfire, and that on no parochial scale. . . ." A year later, in 1946, he returned to his theme of what could be done in Hollywood:

If you are content to be merely realistic about it—to use a strangely perverted word in the only meaning it seems to carry today—I suppose that it wasn't exactly a bad movie year. . . . I am grateful that a few of the many people of ability and integrity who work in Hollywood managed, with God knows what bloodshed and heartbreak, to get on the screen something more than a split-second glimmer of what they have in them to put there. . . .

The foregoing pretty clearly shows the mind of a man who was just as eager to make films of his own in 1946 as he had been nearly twenty years earlier. Agee was to get his chance to make these films, largely because of his association with John Huston, the director who seemed to Agee to possess many of the qualities that he found so sadly lacking in nearly all of the Hollywood directors of the time. It was Huston's care for the way things *looked* as well as his complete trust in the simple and spontaneous that initially endeared his work to Agee. Liking straightforward, unadorned "reality" films as much as he did, it was not surprising that he liked Huston's wartime documentary *The Battle of San Pietro.* He wrote an appreciative review in *The Nation,* indicating just how much it had moved him: "For at one and the same time, without one slip along the line, from the most ticklish fringes of taste to the depths of a sane mind and heart, it accepts the facts and treats them as materials relevant to anger, tenderness, pride, veneration, and beauty."

Despite his genuine admiration for fact/documentary films (he wrote the commentary for Sidney Meyer's *The Quiet One*), Agee was perfectly aware that the greatest possibility for making pictures still lay in the fiction film. When Huston's *The Treasure of the Sierra Madre* was finally released at the beginning of 1948, Agee's highly favorable review started off with his noting that he had been looking forward eagerly to what the director of *San Pietro* would do with his first postwar fiction film. Although he seemed a bit coyly ingenuous when he claimed it to be "not quite a completely satisfying picture," he had no doubt that

Huston, next only to Chaplin, is the most talented man working in American pictures, and that this is one of the movie talents in the world which is most excitingly capable of still further growth. *The Treasure* is one of the very few movies made since 1927 which I am sure will stand up in the memory and esteem of qualified people alongside the best of the silent movies.

During the course of his sixteen years of on-and-off employment with the Luce Publications, at *Fortune* and *Time* from 1932 through 1948, Agee became very much of a living legend to a great many people. The nonstop, all-night writing or talking marathons, the reading-aloud jags, or the just-listening-to-music stints were all experiences that many still clearly remember to this day. There was little that was ever casual in his life. He felt nearly everything with an overwhelming intensity; his passions for books, ideas, films, music, and people were prodigal. His famous "best way" to hear Beethoven's Seventh Symphony (place your head as close to the speaker as you can get it and turn on the volume as loud as it will go) was no jest; he meant very word of it. Everything he ever did, he did to his utmost, including the writing of his screenplays.

The poet Robert Fitzgerald, Agee's old friend from his Harvard days, as well as a fellow writer on *Time* (Books), has written in the memoir that accompanies the *Collected Short Prose* volume he edited what is perhaps the best physical portrait of Agee yet written:

. . . a tall frame, long-boned but not massive; lean flesh, muscular with some awkwardness; pelt on his chest; a long stride with loose knee-joints, head up, with toes angled a bit outward. A complexion rather dark or sallow in pigment, easily tanned. The head rough-hewn, with a rugged brow and cheek-bones, a strong nose irregular in profile, a large mouth firmly closing in folds, working a little around the gaps of lost teeth. The shape of the face tapered to a sensitive chin, cleft. Hair thick and very dark, a shock uncared for, and best uncared for. Eyes deep-set and rather closely set, a dull-gray-blue or feral blue-gray or radiantly lit with amusement. Strong stained teeth. On the right middle finger a callous as big as a boil; one of his stigmata as a writer. The hands and fingers long and light and blunt and expressive, shaping his thought in the air, conveying stresses direct or splay, drawing razor-edged lines with thumb and forefinger: termini, perspective, tones.

It was partially his strong feelings about Huston and his work as a director that drew Agee to work in Hollywood. He quit his job on *Time* late in 1948, after having arranged with the editors of *Life* to write a series of essays for them on Hollywood and the movies. Only two of these were ever written, "Comedy's Greatest Era," and one about Huston, "Undirectable Director." The writing of these two pieces gave Agee a great deal of pleasure, but each took nearly six months to write; even *Life*'s pay scale could not enable him to live on what he got for them. He soon had contracted to write his first *real* screenplay, *The Blue Hotel.*

[3]

"Oh, Christ, Jim, tell me something I can understand. This isn't like a novel. This is a screenplay."
—*John Huston to Agee, quoted in* Picture *by Lillian Ross*

Well, I would not want to change my way of life.
—*Agee, 1951*

Agee's screenplay for *The Blue Hotel* was commissioned directly by the Huntington Hartford Organization in late 1948, at the time Hartford was most actively patronizing all the arts, including film. The work was based on Stephen Crane's famous short story about a suicidal Swede who relentlessly becomes the cause of his own violent death in the bleak town of Fort Romper, Nebraska, at the end of the last century. It is an extremely powerful story, and it is easy to see why Agee would have wanted to do it. The only question a wary producer might well have asked is: "Is there enough here for a feature film?" Agee would have answered yes, but his method of writing this script would have frightened the producer. It was actually written with John Huston in mind as the director, but he proved to be tied up with a variety of other projects, and it has never been produced as a film.

The Blue Hotel is the first of Agee's full-length screenplays. It is written with a great deal more care and precision of language than any of the screenplays written by the other writers in this book. This is so much the case that Agee's film scripts are alone in their having been "honored" by appearing in a book all by themselves, a tribute not yet accorded the screenplays of Faulkner, Fitzgerald, West, or Huxley, and it is indicative of their singularity.

All his scripts are written, *really* written, in such a way that we are never unaware that they have in fact been written by the author of *Let Us Now Praise Famous Men.* There is a genuinely novelistic quality about much of *The Blue Hotel,* in which nearly everything is described with a degree of exactitude that has probably never been approached by any other writer of screenplays. Here is a sample of the way Agee described the character Skully's eating habits at the hotel's dining table:

We pause just long enough to get a glimpse of Skully's character through his eating: a business-like but rather frugal and finicky eater, even a touch of old-maidishness; an old-fashioned and rather cute old guy; absorbed in eating, he loses entirely his Mine Host mannerisms, he's just an aging pappy at home, reloading. Rather frail eyelids and stretched neck when he drinks water; an evidently self-taught but deeply habitual care to take small bites and to keep his lips closed over his chewing; dabby with his fork; delicate at harpooning a biscuit; a suggestion of dental plates which don't quite fit.

There is a *Greed*-like realism about this passage; it will be recalled that Agee very much admired the director of *Greed,* for von Stroheim had the servants in his *Wedding March* wear the Hapsburg coat-of-arms on their underwear. In this next passage Agee slows things down even further by showing how the cowboy eats his meal:

His eating system is to mash whatever can be mashed into malleable material, mix it, load his fork by help of his knife; as heavy as possible, sculpture and trim it with his knife; changes fork to right hand, brings it up to a mouth which opens for it and closes over it as efficiently as a steamshovel, then working his full jaws with a fair amount of SOUND which he keeps reasonably subdued, meanwhile lowering his fork, changing hands, and starting all over again. He swallows as soon as the new load is ready and takes a swallow of water just before shifting the fork to the right hand. . . .

There is still more of this, and in fact a great deal of *The Blue Hotel* is devoted to this systematic method of *slowing things down,* spelling everything out, all for the express purpose of making the director of this film execute what Agee has precisely wanted him to show in every single detail, all and everything.

Still another of his narrative techniques in *The Blue Hotel* involves the camera itself, which Agee never saw as a passive recording device, but rather as a direct participant in the action, jogging, tripping, and sometimes even dancing when the occasion seemed to warrant it. In order to show the Swede's manic self-exaltation after his fight with Johnnie, Agee asks that the camera be used this way:

(A NOTE ON THIS SHOT): It is to be heightened above realism, during the Swede's advance up the boardwalk. When he is still in the deepest distance, we use only every third frame, then every second, then cut every third frame; then every fourth; meanwhile slurring the CAMERA speed a little, fewer frames per second, so that his speed of approach is at all times superhuman and grotesque, but becomes smoother as he approaches. By the time his features become distinct no frames are skipped but the motion, though regular, is fast and dry rather than silky; it is at this time and place that the train is run through. As he comes into full close up, shade back to normal speed, omitting no frames. The SOUND runs smooth, not clipped; it is not recorded on the spot.

He made use of the camera in ways that it has never been used by anyone before or since the writing of *The Blue Hotel.* In the explosive scene in which the Swede catches Johnnie cheating in the second card game, Agee's instructions are these:

CAMERA, starting with a shot past the Swede's head, centering on Johnnie MEDIUM CLOSE, makes, fairly fast and accelerating, steadily tighter and faster and closer, the circling movement by which a tethered heifer winds herself up short around a post. . . . As the CAMERA thus ropes them in they all close tighter and tighter against one center: they come as close as five people can get. . . .

There are those who have found such passages as these simply the overt signs of a frustrated novelist working in an alien medium, but this view would be far from the truth. Some of Agee's techniques often sound absolutely marvelous, but what they amount to is the virtual elimination of all the functions of the director. Agee is not taking any chances of having his intentions or hopes changed in any way: *he* is the director of *The Blue Hotel.*

When Agee had been writing what I have called his cinematic "closet dramas" in the late thirties, he was able to utilize his remarkable command of language as the instrument by which he became not only the writer but also the director and cameraman of his own films. There are many passages in Agee's script for *The Blue Hotel* that show clearly that he had not forgotten those early dreams of wanting to direct, for in this first full-length screenplay he has literally become his own director. Any professional director who would take on *The Blue Hotel* as written would be something of a glorified camera operator, for there would be little else for that person to do. Despite the excellence, as well as the continued availability, of *The Blue Hotel,* no film director has yet taken it on, although it has been televised twice, each time with a different director and cast and with the Agee script cut to the bone, being used only as a guidepost to the story.

By 1950 John Huston was the favorite "young" American director (he was forty-four at the time), or at least he was for those who took their films as seriously as Agee did. There was really very little in the way of new talent in Hollywood in those years, for those who might be called the "old guard" directors (Cukor, Hitchcock, Hawks, and Raoul Walsh) were still quite active. The only genuine competition Huston faced was from Orson Welles, ten years his junior, but his career was very much in doubt. In the four years since the end of the war Welles had completed three films, *The Stranger, Macbeth,* and *The Lady from Shanghai,* all of which seemed to pall before the critical *and* financial success of *Key Largo* and *The Asphalt Jungle,* with *The Treasure of the Sierra Madre* achieving a tremendous critical response despite its lack of success at the box office. With the exception of his *We Were Strangers* of 1949, it seemed Huston could do no wrong.

There has always been something a little larger than life about Huston, something overwhelming enough to befit his nickname of "The Monster," as the man who epitomized the outrageous or the unpredictable in everything. He started behaving that way from the very start, with a professional boxing career while still in his teens, two years in the Mexican Cavalry by his twenty-first year, and the implausible publication of his book *Frankie and Johnny* at twenty-four in 1930. He began working in Hollywood as a writer for Universal in 1930 without much success, soon leaving California to occupy himself for several years in wandering around the world editing magazines and directing plays, as well as acting in them. He returned to Hollywood at the end of the thirties and was hired by Warner Brothers, again as a writer, and wrote a number of extremely popular films for them, including *Jezebel, Juárez, High Sierra,* and *Sergeant York.* Like Howard Hawks and Orson Welles, Huston has regularly taken a hand in the scripts he has directed; these have nearly always been his best films: *The Treasure of the Sierra Madre, The African Queen,* and *The Maltese Falcon.* Like Agee, he too had always wanted to direct, but it was not to be until he convinced Jack Warner that he could really bring off his own script for *The Maltese Falcon,* a picture Warner's had made twice before. The smashing success of this film launched his career as a major director, a career that seemed in full upward flight at the time he first meet Agee.

It was Huston's huge success as writer/director that most attracted Agee to work with him, for at that time only Huston and Welles seemed capable of making this combination work. This may have been possible because they were genuinely men of the theater, with Huston directing the first American production of Sartre's *No Exit* in New York in 1946 and Welles directing his production of *Around the World in 80 Days* the same year.

When Agee went out to California at the end of 1950 to work with Huston on the script of *The African Queen,* he found Huston still caught up in the sad, savage aftermath of the shooting of his *The Red Badge of Courage,* which had entailed

resentments, power plays, and hatreds that effectively destroyed the film that he thought might well have been his best.
Both Agee and his wife, Mia, had been present for a great
deal of the actual shooting of the film, seeing the rushes at the
end of each day's shooting. This story of the making and de-
struction of *The Red Badge* is told with a great deal of narrative
art by Lillian Ross in her book *Picture*. Agee makes a brief appearance in this book, actually a rather foolish one, for he is
depicted as attempting to convince Huston that the voyage of
Rose and Allnutt (Hepburn and Bogart) down the river in *The
African Queen* is to be taken as a metaphor for the act of love;
Huston's reply is given at the beginning of this section, but
Miss Ross also has him saying this: "You've got to demonstrate
everything, Jim. People on the screen are gods and goddesses.
We know all about them. Their habits. Their caprices. But we
can't touch them. They're not real. They stand for something,
rather than being something. They're symbols. You can't have
symbolism within symbolism, Jim."

What Agee replied to this is not recorded by Miss Ross, but
he wrote a letter to Father Flye in early December about his
hopes for the picture:

If everything works out right, it could be a wonderful movie. If
much works out wrong, it can be lousier than most. I think most
likely it will wind up as good, maybe even very good, but not wonderful, or lousy. The work is a great deal of fun: treating it fun-
damentally as high comedy with deeply ribald undertones, and trying to blend extraordinary things—poetry, mysticism, realism,
romance, tragedy, with the comedy. . . .

He succeeded in accomplishing a good many of these things,
for *The African Queen* is truly a triumph of collaborative art,
and the contributions of Hepburn and Bogart are surely just
as important as those of Agee and Huston. The combination
of these four talents within the ambience of C. S. Forester's
novel produced one of the most purely delightful of all American films, one of Huston's very best along with *The Treasure*
and *The Maltese Falcon,* both of these again triumphs of collaboration.

There has been some question as to just how much of *The*

African Queen was written by Agee. In a letter he wrote to the director David Bradley in 1953, Agee was quite specific about his share of the writing: ". . . *African Queen,* 1st draft, was 160 pages. The first hundred were mine and brought it through almost half the story. The last 60, except a few scenes and interpolations, were Huston's; but the playing time worked that his 60 and my 100 amounted to about the same."

Agee and Huston seem to have worked together in a fashion not unlike that of Faulkner and Hawks, with both Huston and Hawks appearing to simply like the *idea* of having these writers around on the scene, often just as *someone there to talk with.* The comparison breaks down, of course, for Hawks was no "Monster," sacred or otherwise, and Faulkner was there only for the money and had little interest in films. But Agee couldn't get enough of this sudden new world of movie-making and loved writing for it, although he needed the money just as badly as did Faulkner.

In the writing of *The African Queen* Agee employed many of the working methods he had developed in *The Blue Hotel,* especially his "slowing things down" effect. This device received a completely justified use in the famous scene when Bogart's stomach starts rumbling during the course of his tea with Rose and her brother (Robert Morley). Here is what Agee wrote at this point:

All of a sudden, out of the silence, there is a SOUND like a mandolin string being plucked. At first the sound is unidentifiable, though instantly all three glance sharply up, each at the other two, then away; in the next instant they recognize what it is and each glances sharply, incredulously, at the other two—and then again, quickly away; then Brother and Rose glance with full recognition at Allnutt, at the instant that he knows the belly-growl is his. At the moment of recognition, he glances down at his middle with a look of embarrassed reproach. He glances up quickly and slyly—hopeful they've missed it—to find the eyes of both still fixed on him. The instant their eyes meet they bounce apart like billiard balls, and fix on the first neutral object they happen to hit. Then Allnutt looks at them again: neither will look at him.

Huston may not have been able to get every bit of this, but he got enough to make of the scene a brilliant occasion of superb comic acting. As a scene it clearly shows that Agee's exquisite care in writing this way was completely justified in the actual practice of making a film.

An example of what some have called Agee's novelistic gifts being carried over into screenwriting occurs in the scene when it appears that Rose and Allnutt seem doomed to die on the hopelessly stranded *Queen*. The camera is described as slowly lifting upward from their unconscious bodies, as if bidding them farewell, as the screen slowly darkens:

The CAMERA STOPS RISING. The dead silence is broken by an infinitesimal SOUND OF RUSTLING. By eye and ear, after a few seconds, it becomes recognizable as the stillest, slenderest kind of rain, splintering downward, very gradually increasing in volume and in richness of SOUND as the darkness deepens, to an immense, peaceful, steady, flooding downpour. The darkness pales into full daylight and the downpour continues, and through it we can dimly see the boat and the prostrate bodies, and after perhaps ten seconds of the new daylight (after maybe fifteen of darkness), the rain begins to abate and the CAMERA BEGINS VERY SLOWLY TO DESCEND.

Agee spent a good deal of his free time, really as much as he could, with Charles Chaplin during his 1951 stay in Hollywood. Chaplin was then completing the shooting of *Limelight* and invited Agee and his wife, Mia, to visit the set on a number of occasions. One of these visits occurred when the sequence involving both Keaton and Chaplin performing their clown act together was being shot. Agee and apparently everyone else who witnessed Keaton's performance were delighted and even staggered by how good he was; Chaplin may have thought so too, for nearly all this footage vanished in the cutting room, and there is only a trace of it left in the release print of *Limelight*.

Both Agee and Chaplin were insomniacs, and many of their long talks occurred in the hours after midnight. Agee wished later that he had kept a journal of these conversations:

I've spent 30 or 50 evenings talking alone most of the night with Chaplin, and he has talked very openly and intimately. The last thing I'd ever do is to make an article of this; the only way it could ever belong on paper, if at all, is in a journal or in letters, the kind of thing which is never public until long after both people are dead. Both because he is the man he is and I so much respect him, and because he's also an intrinsically interesting man, I wish I had kept a record of all of this. But all I've done of it is in a couple or three letters to Mia, and a good deal of it, though all of it interested me so much, I'm bound to have forgotten.

The thing they both remembered is that they were in debt to each other, for Agee was deeply thankful to Chaplin for being not only the great artist he in fact was as an actor but also the greatest American film-maker of his time. Conversely, Chaplin found in Agee not only an ardent defender of his *Monsieur Verdoux* as a great film but also an overall spokesman for him at a time when Chaplin was in serious trouble with his public, the Catholic War Veterans, and nearly everyone else in the United States. There had been violent objections to his left-wing politics, his morals (the Joan Barry paternity suit), and his patriotism (he had remained a British subject). Agee's feeling for Chaplin was close to veneration, for in 1936, at the time of *Modern Times,* he had thought of it "as if Beethoven were living now and had completed another symphony."

Agee suffered his first heart attack in January of 1951, while still engaged in the writing of *The African Queen.* His hospitalization of several weeks prevented him from going along with Huston and his company to Africa where a large part of the film was to be made. Although Agee had still another four years of life before him, he was forced to curtail many of his favorite physical activities (tennis, swimming) and to adopt various health regimens aimed at prolonging his life. It was at this time that he indicated to one of his doctors that he did "not want to change my way of life," which he never really did.

Agee stayed on in California through the rest of 1951, not returning to the East until the spring of 1952. It was during this time that he wrote the screenplay for *The Bride Comes to*

Yellow Sky, again for Huntington Hartford, and again based on a short story by Stephen Crane. This time his script was actually produced, starring Robert Preston and Hartford's very young and pretty wife, Barbara Steele, as the bride. Crane's story is about what happens when the marshal of Yellow Sky goes to San Antonio to bring his bride back to town. In his absence, the town's hard-drinking gunslinger goes on a shooting spree that ends only with the return of the marshal.

The writing in *The Bride Comes to Yellow Sky* is recognizably Agee's, but it is nowhere near as intense and detailed as in *The Blue Hotel,* perhaps reflecting the nature of the story itself. Here is a brief excerpt from it that shows that Agee was still very much concerned with what he could make the camera *see,* as "Scratchy" looks for a tie in a drawer:

CAMERA proceeds into a slow, wobbly DOLLYING PAN, past window and bureau to pegs where Scratch's hand fumbles among his few clothes. Most of them are old and poor but his hands get off the hook a violently fancy pseudowestern shirt on which CAMERA comes into ULTRA SHARP FOCUS. Then one hand, as CAMERA CREEPS IN, FOCUS DITTO, reaches for a real shocker of a necktie, muffs it, and as CAMERA comes into EXTREME CLOSE SHOT, drags it drunkenly, snakily, slithering from its hook. All this time Scratchy is muttering and humming. OVER the slithering tie we

IRIS OUT

IRIS IN

INT. PARLOR CAR—DAY

Center CAMERA on Potter's more conservative tie. Tense and uneasy, he adjusts it.

All this extreme concentration on the ties worn by the drunken Scratchy and the marshal has told us a good part of the story without a single word of dialogue, something Agee had always liked to do; he had never forgotten the example of F. W. Murnau's *The Last Laugh,* the first film he'd ever seen that had totally dispensed with subtitles.

The Bride was produced for Hartford at RKO, with Bretaigne Windust as the director. An atmosphere of good feeling seems to have prevailed during the shooting, with Agee himself playing the small part of the jail's "permanent" prisoner, as well as singing "Bringing in the Sheaves" in a quite passable voice. All this resulted in an extremely charming film of far less than feature length. For this reason, *The Bride* was teamed up with an equally short film based on Joseph Conrad's story *The Secret Sharer.* They were released together in 1952 as *Face to Face,* with nothing approaching the fantastic success of *The African Queen* the previous year.

Throughout the rest of 1951 Agee worked on all sorts of brief polishing and "doctoring" jobs, mostly at Twentieth Century-Fox, but at other studios as well. These early years of the fifties were bad ones for a free-lancer like Agee, for this was a period of uncertainty, even a certain amount of terror, because of the first impact of television on Hollywood. It was actually hard to get regular work, as Agee soon discovered.

Agee was stricken with his second major heart attack at the beginning of November 1951. His difficulties getting screenwriting assignments in Hollywood, plus his deep concern about the neglect of his own writing, combined to make the burden of this second attack even heavier than it might have been:

Today (and yesterday, and the day before) I am quite depressed. . . . I am depressed at being broke and unemployed with no job in sight unless—which will be my very last resort—I go back into *Time.* I am depressed that it is now over three years since I quit regular work in order, at last, to get down to serious business about my own writing—and at how very little of it I've got done. . . .

At the time he wrote these lines to Father Flye he had published his short novel *The Morning Watch* in the previous year; but before that it had been nearly a full decade since he had finished *Let Us Now Praise Famous Men.* All during the late forties he had kept on with what became *A Death in the Family,* but he made it clear that he needed a good deal of "free" time to finish it, along with a number of the other projects he had in mind to write. He referred to this situation in the same long letter to Father Flye: ". . . so that the only prospects of doing work on my own, for a long time to come, are during periods of unwilling unemployment, such as now, and interstitially

with hack work—which I proved to myself by several years' effort I can't do, anywhere near well enough. . . ."

All through the spring of 1952 he kept turning over various
possibilities for original screenplays, including one that would
have had a major storm as the "central character," but nothing
came of this. The NBC television network finally commissioned him to write a series of scripts for them about Lincoln
for their *Omnibus* series, and he returned to the East that
spring to begin writing them.

[4]

*I feel sure you will forgive me if as the writer I infringe on
other territories, including those of the director. I can no
more conceive of a writer's not trying to imagine the film as
a whole, and finished, than your not entering as deeply as
you might wish to, into the writing stage of it.*
—*Agee to Fred Zinnemann, January 1954*

Nearly all of Agee's film work in the last three years of his life
took place either at his house on King Street in New York City
or at his place in the country in Hillsdale, New York. There
were occasional short visits to California for last-minute polishing jobs on various films, but he seemed to do just as well
securing film work in New York as in Hollywood.

He became something of a journeyman film-worker in these
last years, becoming involved in a wide variety of projects. The
NBC Lincoln scripts paid him well, but they were especially
time-consuming, for the completed film ran about four and a
half hours, with Agee appearing on the screen with Allan
Nevins discussing the legendary Lincoln as opposed to the real
one. His health continued to be erratic.

There were still other ways of making money via films. In
1948 he had written the spoken commentary for *The Quiet
One,* the Sidney Meyers–Helen Levitt semidocumentary film

about a disturbed child in Harlem.* Agee's magnificently written commentary did much to make *The Quiet One* a critical success, if not a financial one, and established him as a sort of
"expert" at writing material of this nature. In 1952 he was
approached to write commentary for another film, Albert La-
morisse's *White Mane,* a very lovely film about a young boy and
a wild horse, set in the Camargue region of Southern France.
For Agee, writing these commentaries meant a great many
screenings of the original foreign film, getting the gist of what
had been on the French or Italian sound track, throwing out
most if not all of it, and then writing his own version. *The Sky
Above, the Mud Below* is such a film.

In 1953 he had planned to go to France and Ireland to
work on the screenplay for John Huston's production of *Moby
Dick,* a film project about which he had some very definite
ideas, seeing it as a "Shakespearean poem" that Melville had
not realized in his novel, or at least not for a mass audience.
At one critical point in his dealings with Huston, Agee found
that he would have to make a choice between *Moby Dick* and
an entirely different project of a rather exotic nature. In the
course of performing these various commentary jobs for
foreign films, he had done one for a biographical film made in
the Philippines called *Genghis Khan,* starring that country's
most popular actor, Manuel Condé. Agee got to know Condé
quite well, well enough to have Condé propose and Agee
agree to have them get together for a vast, spectacular film
with Condé starring, Agee both writing and directing, and
James Wong Howe as the cameraman. It was to cost many
millions and was to be shot entirely in the Philippines.

For a brief moment it appeared that Agee's life-long dream
of directing his own film was about to be realized. When Huston discovered that Agee might not be available for *Moby Dick,*
and that he had pledged his word to Condé (with only a hand-
shake) to proceed with this very strange-sounding deal, he was
both shocked and outraged. How could Agee accept some-

---

* *Agee's own voice was recorded for the film, but it was considered indistinct, and a professional
actor's was used. It is now possible to rent the film in either version.*

thing so vague and open-ended? For Agee, however, his word was his word, and he could not go back on it.

Eventually Condé reported that his backers were anxious to replace him as the star of the picture with a "Yul Brynner" type of actor and tacitly advised Agee and Howe to abandon the project. This was the very last Agee ever heard of Condé or anything else concerning the film. There was another disappointment, for Huston was unable to secure the services of the actor he wished to play Ahab at that time, thus postponing the production of *Moby Dick* for at least a year. He finally did get Gregory Peck for the part, with Ray Bradbury as the scriptwriter, but this was all after Agee's death in 1955.

The biggest single project that occupied Agee in 1953 was his *Noa Noa,* a film biography of Paul Gauguin that has never been produced, although it was commissioned, as were all the other Agee film scripts. In some ways it was his most ambitious project, although there are those who have found it to be his most overtly "commercial" script. On the whole, it is a much more conventional piece of work than *The Blue Hotel,* or even *The African Queen.* Unlike all his other screenplays, *Noa Noa* is a completely original work based only on a rather personal view of Gauguin he had formed by reading Gauguin's letters and various novels and biographies, as well as examining the paintings themselves. David Bradley, a young director best known at the time for a cheaply made version of *Julius Caesar* he had produced and directed in Chicago, was to have directed *Noa Noa,* but there were the usual money problems, and while this script has been read as widely as any other script in print, no one has yet risked producing it.

There is a curiously simplistic approach to parts of *Noa Noa,* as in the scene where Gauguin discovers his native mistress, Tehura, so terrified by having been left alone in the dark that she actually assumes the same posture as the girl in his own painting *Spirit of the Dead Watching:*

CLOSE SHOT—TEHURA

She lies belly-down, diagonal on the bed, in the matchlight. We TIGHTEN THIS DOWNSHOT from her nude back, waist-up to a head CLOSEUP. In this light her eyes, enlarged by fear, look phosphorescent, and deeply animal. . . .

There is an earlier scene in the script in which Agee has Gauguin talking about painting with Van Gogh in a way that sounds like a parody of the way art students might imagine painters to have talked:

VINCENT
Painting is the love of God.

GAUGUIN
O, forget religion for five minutes and tend to your business as an artist. Do you want to know the real trouble with you?

VINCENT
Thank you; do tell me.

GAUGUIN
You're a hopeless sentimentalist. Your work's all emotion—hysteria. Don't you *ever* stop to think?

VINCENT
What has painting to do with thought?

He had not given up his old basic notion that things must be *exactly right,* for in the scene depicting the Tahitian King Pomare's funeral, Agee indicates precisely how this music is to be played:

NOTE: The funeral sequence is to be cut rigidly to the music of Chopin's Funeral March. I will indicate the cuts and shots exactly, but serve warning that without the melody to key it to, it will be hard to read, or to imagine the effectiveness of. I will write out and enclose the melody, as a key; the scoring, and performance, should be those of a French deep provincial military band of the period: rather shrill and squeaky, and not very well played; yet with genuine solemnity.

Although there are many magnificent scenes in *Noa Noa* it must have been this stupefyingly precise way of indicating *everything* that turned producers and/or directors from taking it on. The desire to take over the director's function never left Agee, as can be seen from the letter to Fred Zinnemann quoted at the beginning of this section. Agee indicates that he will always take a director's advice about the writing in a script *if* he is permitted to return the favor. This sounds perfectly "fair" on paper, but in practice Agee knew that while he could take on a director's job in a flash, it was most unlikely that Zinnemann or any other director could ever write as well as he could.

Agee's last completed screenplay was for the Paul Gregory production of *The Night of the Hunter,* which Charles Laughton directed in 1955, the only film he ever chose to direct. It is the most melodramatic of all Agee's scripts, and the film as produced is a curious one for a number of reasons. It was based on Davis Grubb's novel about a murderous "Preacher" who is attempting to wrest away the $10,000 a condemned convict has hidden away with his two small children, a boy of nine and a girl of five. To get the money from them "Preacher" marries the children's mother and kills her when she discovers his real purpose. Robert Mitchum was "Preacher," with Shelley Winters the young widow he marries, and Lillian Gish the indomitable old lady who saves the children.

There is a "Tennessee Mountain" atmosphere about the film throughout, most of it handled in a reasonably modern style, but there are sections involving the kind of "warning shadows" or "expressionistic" effects that F. W. Murnau had used back in the late twenties. Agee seems to have deliberately chosen this device to suggest the horrifically evil nature of "Preacher," who has had the letters H-A-T-E tattooed on the fingers of one hand and the letters L-O-V-E tattooed on the other. For show purposes he allows his two hands to engage in combat, with LOVE always vanquishing HATE. The film contains shots of owls and rabbits to symbolize the desperation of the children as they flee from the bloody hands of the "Preacher."

The presence of Lillian Gish in the picture evoked a number of D. W. Griffith films, and Laughton was criticized for having directed the film in a such a variety of styles, but a great deal of this can be found in Agee's script. One critic remarked that Laughton, instead of making his first film in his own style, had "decided to remake everyone else's." It is easy to see why William S. Pechter should feel this way about the

James Agee, taken at King Street, New York City, 1955 (*Helen Levitt*)

film; if Agee had lived through the actual production it is quite possible that the final approach would have been a different one.

In the years from the "private" writing of *The House* in 1936 to his very last complete screenplay, *The Night of the Hunter* in 1954, Agee had learned a lot about writing, some of it directly attributable to the work he did as a screenwriter. Along with Faulkner and West, Agee was able to translate some of his discoveries in film-making into his serious fiction, especially his tremendous faith in the visual above everything else, as in the great passage in *A Death in the Family,* when young Rufus first sees the body of his dead father in the coffin:

The arm was bent. Out of the dark suit, the starched cuff, sprang the hairy wrist.

The wrist was angled; the hand was arched; none of the fingers touched each other.

The hand was so composed that it seemed at once casual and majestic. It stood exactly above the center of his body.

The fingers looked unusually clean and dry, as if they had been scrubbed with great care.

The hand looked very strong, and the veins were strong in it. The nostrils were very dark, yet he thought he could see, in one of them, something which looked like cotton.

On the lower lip, a trifle to the left of its middle, there was a small blue line which ran also a little below the lip.

At the exact point of the chin, there was another small blue mark, as straight and neat as might be drawn with a pencil, and scarcely wider.

The lines which formed the wings of the nose and mouth were almost gone.

The hair was most carefully brushed.

Like Fitzgerald, Huxley, and West, Agee still had films on his mind at the very end of his life. He wrote a long letter to Father Flye on May 11, 1955, which he never got around to mailing, but it was found on the mantelpiece of his house on King Street. In this letter Agee tells his old friend about an idea he has for a film about elephants, those strange, huge, sad beasts that have been so badly treated by men. The con-

Grauman's Chinese Theatre, *circa* 1934

cluding section of it concerns the plight of some circus elephants who have been taught by Balanchine to dance to the
music of Stravinsky. The crowd roars its approval and

. . . the elephants are deeply shamed. Later that night the wisest of
them, extending his trunk, licks up a dying cigar-butt, and drops it
in fresh straw. All 36 elephants die in the fire. Their huge souls,
light as clouds, settle like doves, in the great cemetery back in
Africa—

. . . Almost nobody I've described it to likes this idea, except me. It
has its weaknesses, but I like it. I hope you do.

BIBLIOGRAPHY

Agee, James. *Agee on Film: Five Film Scripts.* New York: McDowell, Obolensky, Inc., 1960.

Agee, James. *Agee on Film: Reviews and Comments.* New York: McDowell, Obolensky, Inc., 1958.

Agee, James. *Collected Short Prose.* Edited by Robert Fitzgerald. Boston: Houghton Mifflin Company, 1968.

Agee, James. *A Death in the Family.* New York: McDowell, Obolensky Inc., 1957.

Agee, James. *Letters of James Agee to Father Flye.* New York: George Braziller, 1962.

Balcon, Michael. *Michael Balcon Presents a Lifetime of Films.* London: Hutchinson, 1969.

Barson, Alfred T. *A Way of Seeing.* Boston: University of Massachusetts Press, 1972.

Bedford, Sybille. *Aldous Huxley: A Biography,* 2 vols. London: Chatto & Windus, 1973, 1974.

Bessie, Alvah. *Inquisition in Eden.* New York: Macmillan, 1965.

Blotner, Joseph. *Faulkner: A Biography,* 2 vols. New York: Random House, 1974.

Blotner, Joseph. "Faulkner in Hollywood." In *Man and the Movies,* edited by W. R. Robinson, 261–303.

Bradford, Roark. "The Private World of William Faulkner." *48: The Magazine of the Year* 2, no. 5 (1948).

Brecht, Bertolt. *Hundert Gedichte.* Berlin: Aufbau-Verlag, 1952.

Brecht, Bertolt. *Mahagonny,* translation by Guy Stern, Album Notes, Columbia Records, New York, 1957.

Bruccoli, Matthew J., ed. *As Ever, Scott Fitz—.* Philadelphia: J. B. Lippincott Co., 1972.

Bruccoli, Matthew J., and Clark, C. E. Frazer, Jr., eds. *The Fitzgerald-Hemingway Annual, 1971.* Washington, D.C.: NCR Micro-Card Editions, 1972.

Bruccoli, Matthew J., and Clark, C. E. Frazer, Jr., eds. *The Fitzgerald-*

Hemingway Annual, 1973. Washington, D.C.: NCR Micro-Card Editions, 1974.

Coindreau, Maurice Edgar. "The Faulkner I Knew." *Shenandoah* 16, no. 2 (Winter 1965), 27–35.

Connolly, Cyril. *Previous Convictions.* London: Hamish Hamilton, 1963.

Coughlan, Robert. *The Private World of William Faulkner.* New York: Harper and Brothers, 1954.

Cowley, Malcolm. *The Faulkner-Cowley File.* New York: The Viking Press, 1966.

Farber, Manny. *Negative Space.* New York: Praeger Publishers, 1971.

Faulkner, William. *The Big Sleep.* Screenplay by William Faulkner, Leigh Brackett, and Jules Furthman. Lincoln Center Library and Museum for the Performing Arts.

Faulkner, William. "The Golden Land." In *Collected Stories.* New York: Random House, 1950, 701–26.

Faulkner, William. *Sanctuary.* New York: Random House, 1962.

Faulkner, William. *The Wild Palms.* New York: Random House, 1939.

Fitzgerald, F. Scott. *The Crack-Up.* Edited by Edmund Wilson. Norfolk, Conn., and New York: New Directions, 1945.

Fitzgerald, F. Scott. *The Last Tycoon.* New York: Charles Scribner's Sons, 1951.

Fowles, John. "Notes on an Unfinished Novel." In *Afterwords,* edited by Thomas McCormack. New York: Harper & Row, 1969.

Fuchs, Daniel. "Days in the Gardens of Hollywood." *New York Times Book Review,* July 18, 1971.

Graham, Sheilah. *The Rest of the Story.* New York: Coward-McCann, 1964.

Graham, Sheilah, and Frank, Gerald. *Beloved Infidel.* New York: Bantam, 1959.

Hemingway, Ernest. *A Moveable Feast.* New York: Charles Scribner's Sons, 1964.

Higham, Charles. *The Films of Orson Welles.* Berkeley: University of California Press, 1970.

Huxley, Aldous. *After Many a Summer Dies the Swan.* New York: Harper & Brothers (Perennial Classic Edition), 1965.

Huxley, Aldous. *Ape and Essence.* New York: Harper & Brothers, 1949.

Huxley, Aldous. *Letters of Aldous Huxley.* Edited by Grover Smith. New York: Harper & Row, 1969.

Huxley, Julian, ed. *Aldous Huxley, 1894–1963*. New York: Harper & Row, 1965.

Kuehl, John, and Breyer, Jackson. *Dear Scott/Dear Max: The Fitzgerald-Perkins Correspondence*. New York: Charles Scribner's Sons, 1971.

Latham, Aaron. *Crazy Sundays*. New York: The Viking Press, 1971.

Light, James. *Nathanael West: An Interpretative Biography*, 2d rev. ed. Evanston, Ill.: Northwestern University Press, 1971.

Loos, Anita. *Kiss Hollywood Good-bye*. New York: The Viking Press, 1974.

MacDonald, Dwight. *On Movies*. Englewood Cliffs, N.J.: Prentice-Hall, 1969.

MacDonald, Dwight. *Against the American Grain*. New York: Random House, 1965.

Mann, Thomas. *The Story of a Novel*. New York: Alfred A. Knopf, 1961.

Margolies, Alan. "F. Scott Fitzgerald's Work in the Film Studios." *Princeton University Library Quarterly* 32, no. 2 (Winter 1971), 81–110.

Martin, Jay. *Nathanael West: The Art of His Life*. New York: Farrar, Straus & Giroux, 1970.

Martin, Jay. *Nathanael West: A Collection of Critical Essays*. Englewood Cliffs, N.J.: Prentice-Hall, 1971.

Maugham, W. Somerset. *Cakes and Ale*. London: William Heinemann Ltd. 1930.

McBride, Joseph. *Focus on Howard Hawks*. Englewood Cliffs, N.J.: Prentice-Hall, 1972.

McCoy, Horace. *I Should Have Stayed Home*. New York: Alfred A. Knopf, 1938.

Meriwether, James B., ed. *Essays, Speeches and Public Letters by William Faulkner*. New York: Random House, 1965.

Meriwether, James B., and Millgate, Michael, eds. *Lion in the Garden. Interviews with William Faulkner, 1926–1962*. New York: Random House, 1968.

Mizener, Arthur. *The Far Side of Paradise*, rev. ed. Boston: Houghton Mifflin Company, 1965.

O'Hara, John. "In Memory of Scott Fitzgerald: Certain Aspects." In *Hello, Hollywood!*, edited by Allen Rivkin and Laura Kerr, 522–23.

Oulahan, Richard. "A Cult Grew Around a Many-Sided Writer." *Life* 55 (November 1, 1963), 169–72.

Perelman, S. J. "The Great (and Invisible) Man." In *Hello, Hollywood!*, edited by Allen Rivkin and Laura Kerr, 75–80.

Powell, Anthony. "Hollywood Canteen." In *The Fitzgerald-Hemingway Annual, 1971,* 71–80.

Princeton University. Fitzgerald Papers.

Rivkin, Allen, and Kerr, Laura. *Hello, Hollywood!* New York: Doubleday & Company, 1962.

Robinson, W. R. *Man and the Movies.* Baton Rouge: Louisiana State University Press, 1967.

Ross, Lillian. *Picture.* New York: Rinehart & Company, 1952.

Rosten, Leo C. *Hollywood: The Movie Colony, the Movie Makers.* New York: Harcourt, Brace & Co., 1941.

Samsell, R. L. "Six Unpublished Letters to Hunt Stromberg." In *The Fitzgerald-Hemingway Annual, 1972,* 9–18.

Sanford, John. "Nathanael West." In *Hello, Hollywood!,* edited by Allen Rivkin and Laura Kerr, 527–30.

Schwartz, Delmore. *Selected Essays.* Edited by Donald A. Dike and David H. Zucker. Chicago: University of Chicago Press, 1970.

Schulberg, Budd. *The Disenchanted.* New York: Random House, 1950.

Schulberg, Budd. *The Four Seasons of Success.* New York: Doubleday & Company, 1972.

Sidney, George R. *Faulkner in Hollywood.* Albuquerque: University of New Mexico, 1957.

Stewart, Donald Ogden. "A Recollection of Fitzgerald and Hemingway." In *The Fitzgerald-Hemingway Annual, 1971,* 177–89.

Stravinsky, Igor, and Craft, Robert. *Dialogues and a Diary.* New York: Doubleday & Company, 1963.

Turnbull, Andrew. *Letters of F. Scott Fitzgerald.* New York: Charles Scribner's Sons, 1963.

Turnbull, Andrew. *Scott Fitzgerald.* New York: Charles Scribner's Sons, 1962.

Viertel, Salka. *The Kindness of Strangers.* New York: Holt, Rinehart and Winston, 1965.

NOTES

Page

34   Hemingway, 179; Bruccoli, 330; Bruccoli, 403; Letter, Daniel Fuchs to Tom Dardis, May 1975.

36   Balcon, 109.

37   Princeton, Fitzgerald Papers, *A Yank at Oxford, Analysis, Treatment, and Dialogue,* July 26, 1937, 1.

39   Turnbull, *Letters,* 564; Margolies, 31.

40   Princeton, Fitzgerald Papers, Telegram, Joseph Mankiewicz to Fitzgerald, September 9, 1937.

41   Princeton, Fitzgerald Papers, *Three Comrades,* September 1, 1937, 31; Turnbull, *Letters,* 17.

43   Princeton, Fitzgerald Papers, *Three Comrades,* September 1, 1937, 52–53, 156.

44   Princeton, Fitzgerald Papers, *Three Comrades,* February 1, 1938, 114–15, 123; Letter, Fitzgerald to E. E. Paramore, October 24, 1937.

46   Princeton, Fitzgerald Papers, Letter, Fitzgerald to Joseph Mankiewicz, January 20, 1938 (the sentence "I had an entirely different conception of you" was not included in Turnbull's transcription of this letter); Turnbull, *Letters,* 23; Graham, *Beloved Infidel,* 176.

48   Perelman in Rivkin, 80.

51   Bruccoli and Clark, *1973,* 13; Princeton, Fitzgerald Papers, *Infidelity,* September 3, 1938, 18–20.

52   Latham, 194.

53   Bruccoli and Clark, *1971,* 188.

54   Bruccoli, 403; Princeton, Fitzgerald Papers, in "Pictures" file; Graham, *Rest of the Story,* 16.

55   Turnbull, *Letters,* 102.

56   Turnbull, *Letters,* 39.

57   Letter, Nunnally Johnson to Tom Dardis, December 1974; Bruccoli, 379, 379–80.

58   Bruccoli, 381; Letter, Nunnally Johnson to Tom Dardis, November 1974.

59   Letter, Nunnally Johnson to Tom Dardis, November 1974; Kuehl and Breyer, 255.

62   Mizener, 317; Schulberg, *The Disenchanted,* 347; Turnbull, *Scott Fitzgerald,* 296; Fitzgerald, *The Last Tycoon,* 152.

63   Turnbull, *Letters,* 127.

65   Turnbull, *Letters,* 62; Letter, Nunnally Johnson to Tom Dardis, December 1974.

Page

67   Bruccoli, 397, 400, 400, 403.
68   Bruccoli, 408.
69   Turnbull, *Letters,* 112, 68.
70   Princeton, Fitzgerald Papers, Letter, Fitzgerald to Lester Cowan, dated "Monday Night."
71   Princeton, Fitzgerald Papers, *Cosmopolitan,* August 13, 1940, 132–33.
72   Turnbull, *Letters,* 84, 122, 124.
73   Turnbull, *Letters,* 551, 127.
74   Bruccoli, 361; Kuehl and Breyer, 256; Turnbull, *Letters,* 61.
75   O'Hara in Rivkin, 522; information supplied by Kenneth Littauer, New York, May 1967.
76   Turnbull, *Letters,* 128, 132; Bruccoli, 423.

WILLIAM FAULKNER

79   Robinson, 287.
80   Letter, Nunnally Johnson to Tom Dardis, November 1974; Letter, Daniel Fuchs to Tom Dardis, May 1975.
81   Faulkner, *The Big Sleep,* 5.
82   Farber, 6; McBride, 21.
83   Information supplied by Leigh Brackett, Medford, Oregon, June 1973.
85   Meriwether, 177, 178; information supplied by Edith Haggard, New York, August 1974.
86   Blotner, vol. 1, 749.
87   Information supplied by Edith Haggard, New York, September 1974.
88   Robinson, 269.
89   Robinson, 266–67.
90   Robinson, 269; information supplied by Edith Haggard, New York, September 1974.
91   McBride, 24.
93   Farber, 114; Faulkner, *Sanctuary,* 241–42.
94   Sidney, 260; Robinson, 267.
95   Robinson, 269, 270.
96   Meriwether and Millgate, 241–43.
97   Blotner, vol. 1, 802.
98   Robinson, 272.

Page

99   Faulkner, *Collected Stories,* 719; Robinson, 272; Letter, Nunnally Johnson to Tom Dardis, November 1974.
101   Blotner, vol. 1, 919.
102   Blotner, vol. 1, 920.
103   Bradford, 92.
104   Blotner, vol. 2, 915.
105   Sidney, 54.
106   Blotner, vol. 2, 921.
107   Coindreau, 30; Sidney, 79, 161.
108   Meriwether and Millgate, 57; Schwartz, 274.
110   Blotner, vol. 2, 934.
111   Blotner, vol. 2, 945.
112   Sidney, 151.
113   Meriwether and Millgate, 33–34; Blotner, vol. 2, 1107; Letter, Daniel Fuchs to Tom Dardis, May 1975.
114   Faulkner, *The Wild Palms,* 209.
116   Blotner, vol. 2, 1044, 1066, 1068, 1106.
117   Blotner, vol. 2, 1107.
118   Sidney, 45; Bessie, 105–6.
119   Sidney, 50.
123   Sidney, 187.
125   Sidney, 190, 193–202.
126   Sidney, 177.
127   Blotner, vol. 2, 996–97, 1154.
128   Meriwether and Millgate, 241.
129   Agee, *Reviews and Comments,* 121–22.
131   Farber, 186–87, 21–22.
133   Coughlan, 109.
134   Sidney, 105; Bessie, 111.
135   Robinson, 287.
136   Coughlan, 116; information supplied by Daniel Fuchs, Hollywood, December 1975.
138   Blotner, vol. 2, 1149.
141   Robinson, 293; Letter, Daniel Fuchs to Tom Dardis, May 1975; Letter, Nunnally Johnson to Tom Dardis, November 1974.
142   Blotner, vol. 2, 1184.
143   Cowley, 106.
144   Agee, *Reviews and Comments,* 167; Blotner, vol. 2, 1191.

Page

147   Blotner, vol. 2, 1188; Cowley, 82, 91, 97–98.
149   Blotner, vol. 2, 1197, 1534, 1538, 1677.

NATHANAEL WEST

152   McCoy, 1; Martin, *Collection of Critical Essays,* 26.
153   Martin, *Collection,* 21.
155   Martin, *Art of His Life,* 149.
156   Martin, *Art,* 208.
157   Martin, *Collection,* 26; *Art,* 207.
159   Letter, John Sanford to Tom Dardis, April 1975.
160   Perelman in Rivkin, 528.
161   Princeton, Fitzgerald Papers, Letter, Nathanael West to
       Fitzgerald, September 11, 1934.
162   Martin, *Art,* 245, 268.
163   Martin, *Art,* 306.
167   Letter, John Sanford to Tom Dardis, May 1975; Letter,
       Daniel Fuchs to Tom Dardis, May 1975.
168   Rosten, 384.
169   Martin, *Art,* 277–79.
170   Letter, John Sanford to Tom Dardis, May 1975; Martin,
       Art, 313.
173   Martin, *Art,* 294–95.
174   Martin, *Art,* 302, 338, 341.
176   Light, 160.
177   Martin, *Art,* 365.
178   Princeton, Fitzgerald Papers, Letter, Nathanael West to
       Fitzgerald, April 5, 1939.

ALDOUS HUXLEY

184   Huxley, *Ape and Essence,* 62; Stravinsky, 42.
185   Huxley, *Ape and Essence,* 61.
186   Huxley, *Ape and Essence,* 62, 72.
187   Huxley, *After Many a Summer,* 24.
188   Huxley, *Letters,* 593.
189   Huxley, *Letters,* 423.
190   Huxley, *Letters,* 428, 432, 272.
191   Maugham, 128.

Page

192   Bedford, vol. 1, 360.
193   Huxley, *Letters,* 437.
194   Bedford, vol. 2, 17.
195   Huxley, *Aldous Huxley, 1894–1963,* 154–55.
196   Huxley, *Letters,* 446; Loos, 154–55; Huxley, *Aldous Huxley, 1894–1963,* 95.
197   Huxley, *Letters,* 450.
198   Huxley, *Letters,* 447.
199   Bedford, vol. 2, 13–14.
200   Bedford, vol. 2, 8, 20. In 1933 Goetz had borrowed money from his father-in-law, L. B. Mayer of MGM, to create Twentieth Century Pictures, which became Twentieth Century-Fox in 1935.
201   Huxley, *Letters,* 458.
202   Higham, 2.
203   Huxley, *Letters,* 471; Huxley, *Aldous Huxley, 1894–1963,* 155; Huxley, *Letters,* 502.
204   Huxley, *Letters,* 510; Bedford, vol. 2, 88.
205   Huxley, *Letters,* 537; Bedford, vol. 2, 65; Huxley, *Letters,* 537, 535.
206   Huxley, *Letters,* 539.
207   Bedford, vol. 2, 77.
208   Huxley, *Letters,* 549–50; 565.
209   Huxley, *Letters,* 572, 576.
210   Agee, *Reviews and Comments,* 294; Bedford, vol. 2, 103.
211   Stravinsky, 42.
213   Huxley, *Letters,* 632, 644–45.
214   Huxley, *Letters,* 875; Letter, Aldous Huxley to Tom Dardis, July 1, 1963.

James Agee

218   Letter, James Agee to Dwight MacDonald, July 21, 1927.
219   Information supplied by Mia Agee, New York, July 1975; Agee, *Collected Short Prose,* 50.
220   Letters, James Agee to Dwight MacDonald, July 21, 1927, June 26, 1927, April 24, 1929; MacDonald, *On Movies,* 14.
221   Agee, *Letters,* 46.
222   Agee, *Collected Short Prose,* 157; information supplied by Jay Leyda, New York, September 1975.

Page

223   Agee, *Collected Short Prose,* 166.

225   Agee, *Collected Short Prose,* 216; Agee, *Reviews and Comments,* 67, 136.

227   Agee, *Reviews and Comments,* 29, 77, 204.

228   Agee, *Reviews and Comments,* 295, 262.

229   Information supplied by Eleanor Keaton, Hollywood, December 1975; Agee, *Reviews and Comments,* 155.

230   Agee, *Reviews and Comments,* 188, 164.

231   Agee, *Reviews and Comments,* 290; Agee, *Collected Short Prose,* 41–42.

232   Ross, 147; Oulahan, 71.

233   Agee, *Five Film Scripts,* "The Blue Hotel," 400, 401.

234   Agee, *Five Film Scripts,* "The Blue Hotel," 464, 440.

237   Ross, 147; Agee, *Letters,* 185.

238   Barson, 170; Agee, *Five Film Scripts,* "The African Queen," 157.

239   Information supplied by Mia Agee, New York, August 1975; Agee, *Five Film Scripts,* "The African Queen," 372.

240   Agee, *Letters,* 191–92.

242   Agee, *Letters,* 194.

243–44   Agee, *Letters,* 194; Barson, 169; information supplied by Mia Agee, New York, August 1975, and by Jay Leyda, New York, September 1975.

246   Agee, *Five Film Scripts,* "Noa Noa," 79, 60.

249   Agee, *A Death in the Family,* 308.

251   Agee, *Letters,* 231–32.

INDEX

PS
129
D3

Dardis, Tom.
    Some time in the sun.